Published by the
UNIVERSITY OF MINNESOTA PRESS · Minneapolis
LONDON · GEOFFREY CUMBERLEGE · OXFORD UNIVERSITY PRESS

JAMES GRAY

on second thought

The author and the publisher wish to thank the
St. Paul Pioneer Press and Dispatch for permission
to reprint freely from the reviews Mr. Gray
wrote for their columns.

Table of Contents

on second thought

Did I Say That?

THAT suave and silken ironist, Somerset Maugham, made the suggestion in *Cakes and Ale* that to become august, in British eyes, a man has only to survive for more than the ordinary number of years. To the uncritical majority of humankind, longevity and venerability are, Mr. Maugham suspects, synonymous.

This is one of those unobtrusive and mouselike bits of cynicism that scurries busily through the mind, gnawing at the basic structure of one's faith in the dignity of the human spirit and in the significance of any effort. But perhaps the philosophers of negation serve a useful purpose in dissuading the suggestible from being content with standards of excellence that are low or loose or flimsy. The dignity of the human spirit deserves to be enshrined in nothing less noble than a temple which revolutions of thought cannot shake. Less solid structures should have their foundations undermined and nothing should be done to prop them up artificially.

A corollary to Mr. Maugham's implied warning to critical intelligences may be that persistence of effort is not identical with worthiness of effort. "Steadfastness of purpose" is a phrase often on the tongues of self-conscious moralists, who seem, sometimes, not to be at all embarrassed by the reflection that many people are steadfast in the lightly disguised purpose of being ungenerous, mean-spirited, or merely tedious.

So, in appropriate humility of spirit, I would warn readers of this volume that it contains writings which are of interest partly because they are the result of a continuity of effort that has persisted for twenty years. Day after day, through various

3

phases of the world's sad passion—through a frenzied ecstasy of faith in an economic millennium; through panic and collapse; through depression and the universal paralysis of fear; through rumors of wars and wars themselves; through the bitterest of disillusionments about the perfectibility of man— the author of these essays has sat himself down to brood over a fragment of the recorded experience of the race. In the midst of so furious a drama it seemed sometimes ludicrous to be concerned about the tiny containers of sorrow and wrath that even the most ambitious books end by being.

But even when his life is shadowed by momentous happenings, a man must continue to earn his bread and do the job to which circumstance and his training have assigned him. Mine during all this tempestuous time has been to read a book between eight o'clock and noon of a morning and, between one and five of an afternoon, to write out an estimate of its worth as a contribution to the history of the humanities.

Visitors to a reviewer's place of work have two characteristic reactions. One is to marvel, with obvious envy, as they see this lethargic creature surrounded by shelves showing the handsome backs of red and blue and green books, that anyone's life should be so soft and sybaritic. The other is to feel a wave of awe that anyone should have the temerity to attempt to make his way through such a jungle of expressiveness.

About neither the softness nor the awesomeness of his way of life does the reviewer ever think at all. Though he is required by the rules of politeness to parry many gentle insults about his laziness and to seem to be prettily abashed by tributes to his energy, he never thinks of himself as being either physically slack or mentally virile. At his best, when his metabolism is good or the vitamin pills are managing to prop up his spirit, he thinks of the delight it is to be allowed to spend his days doing something he likes so well to do. In his worst moments, which come with crushing regularity, or his next to the worst, which always threaten, he thinks of

4

the drudgery of his work; of the dismal certainty of knowing what a mediocre writer will say before he has long-windedly managed to say it; of the appalling possibility of being unfair; and the even more grim probability of having no real opinion at all.

But a day is only twenty-four hours long and books seldom stretch indolently beyond a thousand pages. These measurements of time and space can be conquered by technique. A reviewer learns to make his genuine enthusiasm for the art of letters fill in the chinks of his vitality, so that each sun sets on the minor accomplishment represented by another thousand words of typescript.

Then one day the suggestion of an editor that there may be something of all that effort worth preserving in more permanent form makes him wake to the realization that he has been doing the same job over and over again for twenty years. That is such a vast stretch of time as the young man can never really believe is before him and the middle-aged man grieves to think is already behind him. Vanity prompts the latter to hope that out of the mountain of his printed work a molehill of significant comment may be sifted.

The relationship of the newspaper reviewer to the art of letters is a curious one. Opinions are produced in reckless submission to the demand of journalism, which is that the timely topic must be wrapped up in glib and authoritative finalities and tossed at the front doors of all the literate citizens of the neighborhood no later than five o'clock of each afternoon. There is no time to roll judgment under the tongue, to test its flavor for either cloying sweetness or tart imprudence. The newspaper god of immediacy must be served in the knowledge that he is indulgent toward critical caprice but implacable in his distaste for critical uncertainty.

So the reviewer's judgments are thrown off as though by the centrifugal force of the newspaper world's daily spinning. They disappear into oblivion along with the paper itself.

Occasionally they reappear together in curious and unexpected places. I have seen my strictures against the decaying art of Edith Wharton serving as a bed for the corpses of two pickerel lately plucked from a Minnesota lake, and an estimate of the importance of Thomas Wolfe protecting an old sweater from an invasion by moths. It is sometimes difficult to recognize these ghostly fragmentations of oneself. Once when I was gathering together old newspapers for a salvage drive, I sat for hours on the very cold floor of my basement reviewing a long parade of these adumbrations of a mind that I should know reasonably well, murmuring over and over again, "Did I say that?" It is startling to be in the company of a great many opinionated people, whose outlines except on this one point of expressiveness are shadowy, and then to realize that they are all oneself.

But such a reunion with one's various critical selves does result in the discovery that there has been a certain design to the experience. Anyone who has contemplated the development of English letters steadily for twenty years finds, in retrospect, that he has seen significant things happen. He has, for example, watched the first American writers embark on a return trip to the Old World to receive the bounty of Sweden as winners of the Nobel prize. He has observed the mass movements of the literary population, as one group stampedes into the camp of the "proletarian" artists and another disperses over the face of the land in search of "regional" material. He has been startled and disturbed to see serious fiction passing in England under the protection of a sort of matriarchal society, while the male novelists have been content to be either eccentric champions of philosophic nihilism or whimsical designers of vague new faiths. He has examined that weirdest phenomenon of decadence which makes it possible for Aldous Huxley to entertain these mutually exclusive attitudes at the same time. He has noticed with dismay that some of the talents which owe their youthful inspiration to the last years of the nineteenth century have clung tenaciously to their originality and audacity, while some of the talents of the twentieth century have flowered and gone to seed within a pitifully short time.

And he reaches the conclusion in the end that if there is such a thing as a literary age of complete sterility and charmlessness, his own has not been one. Rather, it has been crowded with brash, assertive new interests; gusty, egocentric talents and ones dedicated to the service of the public good; explorative expeditions into the terra incognita of the mind; movements with more liveliness than dignity and causes with more honesty of purpose than of artistic fastidiousness. Much of it has been engrossing and some of it will survive as a part of the heritage of the race.

Within this drama of creativity there is always the depressing scene of the individual's decay and collapse. The reviewer who has watched the parade of literary figures through twenty years has witnessed over and over again the inevitable cycle of growth, fulfillment, and decay. But it should not have depressed him unduly, for always there are bright newcomers to take the place of those who have faded and become drab. In the world of letters when the half-gods go, perhaps the gods do not appear; but at least other half-gods crowd over the threshold.

Having observed so much of "change and decay" in the work of other men, the reviewer tends to become almost morbidly conscious of weakness in himself. He knows, to his sorrow and chagrin, that all too often discernment will fail him. There is the pathetic little crisis of servile acceptance when one rushes out to embrace the languorous sensibility of a talent that later proves to be completely meretricious. Black indeed is one's mood of self-accusation when it becomes painfully clear that in a time of niggardliness one has failed to acknowledge the richness of a major literary skill. Perhaps the most deflating experience of all is to discover that one has

7

been overwhelmed, that one's judgment has been crushed, by the sheer bulk of a literary product. In newspaper offices, a city editor sometimes will hold up for display the copy of an inexperienced reporter, saying derisively, "Must be good! See how long it is!" Yet in a world where many rewards go to stubborn industry, it is difficult not to be impressed by copiousness. To discover that, despite all warnings to oneself in advance, one has succumbed still another time to the childish delusion that a work of six hundred pages must of necessity be three times better than one of two hundred pages—this is the sort of experience that makes a reviewer continuously conscious of his frailty.

For all these reasons, the author of a daily column devoted to books has very little impulse to say, "I am Sir Oracle. When I open my mouth, let no dog bark." Even if there were no derisive echoings from his own heart, there would still be the warnings offered by conspicuous examples of critical stumbling. The late Alexander Woollcott, at the time when he was arbiter of the elegances for a huge American public, seldom sat down before the microphone, on a national hookup, without working himself into hysterics over something flagrantly and flamboyantly third-rate. Even the great Edgar Allan Poe, whose taste was usually fastidious and exacting, had his unfortunate moments of flinging away the armor of his critical judgment to dance a wild, swooning measure or two with some entirely forgotten lady poet who happened to catch his fancy.

The state of being infallible would be a lonely one, a bleak and forbidding eminence on which there would be no one with whom to wrangle. That alone would make it completely unsympathetic to the average reviewer of books, who likes above all things to compare notes with others of his kind.

Yet this much a man may be permitted, perhaps, to say about his work. If he has taken his task seriously and struggled with it for a long time, he is likely to have developed a kind of consistency of outlook. He should have discovered, at last, a set of principles which, however faulty many individual tenets may be, still has the value of throwing the light of one mind, steadily and concentratedly, on an important aspect of human effort.

It is to try to follow such a thread of consistency through twenty years of critical writing that these essays have been brought together. The scope of the book is limited, in certain obvious ways, by the perceptions of its author. He has ignored some conspicuous figures because they happen to have stirred in him neither enthusiasm nor distaste. He has grouped writers in a fashion that may seem whimsical to certain readers. Sometimes he may have skimped giants to concentrate on dwarfs. For these faults, apology is hereby offered to those who, looking for firm boundaries to an outline of contemporary literature, find here many holes in the fence.

The newspaper articles on which these essays are based are the ones which interested me most when I began to turn them over in the files of the public library and in the borrowed scrapbooks of loyal readers. They are the ones also with which I still find myself, on second thought, largely in agreement.

Let the book stand, then, as a casual summing up of a long discursive conversation about the literary impulse of our time.

Publisher's Note. To distinguish between Mr. Gray's earlier opinions and his current comments, without unduly interrupting the continuity of his "summing up," we have used leaf devices, like the ones enclosing this paragraph, at the beginning and end of each republished review or excerpt from a review.

9

Gods by Adoption

THOSE talent scouts for posterity, the directors of the Nobel Fund, had not, before the year 1930, found an American writer worthy of consideration as a candidate for the prize in the field of literature. The tremendous prestige of the award, which makes of the ordinary earnest, worried scrivener a god by adoption of the Swedish Academy, had shone into various obscure corners of Europe but had left the continent of North America still in outer darkness.

The official attitude of the European world of letters was still that expressed, with sweeping dismissiveness, by Sydney Smith in a review of Seybert's *Annals of the United States*, 1820.

"In the four quarters of the globe," sniffed this fastidious but parochial observer, "who reads an American book, goes to see an American play, or looks at an American picture or statue?" It was an unfortunate myopia that made such witnesses unable to discern the importance of the six volumes of the works of Benjamin Franklin that had been put into print before 1820 or the historic and artistic interest of the paintings of Gilbert Stuart, who had worked industriously for many years before his death in 1828.

In the course of the next century, American books penetrated into far corners of the European world. Victoria, the *hausfrau* queen, treasured the improving sentiments of Mr. Longfellow; the works of James Fenimore Cooper were dear to the sentimental sadists of Germany; and later the psychological searchings of Jack London pleased the Russian soul.

The admission during the 1930's of three American writers into the rights and privileges of the Nobel alcove of eternity gave for the first time a sort of official endorsement to the curiosity that Europe had always felt about the fabulous lives of Americans.

Sinclair Lewis

THE choice of Sinclair Lewis as the first American to win the Nobel prize for literature startled America as much as it is said to have surprised the jaunty "Red" himself. He was known to an already large public as an extraordinarily skillful improviser, able to produce a satisfactory serial for the *Saturday Evening Post*, a narrative suitable to be made into a scenario for an ingénue madcap of the screen, or a bright and provocative piece of journalism on the spirit of the times. *Main Street* and *Babbitt* had presented hearty caricatures of village and small-town life. Their obvious cleverness recommended them to all lovers of boldness, but the discerning saw that Lewis' satire was not a precision instrument. It was designed for use against the pachydermous covering of American complacency. If there was more cruelty than compassion in the novelist's surgical method, such an attack was assumed by a large company of intellectual masochists to be no better than the beast deserved.

In *Arrowsmith* Lewis seemed to be allowing his sympathies to broaden and his insights to penetrate deeper into the jungle of American temperament. But in essential impulse he was too eagerly the exhibitionistic wooer of his audience to be willing to undertake long hard chores of psychological exploration. He wanted the quick effect, the immediate reward, quite as much in his role as literary artist as he wanted it in his role as mimic and monologuist at dinner parties. So, after *Arrowsmith*, he returned to the level of superficial enthusiasm and vituperative rejection. There he has remained ever since.

When Sinclair Lewis won the Nobel prize I wrote for my newspaper column a modest little fantasy, intended to suggest that a close affinity existed between Babbitt and his creator. An overtone intimates that there may be Swedish Babbitts, too, whose influence prompted Lewis' nomination for immortality.

The stunning news that Sinclair Lewis has been awarded the Nobel prize for literature has in the past few days penetrated to the region about which he has written so extensively.

Wishing to express the reaction of its members, I ran over in my mind the names of men best qualified to speak of Lewis' worthiness. Suddenly it occurred to me that no one knows Sinclair Lewis better than George Babbitt. The two are intimates. Lewis has even written a book about his friend.

So I drove out to Zenith. (It is a delightful trip from St. Paul, just over the state line. There are excellent concrete roads all the way.) Mr. Babbitt was in conference, but after an hour I was admitted to his private office.

This sanctum looks much as it looked in the period of the novel—imposing and full of massive furniture. I noticed a few modern touches. A Covarrubias caricature of Sinclair Lewis hangs over Mr. Babbitt's desk, and near it is a striking etching by Clement Haupers of St. Paul. Otherwise the office is unchanged. Nor has Mr. Babbitt himself aged perceptibly. He is still plump and genial. The worried look of his harassed years is gone, and in its place has emerged once more his irrepressible exuberance, the gift of shrewdness mixed with naiveté.

I told Mr. Babbitt why I had come to see him.

"Yeah," he said, leaning back in his swivel chair and offering me a cigar, "I saw in the paper where that fella Lewis had got the Nobel (he pronounced it *Noble*) prize. I sure was glad to see it. You can quote me as saying that he's just about the best inkslinger we got around here.

"You know he wrote a book about me once." Mr. Babbitt leaned forward and his eyes shone with what I suddenly realized was pride.

"A lotta my friends," he continued, "thought Lewis took a coupla nasty cracks in that book. But it didn't get me sore. Heck, I knew Sinclair too well. We got on great together. Whatever he said was just in fun. I can stand a little criticism, I guess. You can't be thin-skinned in my racket.

"Besides, Sinclair is just one of the fellas. Why, when he lived in Zenith I used to take him to my poker club every Saturday night. He talked just as plain as any of us. And laugh! Say, his wheezes were great! Of course, some of the others got a little sore when he put all that stuff in the book. But what the heck! That's life, ain't it? Why shouldn't he? We all thought he was a regular guy then and I still do.

"Didya ever see Sinclair do his imitations? Boy, you missed something. He coulda made a mint of money in vaw-de-ville. I never saw such a guy for taking people off. I usta split my sides laughing. Well, I laughed at Red when he did his act about Bill Connors calling up his wife from a poker game. I can laugh when he's a little rough on me.

"Not that I don't take Red serious. I think his books have done a lotta good. What was the one about this Gantry guy? Say, was he a skunk! Well, I think them birds oughta be showed up. Where do they get off, preaching to us on Sundays and then boozing all through the week. It took courage to write that book. You gotta hand it to Red.

"Some of the boys in the poker game usta think Sinclair was pretty crazy about Sinclair. But heck, look at what he's made out of himself. Just a local boy, but now he's famous all over the world. You don't get that way for nothing, lemme tell you. He's gotta right to be proud. I respect him. And how!"

Mr. Babbitt lit a fresh cigar and leaned toward me earnestly.

"You know, I never could get this Nobel prize stuff before. Clear outa my depth. This Bernard Shaw and Anatole France! They may be great, but I don't get them. I'm real glad if people in Sweden have waked up to the fact that real people are leading real lives in this little old world and that Sinclair

13

Lewis is writing about real stuff. That highbrow hokum don't go with me and a lotta my friends feel the same way. Some in Sweden, too, I guess. I'm glad that for once they've given that prize to a regular he-man with red blood in his veins.

"A lady I know told me she thought this man Dreiser that wrote *An American Tragedy* oughta had the prize. Golly, that stuff! Two volumes! I tackled it, but gosh! What I say is there's enough sadness in life without faking it. Lewis gives out with the straight dope. It ain't sweet and Pollyanna-ish. And yet you know the birds he writes about is live ones.

"Of course, Lewis writes a lotta stuff just to make money. Why wouldn't he? He's got to capitalize on his investment, hasn't he? I just read a piece of his in the *Cosmopolitan* magazine.'Go East Young Man' it's called. Nothing to it much. Just a young man that goes to Paris thinking he's an artist. Well, he gets sense and comes home. Don't amount to much— the story, I mean. But you can read it, every word! And that's more'n you can say for a lotta these guys."

I rose to go. I understood clearly that Babbitt liked Sinclair Lewis and why. I also understood why 1,300,000 copies of his books had been sold in America.

"Say," exclaimed Mr. Babbitt cordially as I left, "why don't you come over for the poker game Saturday night? We'll give you a good run for your money. You can ask the other boys what they think of Red Lewis. But I can tell you what they'll say. He ain't a highbrow that sits up in a studio somewhere and writes about life the way he thinks it oughta be. Of course he'd like to make it better if he knew how. But he don't have fancy ideas. He's just as common as you and me. He'd be a whirlwind at anything. Business! Boy, he woulda been a knockout! He understands publicity for one thing. Maybe that's why he's a knockout in literachoor." &

One of Lewis' brisk journalistic impulses took possession of his mind in 1935 and jerked him out of a long preoccupation with commonplace and unrewarding material. *It Can't Happen Here* is the best book of his middle period. Not that it is a work of art or of much imagination. Lewis merely translated into American slang the history of other dictatorships, and his characters are imported terrorists thinly disguised in native American dress.

The legend is that the book was finished in six weeks. It may well have been. Written with the blunt I'm-telling-you manner of the political arena at its most vehement, it has the brusque emphasis of something shot from a gun. But with all its obvious faults, it is much to be preferred to the lamentable *Work of Art* and *Ann Vickers*, which preceded it.

In the late 1930's Lewis had the rather desperate misfortune to become stage-struck. He had always been on the verge of such a disaster. A certain facility as entertainer which had turned the limelight of private and public dinner parties stimulatingly upon him had made him yearn for grease paint at a moment when he had to think of toupees as well. Lewis wrote for the stage, acted upon the stage, directed and financed theatrical adventures. The novel called *Bethel Merriday* was the regrettable end result of all this passion.

◄§ Bethel Merriday was a pretty, good-natured child from Sladesbury, somewhere in New England. She wanted to be an actress and, after playing the lead in a college production of *A Doll's House*, went as an apprentice to one of those resort theaters called by the trade "the straw hats." She painted scenery, constructed "flats," ushered, and played small parts creditably. In classes she was scolded for overacting, but there was a vague conviction in amateur circles that she "had something."

After this experience in summer stock, Bethel's parents indulged her in a fling at New York. Presently she went as understudy to the star in a modern-dress production of *Romeo and Juliet*. The tour was badly handled by a gallant young amateur actor-manager and after a few months—mostly of one-night stands in the Middle West—the play closed. Bethel could have married the young actor-manager, but she preferred a tempestuous rebel who had been playing Mercutio. The two of them went back to New York and got jobs in a production called *Alas in Arcady*.

I am not, I think, unfair to Sinclair Lewis in this bald recital of the principal happenings of his novel. It is just as routine and commonplace as the outline makes it sound. Lewis cannot hope to justify his effort by pointing out that each year hundreds of Bethel Merridays follow exactly the course he has charted. So, each year, do hundreds of ingénues devote their days to running elevators up and down in bank buildings. The existence of either the actress or the elevator operator might be made interesting, but the dogged rehearsal of the events in the daily life of either is not in itself significant.

What Sinclair Lewis' novel lacks is any sort of point of view toward his characters or toward the theater. Despite the fact that he resorts to the old-fashioned device of chatting about Bethel behind her back, Lewis never succeeds in making her anything but a nattily turned out type. Worse still is his failure with Zed Wintergeist, who as a dashing innovator and a disarming egotist bears a superficial resemblance to Orson Welles. Lewis need not have bothered to explain that none of his characters was drawn from life, because life is so much more vivid. Upon Zed he has been unable to fix even one of the amusing, definitive eccentricities of mind which Mr. Welles has in embarrassing abundance.

Worst of all is the absence of any attitude toward the theater either as an art or as an industry. Lewis takes a few casual sideswipes at the monstrous way in which the young are exploited by the cynical in the theater; he is contemptuous about incompetence among dreary little actors who assume that by calling themselves artists they have acquired special privileges in the world; he dislikes the incompetence of managers even more. But it is all on the level of Times Square gossip. Nothing resembling a philosophic attitude toward the place of entertainment in our civilization is to be discerned in *Bethel Merriday*.

Our Nobel prize winner is fascinated by the trivia of the theater: by the way in which actors fling endearments at one another with languid indifference to any meaning; by the shady tricks which enable one mean-spirited player to steal a scene from another; by the endless shop-talk which goes on backstage; by the blend of affection and spite which gives the community life of the theater its peculiar tone.

But unless all this is revealed through the minds and hearts of vital people, it has no more interest for the intelligent non-expert than a book devoted to the private mores and jargon of bricklayers or morticians would have.

Sinclair Lewis is a brilliant conversationalist. He cannot cover four hundred pages without tossing off many of the same bright ideas that explode in his casual talk. He makes one laugh outright with such an unexpected bit of malice as is contained in the description of a worried young man who felt so guilty about not being a Communist that he had to go to a psychoanalyst. But in general Lewis' satiric method seems heavy-handed. It consists of giving people funny names, of prodding them into grotesque attitudes, of eavesdropping upon their worst banalities.

I think Mr. Lewis must have felt the hot breath of banality on his own neck quite constantly as he wrote this story. He has tried hard to escape from the routine pattern of the backstage novel. How? Why, when the understudy gets a chance to play the star's part she does not make an instantaneous hit; she does not save the day. That is the best Mr. Lewis has to offer in the way of brave innovation.

Bethel Merriday is not the work of distinction we have a right to expect from a Nobel prize winner. ৪৯

The theater is famous for its sluttish ingratitude. Nothing that Lewis did for the most glamorous but least reliable of the Muses added to his reputation; nor could he force the light of his literary prestige to give reflected glory to his inept efforts as a man of the theater.

Presently he surveyed this dismal chapter of his professional history and accepted the blighting judgment that he had perversely reduced himself to the standing of an amateur as an artist. His retort to those who imagined that on this level he would live out his days was to write *Cass Timberlane*, in which he managed to turn back the clock and return to the era of the 1920's, dragging his surprised but not wholly displeased public after him.

⊸§ Now this is a stimulating sight. After many years of seeming like a groggy old fighter, fumbling his way with a kind of bewildered ferocity through a struggle the basic rules of which he had forgotten, Sinclair Lewis has come back to his favorite arena, rejuvenated, confident, and full of superb swagger. His mind is clear, his style aggressive, and his technique, if not precisely lethal, is at least briskly punitive.

His new novel, *Cass Timberlane*, is much the best thing he has done since that moment in the 1920's when it seemed impossible for him to write anything that did not contain a buoyant, boyish, brassy sort of challenge. Indeed the book invokes the mood of the 20's and, without seeming either wistfully nostalgic or lamely old-fashioned, restores to life the temper of those times.

One reason why Sinclair Lewis has been able to make this retreat without dating himself is that he has caught up a universal theme. The relations of men and women will continue to be the subject of polite, and impolite, discussion as long as the two-party system in the domain of sex endures. There is a typical Sinclair Lewis flavor to the tone of the discussion in *Cass Timberlane*, and it is also a typical 1920 flavor. But it is a pungent and a lingering flavor, which one is delighted to roll under the tongue.

Sinclair Lewis believes that the American husband is desperately afraid of the American wife. Margot Asquith and the visiting lecturers from the Continent used to say that sort of thing and so did Mencken and Nathan. Unduly humble and apologetic, the American Adam has eaten of whatever fruit the American Eve has put before him. Sometimes these dishes have been sour and unappetizing affairs, but the uncomplaining husband has accepted them as the only meal he deserves.

Brazenly voting themselves special virtues of taste, American women have continued to be petty snobs; voting themselves special virtues as ethical beings, they have continued to be petty racketeers who take everything and give as little as possible.

This sounds rather as though Mr. Lewis were smiting about him hip and thigh in the undiscriminating manner of *Elmer Gantry* and *Gideon Planish*. But that, fortunately, is not true. He is a much more mellow satirist than he has been at any other moment of his career except when he wrote what is certainly his best book, *Arrowsmith*. He might easily have fallen into the error of making the wife in this case history a sort of all-American brat. But he has not done so.

Though his study of the marital relationship is candid, unsparing in its emphasis on the misery of intimacy, still an even-tempered, genuinely humorous concern for the rules of sportsmanship seems to preside over the discussion. Though he doesn't presume to be God, loving those whom he chasteneth, he does allow himself the attractive role of the good fellow who is, in retrospect, rueful about the bruises he has caused. . . .

I have the haunting impression that in this book Lewis meant to justify the spirit of the 1920's. Not only do I catch overtones of Mencken's voice, but I find also a kind of retrospective reverence paid to the memory of Sherwood Anderson.

Between the chapters dealing with the troubled relationship of Judge Timberlane and his young wife there are sketches of other partners of despair who torment each other in and out of marriage. I do not suspect Lewis of imitating *Winesburg, Ohio*; yet the surgical technique used in probing these wounds of the spirit shows many features of the typical Anderson operation. It seems to me that at least one of these sketches, that of Virga Vay and Allan Cedar, is a masterpiece of bitter tragi-comedy.

The last chapters of *Cass Timberlane* reveal the author caught in an insolvable dilemma, out of which he jauntily elbows his way by contriving a trick denouement as obvious as any in which a popular Broadway playwright ever indulged. But the novel as a whole is lively, witty, believable, and very often curiously touching. It catches up the threads of Sinclair Lewis' talent, which he has lately allowed to fly so loose. Published a quarter of a century late, it is nonetheless one of the best novels of the 1920's. ɞ

Sinclair Lewis is a striking manifestation of the spirit of our time, but it is difficult to accept him as a major figure of world literature. One suspects that at the time when he was chosen as the first American winner of the Nobel prize, extra-artistic considerations influenced the decision of the jury.

In 1929, when the jurors were met in momentous conference, all Europeans had a confused view of America, one distorted by both envy and fear. Uncle Sam, having not yet faced the stern discipline of depression, was still Europe's Uncle Shylock. The riches of America were so dazzling and its own bland assumption of supreme importance in world affairs was so infuriating that it comforted the European a little to believe the typical citizen of the blatant republic was trivial and thoughtless, debased by a shameless pursuit of shoddy values.

Europe, forced to accept the significance of America's role in the society of nations, was determined nonetheless to think ill of her in all possible ways. The novels of Sinclair Lewis confirmed the Old World in a soothing prejudice. It was only proper courtesy and proper strategy for the Old World to turn about and confirm the significance of the testimony of Sinclair Lewis.

The disturbing conviction that Lewis has had more than his due has made American reviewers peculiarly impatient with the crudity of his style, the superficiality of his thought, the distortions of his emphases. But it should be remembered, perhaps, that it was Lewis' task to reflect, not the steady faith of an age of greatness, but the confusion of a day in which doubts, fears, betrayals, and retrogressive impulses defined the social life. His protests, blatant and boyish as they have seemed always to be, came nearer to being pleas for honest values than his impatient critics—I among them—have been willing to admit.

Eugene O'Neill

IT WAS inevitable that Eugene O'Neill should make his way with the heavy tread of utter solemnity and unwavering resolution into the inner sanctum of the Swedish Academy at Stockholm. He was the first American dramatist to influence, or even very much to interest, European writers. Even before he produced his two inescapably noticeable plays, *Strange Interlude* and *Mourning Becomes Electra*, he had been a favorite playwright in the art theaters of London, Paris, Berlin, and Moscow. Some of the finest actresses of our time, including Greta Garbo and Ingrid Bergman, have played Anna Christie, and stage technicians everywhere have rushed forward happily to meet the challenges presented by the special dramatic devices of *The Great God Brown* and *Desire under the Elms*.

O'Neill, the product of a theatrical background, knew enough about commercial drama to utilize its resources and to reject its limitations. He hated and resented the romantic tradition of which his father, James O'Neill, had been the too glittering, too complacent, exponent. The playwright sought a harsher initiation into reality than was available to a member of his father's company and found what was, for him, a rewarding approach to wisdom in the forecastles of ships and the back rooms of Greenwich Village bars.

Writing in a time when the American producer with shameless servility undertook to titillate the tastes of those who said (*ad nauseam!*) that they "went to the theater to be amused," O'Neill had the stubborn, slightly sullen, hardihood to regard the drama as an art and himself as an artist. He seized upon bold themes; he invented an idiom for the theater that blended naturalism with a kind of folk poetry; he experimented with new devices in technique. His plays, produced at first on the windy wharf of Provincetown and later in the dusty, makeshift theaters of Greenwich Village, came at last to be recognized as the work of a unique figure in the American theater.

Reviewers who had been seeing the same pleasant inanities over and over again for years were grateful for the length, breadth, and psychological thickness of *Strange Interlude*. My review was the excited comment of a young lover of the theater who saw the drama being reborn before his eyes.

⏀ *Strange Interlude*, Eugene O'Neill's solemn giant among dramas, has stalked into the theater and worked a fine miracle by persuading theater-goers to listen very attentively for a very long time to a very serious discussion of what it is to be a human being living this human life.

It is chiefly by his intense earnestness that O'Neill manages to isolate himself from the great army of his fellow playwrights. The job he has undertaken is tremendously important to him.

He has looked at the human scene and discovered it to be confused, blurred, and hazy. He has watched human relations and found them to be tangles of cruelty and generosity, stupidity and comprehension, folly and fineness. He has wondered why and in his own way groped toward an interpretation, in dramatic terms, which may clarify these puzzles.

The theater of this day has very generally taken a humble and shabby view of its rights and duties. It has been content for the most part to tell, often with facility and grace and cleverness, artificially smooth little stories, baited with pleasantry and concession. Larger themes and longer records have been resigned to the novel. O'Neill has the individualist's contempt for limitations. He declines to admit that they exist for the theater. To tell anecdotes does not satisfy him, and he has set to work to make certain minor modifications of the technique of drama which permit him to tell on the stage the life story of a woman from youth to old age.

He has chosen to write of a neurotic woman. The advantage of making her so should be obvious. A highly sensitive person reflects more easily and more completely the influences that touch all life. Nina Leeds, therefore, is presented as one of those creatures of rare vitality who attracts life and through whom life reveals its essential quality. Such persons exist, and to the dramatist they are the world's most important, most revealing individuals.

O'Neill picks up Nina's story at the moment when she is floundering in resentful grief over the death of the fiancé whom she was not permitted to marry when he went to war. In flight from this feeling of defeat and frustration, she takes refuge in promiscuity. Emerging disgusted from this phase, she marries her harmless admirer so that she may have children and the good things of security. The convenience of the marriage collapses when she learns that a child by her husband would have an inheritance of mental disease. She chooses another father for her child, conscientiously believing that the relationship can be kept impersonal. But human need defeats eugenics, and in the following scenes the lovers struggle in an effort to hold both their own love and the loyalty they feel to the pathetic and entirely innocent husband. In the end, age and the slackening of all need for life and experience defeat their love, and they are left passive and even calm in the midst of their failure.

Merely to tell this story would not have satisfied O'Neill. He is driven by the desire to discover what is meaningful and significant in these events. What concerns him is to trace out the multiplicity of impulse behind the spoken word and behind the act. The interest of the story increases many times over as the mental war behind the puckered forehead of each character is revealed. In the relations of a wife to her husband pity half masters contempt, but contempt keeps the mind stirred into a tempest. In the relation of a father to his daughter, love is touched with selfishness and jealousy, while a thousand petty motives scratch their little pin pricks on the smooth surface of the emotion.

In order that he may uncover these scores of mental excursions and alarums, O'Neill has revived the old stage convention of the aside in which the character speaks his thought. Undoubtedly the aside enriches the vitality and interest of *Strange Interlude*. Sometimes these emotional parentheses are repetitious, stating what the understanding person has already grasped. Again they reflect the author's acceptance of a school of psychology which is already dated. They reveal the worst as well as the best of O'Neill's writing quality. Occasionally these passages are too purple, too obviously tricked out with verbal splendor. But for the most part they reflect the richness and beauty and poetry of which the intuitive mind is, in isolated flashes, capable. I would not want them eliminated or very much modified.

Strange Interlude is one of the few contributions to the living theater of today. Its importance is that it takes the trouble to be intelligent about emotions. It dares to make human life seem important in defiance of the facile, covert cynicism of so many dramatists. Robust and ambitious, it has pushed back the frontiers that have bounded the field of the drama. ટે≈

Enthusiasm began to be a little less ardent as one realized that though a dramatic revolution had taken place with the production of *Strange Interlude*, it had managed perversely to shelter counterrevolutionary tendencies within itself. O'Neill the innovator seemed in *Mourning Becomes Electra* to take a backward look at the satisfying qualities of the old ranting stage. The son of the star who had struck so picturesquely the attitudes of the Count of Monte Cristo was himself touched with the fever of romantic extravagance. Indeed, he was himself a melodramatist.

≈કૃ In the play which all the piping and sonorous voices of American criticism have joined in saluting as Eugene O'Neill's masterpiece, the playwright has borrowed his characters from the classic Greek drama; he has carried them across the centuries and across the world and set them down on the soil of New England. There in the period of the Civil War they live out once more their troubled, tragic story. They love one another with sullen, sulphurous fervor through fourteen acts; they kill each other out of motives in which righteousness and jealous rage are mingled; and in the end they destroy themselves completely.

Staggering under a burden of unholy impulses such as few people in drama have ever had to bear before, they go through the awful maneuvers of homicide, suicide, and thwarted lust. A mother kills the husband who would have separated her from her lover; a son and daughter kill the lover. Defeated and defenseless, the mother shoots herself. The son and daughter, bound together by the shared knowledge of the mischief they have done, draw apart from the world. Their intolerable intimacy finally drives the brother to suicide and

25

the sister to shut herself up in her house and live out a terrible destiny of endless mourning for those she has loved and destroyed.

This is the pattern on the surface. Below is a tangled undergrowth of dark desires. The imagination must deal at various times with the problem of a daughter in love first with her father, then with her mother's lover; with the problem of a son first in love with his mother, then with his sister. The play achieves a sort of unity through the fixity with which it glares at the abnormal.

It is quite improper to try to dictate to a dramatist what material he shall choose. It is even improper to ask him for meanings. He wishes only to represent a kind of life, a development of human character. It is quite clear what O'Neill wished to do in this play. He wanted to show fate brooding horribly over the house of the Mannons, putting into its members a force that drove them to evil beyond their own power to resist. We need not look beyond this to discover the cause of his complete failure.

Tragedy on the heroic scale should deal with people of heroic proportion. If man is to do battle with fate, he should be touched with magnificence in order to make the conflict interesting. Though his defeat may be a foregone conclusion, at least the struggle should be superb. O'Neill has not succeeded in creating stage figures of splendid size. They are petty, venomous, querulous, luckless weaklings. They babble cliché-ridden rhetoric at one another. Death releases each from a graceless, emotionally shabby existence. The observer is neither moved nor terrified. As one by one the figures of the drama drop away, the only necessary comment seems to be that maybe it's all for the best.

The fault is O'Neill's own. He does not even persuade me that it is fate that hovered in the background of the play. The figure shadowing the action is the playwright's own. He maneuvers, he manipulates, always a little slavishly under the direction of Dr. Freud. The writing has a sort of surly, growling quality, unwarmed by compassion, unlighted by a single moment of radiant perception.

One scene of bald, unabashed melodrama (let us define it as the poison-on-the-dead-man's-chest episode) perilously approaches the grotesque. Two comic interludes are absurdly inept. Only in the end does O'Neill approach splendor. That is in the final scene when the daughter, at last aware of how completely she is infected with her own poison, puts up the shutters, closes the door on life, and disappears to live with death.

Mourning Becomes Electra is not in any way to be compared with *Strange Interlude*. The earlier play had many fine qualities. It pushed back the limitations of the stage. It was a sort of challenge to the modern theater to occupy itself with serious themes. But I am afraid we too eagerly saluted O'Neill as a giant. He is a man of courage and intense seriousness who fumbles awkwardly with his bold concepts. ❧

After writing *Mourning Becomes Electra* O'Neill forsook, temporarily at least, his close scrutiny of the genetics of giantism. He wrote a series of plays which confined themselves to the "two hours' traffic of the stage." They proved to be little plays in a sense that no dramatist ever means his work to be. *Dynamo* whirred noisily but its labor failed to bring forth even a mouse of meaning. *Ah, Wilderness!* was an agreeable but wholly undistinguished study of adolescence; it showed Eugene O'Neill edging wistfully into the preserves of Booth Tarkington and making less than a fine art of poaching. *Days Without End* was the most woeful disappointment of all. Its theme was hazy; the characters were unrealized; the technique suggested a faltering beginner rather than a man of wide experience in the theater.

It is by his big plays that O'Neill will be judged in the end, for it is they that contain what he has had to offer of boldness and originality. And the best perhaps is yet to be. As these lines are written, preparations are being made to stage a new play, *The Iceman Cometh*, which after many years of silence O'Neill has finally released. Certain privileged critics who have seen the work in manuscript consider it to be a major contribution to the poetic, as well as to the dramatic, tradition of American letters. It is, these authorities believe, a play that dwarfs O'Neill's own *Strange Interlude* as impressively as *Strange Interlude* seemed in the season when it was first produced to dwarf all other efforts of the day.

The bigness of O'Neill has fascinated the world of the theater. He looms on our horizon like a great natural phenomenon, as curious and colorful and dramatic as the Bad Lands or the Grand Canyon. But perhaps his bigness contains little in the way of positive value. He has not nagged at our minds with a thousand waspish hints of doubt about our virtue and even our sanity, as has Bernard Shaw. He has not released in drama the haunting, disturbing fragrance of a strange philosophy, as did Pirandello.

It is bigness chiefly that distinguishes him from many another intelligent modern writer who has taken up the psychological theme. O'Neill has turned it into melodrama. The giant he sends shuffling across the stage is often inept and clumsy. The playwright lacks the critical faculty that should have saved a man of his talent from making the worst of his blunders. The same humorless failure of perception has kept him from being aware that, after hating his actor father for being an exhibitionistic romantic, he himself has become an exhibitionistic romantic. But his figure nonetheless bulks large in the writing history of our time.

Pearl Buck

PEARL BUCK is one of the literary phenomena of our age. Today she occupies a position a little like that of George Eliot in relation to the circle of intellectuals she dominates. Not only has she an art and a salon at her disposal for the promulgation of her ideas; she has also a publishing house the chief purpose of which, at present, is to provide a channel for the flow of ideas in which she believes. With her husband, Richard Walsh, Miss Buck collaborates closely on the choice of manuscripts to be sponsored by the firm of which Mr. Walsh is president.

The work to which Miss Buck has devoted the decade and a half of her literary career is that of providing in the illuminated center of her own intelligence a meeting place for East and West.

Born to parents who were missionaries in China, she lived much of her childhood in the East and became herself a teacher in a succession of educational institutions at Nanking. When the literary impulse took possession of her vigorous intelligence, Miss Buck inevitably became an interpreter of Chinese culture. With resolution and insight a Western mind undertook to dramatize the quality of Eastern life, not from the point of view of an outsider glancing roguishly and a little skittishly in upon the mysterious and the quaint, but from the point of view of the Chinese themselves, firmly established on the inside of a solid way of life.

This has been done before with varying degrees of success by other travelers. But the blessing of destiny seemed to be upon Miss Buck's undertaking. For she became the interpreter of China at the moment when that vast land began to emerge out of the half sleep in which its leaders and exploiters had encouraged it so long to lie. She was present at the very instant when China came fully alive as a modern state. It was as though Miss Buck had become an energetic and idealistic American governess to the whole Chinese people just when they needed to be taken by the hand and led toward the future.

When *The Good Earth* appeared in 1931, the average American knew no more of China than he could glean from a Burton Holmes travelogue or from the lurid corruptions of fictitious thrillers.

◄§ The Occidental world has curious ideas about the Oriental. We don't really believe, for example, that China is populated by men and women. It is a nightmare place inhabited by the slithering, sinister, yellow-fingered creatures of the bad movies and plays we have seen.

The stage Chinaman is a completely stereotyped figure with his nasal chirpings, his robes embroidered with dragons, his incense, and his penchant for dying very elaborately of poison, drunk from a golden goblet. Say *China* and the average, untraveled American thinks of childish melodrama and of very little else.

But at last we are unburdened of that misunderstanding. Pearl Buck has written a novel called *The Good Earth*, and in it for the first time all the nonsense and sentimentality and air of perfumed mystery has dropped away from a group of Chinese characters. They move through the events of a story imagined with amazing power and vigor, never once losing their complete actuality.

Here is the Chinaman living on his soil; taking his food from it and loving it; marrying; rearing sons and daughters; prospering for a while; falling victim to the famine; wandering as a beggar with his wife and children; profiting by one of those sudden changes of the fortune which the revolutions have made possible; returning to his land; making it yield richly; becoming the important man of the village; buying the home of the decadent aristocrat whom in his youth he has admired and feared; adopting the ways of a decadent aristocrat himself; seeing his sons stray from the land and involve themselves in the pleasures and the quarrels of the mighty; coming at last to the end of his days with the demoralizing fear that his children will uproot themselves from the soil and perish as he has seen the other great family perish and go down into oblivion.

This is an outline that anyone can understand and appreciate. You need no codebook or glossary to overcome any feeling of unfamiliarity. The emotions of these people are the simple ones that all men and women share; their needs are the fundamental needs that all human beings have felt.

One lives intimately with these men and women. They are not sentimentalized or enveloped by misty glamour. They are not wholly admirable, but they are wholly believable and entirely appealing.

A pathetic emotional situation gives a solid basis to the bulk of the story. When the book begins, a young peasant farmer is about to take as his wife the slave girl his father has chosen for him from the great household of the village. She is not beautiful, but she serves. Her feet have not been bound because she has been sold into slavery too young, but lacking that essential of loveliness, she is better able to work with her husband in the fields, to interrupt her service only for a few hours at a time to bear her children. She is inarticulate but cunning, and enormously useful. In a strange way these two are devoted to each other.

The tragedy comes when the husband has grown wealthy. It is a common story, but one that is made new by the setting and tremendously touching by the treatment. The wife with her great feet becomes repulsive and is replaced in her husband's favor by a delicate, delicious creature. The man behaves badly, flouts his old loyalty in ruthless, brutal ways. He hates himself for it and continues to behave badly. Even when the first wife dies he cannot love her.

Miss Buck knows and understands these people extremely well, and all her effort is directed, as an artist's should be, toward communicating her knowledge. She is never for an instant distracted by the desire to shine in such bits of tropical writing as have blossomed luxuriously on the pages of nearly everyone who has previously written about the East.

It is even likely that as one turns the pages of *The Good*

Earth the Chinese background will be forgotten. Though the merely local conditions and customs do importantly affect the story, it is essentially one that deals with fundamental universal problems. ¿♥

When, only seven years after her first distinguished success, Miss Buck was awarded the Nobel prize, there were many who complained at what seemed to be a premature elevation to the company of our modern Olympus. While Dreiser, Robert Frost, and Willa Cather still toiled up the mountainside, it was startling that a writer who had been before the public for less than a decade should have been whisked into immortality. I undertook to explain the ways of the Swedish demigods to American readers.

✍§ Since it is too late to instruct the members of the Nobel prize jury in their duty, we may as well try to conquer our irresponsible American impulse to kill the umpire and reverse his decision. There are reasons why Pearl Buck appealed to the collective imagination of the Nobel jury, and they should be carefully examined.

Probably the most important is that Miss Buck is by way of being an internationalist. She went from her own country into the East to become the interpreter of China's character and culture before all the Western world. The great essential merit of *The Good Earth* was that it stripped away that Oriental mask which we Westerners have somehow managed to admire ourselves for finding inscrutable. Miss Buck insisted upon our seeing that a Chinaman is not, in his own estimation, a yellow menace or a clown speaking gibberish in a ridiculous falsetto. Rather, he is a man who loves, fears, and hopes as we do, who needs to nourish his senses, his body, and his mind in the same ways that Westerners have imagined to be their exclusive privilege.

As a woman who went out from her own country, in the role of missionary, to carry her own philosophy to a foreign people and who had insight and sympathy and wit enough to be charmed and moved by the philosophy she found in that foreign land, Miss Buck naturally would appeal to a jury of men whose commission it is to recognize the best that the human brain in countries other than their own has produced. When Miss Buck translated the Chinese classic *All Men Are Brothers*, she was unconsciously wooing recognition of the kind she has just had. For a creative artist to take time away from his own absorbing labors to make that kind of gesture of international good will is in itself a remarkable demonstration of a superior quality of conscientiousness.

Miss Buck has demonstrated the irrepressible vigor of her creative impulse by producing sometimes one, sometimes two, very solid pieces of work a year. She rounded out her story of modern China with *Sons* and *A House Divided*, completing the significant family record begun in *The Good Earth*. If the later books seemed less distinguished than the one on which Miss Buck's reputation was based, it certainly could not be denied that the trilogy considered as a unit gave a detailed picture of modern China, one on which informed people are still drawing to fill out their understanding of the present crisis in the East.

A curious and highly successful experiment was the telling of her mother's story in *The Exile*, letting her father appear in the fictionized biography as a minor character, and then turning about to tell her father's story in *Fighting Angel*. These companion pieces offer a complete and touching picture of a transplanted American family.

Of the other volumes with a Chinese background—*The First Wife, House of Earth*, and *The Mother*—the last is perhaps the most significant in its direct, simple, and unsentimental interpretation of a universal theme. I never have heard it said by even the sternest scholar that Miss Buck "Europeanizes" her Oriental studies in sentiment. That in itself is a significant comment on her integrity, both as observer and as artist.

33

The Nobel prize committee has saluted a comparatively young artist with the strength in her still to change and grow. It was a daring thing to do and one likes it for its very recklessness. ৶৯

In 1942, in the novel *Dragon Seed*, Pearl Buck returned, wisely I thought, to the special literary task that had given her distinction. Her stories of Americans in an American setting, though they were lacking in neither dignity nor interest, could have been written just as well by a dozen other shrewd and critical observers, but in her fine interpretive stories of China, Miss Buck put on uniquity. In *Dragon Seed* she gave Americans a picture of China being reborn in the midst of the turmoil of war, of the Chinese people drawing upon the enduring patience of their centuries of quiet persistence to build a wall of resistance against the enemy.

The Second World War ended with the complete justification of those who held stubbornly to their hopes for the evolution of a modern East. In a half century China has ceased to be a strange souvenir of the culture of the ancient world, showing its typical mixture of squalid primitivism and perfumed decadence; she has become a vital and important part of the twentieth-century world. Those of us who passed our student days, when the century was in its teens, thinking of China as a vast, vague region lying somewhere beyond the horizon, well outside the realm of probability, have emerged from the experience of the war finding it not in the least remarkable that China should be numbered among the four great powers of the world.

A full share of the credit for that change of mood on the part of the Western world must go to Pearl Buck. Her series of books helped to change our minds, moving them in the direction of sanity, compassion, and understanding.

If the tone of Miss Buck's writing has changed too, if it has tended to take on oracular overtones, this is almost inevitable with a talent that has proved to be so conspicuously useful in the service of a great cause. World history may have collaborated with Miss Buck's ambitions, but Miss Buck's ambitions have never wavered from the stanch support of history's briskly accelerated march toward ideals of justice and equality.

It should be noted, too, that as Miss Buck has passed into the temple to anoint herself as a seeress, she has not failed to take the artist along. Her style, showing the powerful influence of the stately rhythms of the King James version of the Bible, upon which she was reared in the home of her missionary parents, is still strong and flexible. Her writing career has demonstrated that a storyteller can lend his talent to the great issues of the day and still preserve a fastidious concern for the interests of art, restoring to propaganda the dignity of a passionate moral concern with ideas and profound human values.

Nothing is clearer about the history of writing in our time than that the career of Pearl Buck has had the dignity, the esthetic integrity, and the significance we look for in the record of a winner of the Nobel prize.

Four Rich Uncles

In one of her engaging essays, characterized, as so much of her work has been, by a combination of impudence and insight, Rebecca West referred to "the four uncles" of contemporary English letters: Bennett, Galsworthy, Wells, and Shaw. Upon everyone of the generation that came to maturity at the close of the First World War these conspicuous representatives of the culture of our time exercised a kind of familial influence. Whether or not one greatly admired them, they were ubiquitously present in the consciousness of all who took the art of letters seriously. One's mother and one's aunt spoke of them with a blend of intimacy and awe that is reserved for the member of the family who has made good in a spectacular and dramatic fashion. There might even be a slight tincture of disapproval to spice the reverence, and yet Uncle Enoch, Uncle John, Uncle Herbert, and Uncle George occupied positions that made them immune to censure. Though their private morals left something to be desired, their talents lifted them above any criticism that even the most sharply arched eyebrow could imply.

A social world that still suffered slightly from a guilt complex of Victorian origin overlooked the marital irregularities of the first three uncles and the verbal audacities of the fourth to give them everything that writing men could hope to gain. The uncles had prestige, security, money, and (all but the severely monogamous Shaw) a succession of glamorous mates. Two of them were awarded the Nobel prize and one might have had a knighthood if he had cared to accept it. Nothing in the recent history of letters has succeeded like their record of success.

Today their influence is still great. Though two of the four have been dead for many years, their names are mentioned with an instinctual lowering of the voice, as though elevation to the sainthood might presently be expected. Upon readers of books, though not upon writers of them, they exercise an uninterrupted fascination, making their admirers faintly dissatisfied with all that has happened since the time of the uncles' greatness. The enduring interest of their work is therefore worth re-examining.

Arnold Bennett

ENOCH ARNOLD BENNETT was the first to quit the scene. Twenty years ago the bulk of his important work was already behind him—all the novels of the Four Towns, including that giant among them, *The Old Wives' Tale.* Yet young men in college and just out of it were reading his books avidly, unconsciously aware that he, of all the uncles, had the most to teach them about the technique of writing.

He himself had learned his craft slowly. An *arriviste* determined to get on in the world that attracted him, Bennett had served as editor of a magazine for women, and while he put commas in the proper places to lend a moment's readability to articles on homemaking, he studied the fundamentals of writing. His logical mind sought to identify the qualities that must be present in a satisfying work of art. Though his own essentially shallow temperament had little room for these large and often untidy gifts of heart and mind, he learned to recognize them, and to distill their essence into his work by a science of his own. Assuming virtues that he lacked and yet had the wit to admire, he became a self-made artist.

Even in his late years, given over chiefly to the manufacture of skillful, meretricious stories of the rich, prominent, and powerful, he occasionally indulged himself in the production of a beautiful and moving novel. *Riceyman Steps* was such a book. In it Bennett explored the sensibilities of four utterly unimportant people with a compassion and insight that would seem to be quite beyond the scope of the Bennett who wrote the carelessly flung together potboilers.

Arnold Bennett deliberately achieved a split personality which allowed the vulgar, time-serving, success-loving self to function most of the time on its comfortable level and permitted the artist occasionally to climb to a peak of discernment and distinction.

As a youthful admirer of Bennett's *The Old Wives' Tale* and *Riceyman Steps*, I think I felt a shock of delight almost like that associated with one's first highball when I discovered in his posthumously published journal the startling mixture of his traits. I wrote my review of it in the mild exhilaration of disillusionment which the young, contrary to general opinion, accept so happily.

✇§ Arnold Bennett once wrote an amusing potboiler called, in this country, *Denry the Audacious*. It was, in a sense, a self-portrait. For Denry got on tremendously and Arnold Bennett got on tremendously. They shared an ideal, and they shared also an exuberant delight in the satisfying of it.

The Journal of Arnold Bennett, just published in a complete version of a thousand pages, paints another portrait, one of careful detail. But it is substantially the same. The getting on is the thing that Bennett unconsciously stresses.

He is still a sub-editor of the magazine *Woman* when the daybook starts in 1896. He is writing his first novel and meeting immediately with a sort of success. But it is not what he means to have. What he wants is the great world of rich Bohemians. He loves the gossip about their doings long before he has been invited to share in them. Gardner, his editor-in-chief, brings him the chitchat of Charles Wyndham and Beerbohm-Tree, and Bennett admiringly sets it down. He is outside looking in, but he is not envious because he intends to be on the inside eventually and already his loyalty is to this group.

And in the end he is firmly entrenched among the people he has always wanted to know. He has three or four engagements a day with them. Elinor Wylie comes to luncheon and Bennett dines with the Prince of Wales. People actually make a shrine of his home and rap humbly on his door. The village boy, with no background worth mentioning, has arrived. He knows everyone and goes everywhere. That is as it should be. It is, as Max Beerbohm once suggested, all according to the original Bennett plan.

I do not exaggerate this obsession with the objective evidence of success. One of the most revealing passages is that in which he comments upon the funeral of Jane Wells, the wife of H. G. Wells. Bennett writes of it as though it were merely a public function, and the public reaction is what interests him. "Number of A-1 people very small; which shows how Wells kept out of the 'great world' and how the great world is not particularly interested in Wells." There is no word of affection for a lost friend, no sympathy for her husband. Bennett is interested, so to speak, in the gate receipts.

His reaction to the death of Hardy is almost hilariously inept. He goes to the funeral in the Abbey. "Music good. South transept not full. In the morning I had written a letter to the Daily Express animadverting upon the distribution of tickets for this affair." It might have been a prize fight for all the show of sensibility it elicits from Bennett.

It is not in the least that he is stupid or unaware. In his literary notes, of which the *Journal* is full, he comments frequently upon the literary virtue of compassion. He could employ it very artfully indeed, as he did in the treatment of Elsie in *Riceyman Steps*. But apparently it was a matter of technique with him. His private personality was very different from his personality as a writer and distinctly inferior to it. I know of no other instance so brilliant of the man's dwindling in comparison with the best of his work.

The elderly tea-taster of the last years is far from being un-

attractive. Indeed, he is continuously amusing as he dashes
with the feverish enthusiasm of a worldly Peter Pan from
first-night to late party; from weekend excursion to a yachting
trip. He is pleased with his popularity, with his literary pro-
ductiveness, with the fact that he has become a father in his
late years. All these facts testify to his importance. He gets
almost as much gratification out of a house suit from Sulka's
as he does from the precocity of his small daughter. Both pos-
sessions redound to his credit and he innocently, happily, records his satisfaction in them. . . .

The low emotional vibration of Bennett's life was in some
ways, of course, an advantage. He never made himself absurd.
When it became necessary to separate from his French wife,
Marguerite, he could do it with dignity and keep his poise
and friendliness even when she wrote a tasteless little book
about him. His decent, generous relationship with his second,
common-law wife (the mother of his child), whom he could
not marry because Marguerite refused him a divorce, is also
dignified and orderly.

But it is strange to find him so frivolous, so completely
taken up with trivialities: the celebrity of the moment, the
restaurant of the moment, the fad of the moment. I'm sure
no clever person ever managed to make a diary so utterly
superficial.

How could this strutting, busy, unmeditative man write
two books as fine as *The Old Wives' Tale* and *Riceyman
Steps*? Probably it is simply the old phenomenon of the great
craftsman's getting above himself, doing work better than he
is really capable of doing. ॐ

John Galsworthy

JOHN GALSWORTHY has been dead twelve years. In the interval
that separates him from us the world has undergone a startlingly dramatic change, and no part of it has changed more

than Galsworthy's England. Indeed a statue of that mild, conscientious, cultivated, but completely negative man might well
be set up—say in Hyde Park—as a monument to the England
that is also dead.

The theme of all Galsworthy's novels and plays was the
right of the ruling class to dominate the lives of lesser folk.
The pious contention that the members of this group are
under a moral obligation to do so is examined with a certain
skittish skepticism. But timorous good breeding was always
the trademark of Galsworthy's work and in the gentle blur of
concession which brought each of his works to an end, though
never to anything so vulgar as a conclusion, the ruling class
was left ruling. In his play *The Skin Game* he made one of his
well-born characters remark at a moment when she found herself involved in a sordid and trying quarrel with a pushing
"new man," "We know we are the best people." Galsworthy
knew it too, and his popularity was based on the sly flattery
that the very weakness of his pretended doubts offered to the
prejudices of the comfortable and secure.

In an English world that dared to vote Winston Churchill
out of office at a moment when his dynamic dramatization of
the attractions of the ruling class might have been thought
to be unchallengeable, Galsworthy's philosophy and his work
would be sadly anachronistic. He was the embodiment of the
inept, uncertain temporizing that helped to bring on the
Second World War. Churchill would have been his master,
but Chamberlain would have been his intellectual brother.
For Galsworthy understood the formula of appeasement long
before it was introduced into diplomacy.

When Galsworthy was awarded the Nobel prize, I permitted
myself the satisfaction, so treasured by all democrats, of reviewing the decision of the jury with impatient distaste.

◄§ There must always be the small dissenting voice and I
have the temerity to raise it. The choice of Galsworthy for

the Nobel prize seems to me almost incredibly inept. If he had remained where he belongs, in the position of a facile second-rater, one's objection to him would not be in the least bitter. For he has a certain mannerliness in the ordering of small events that puts him above the majority of second-raters. But when he is initiated into the company of giants, his pettiness and triviality become brilliantly apparent. He is deficient in creative imagination. His mind is restless and superficial. As an observer he is always intent upon the obvious and the theatrical. His characters are insufficiently individualized or not individualized at all. He has even offered the apology for Irene in *The Forsyte Saga* that she was not intended to be real but only a "symbol of beauty." He neglects, however, to explain what business a symbol of beauty has got wandering ubiquitously through the pages of a realistic novel. Finally, his moral issues are always thin and formal like those that parade through the gossip of old wives. He is the most anemic of creative artists. . . .

What is happening to literature if Galsworthy is the only candidate the Nobel committee could agree upon? Or what is happening to the Nobel committee? ❧

I was still in the same unregenerate state of mind when Galsworthy died, and in my newspaper column appeared an irreverent obituary.

❧ Few men die at precisely the right moment. Galsworthy did. He had reached the peak of his popularity as a novelist. He had just been awarded the Nobel prize for literature. Nothing could have been added unto him. There was more of subtle drama in his exit than in anything else he did in the whole of his life.

He did not have to see his reputation decline. That it will decline I have no doubt. Galsworthy was so overrated in his own time that he is certain to be underrated afterward. His last trilogy, in which the novels called *Maid in Waiting*, *Flowering Wilderness*, and *Over the River* are grouped under his own title, *End of the Chapter*, reveals more clearly than ever before his weakness for which a few critics have refused to be reconciled to him and for which many will reproach him in the future.

The difficulty is chiefly this: For all his seriousness, for all his bright-eyed curiosity, the man was essentially trivial. His imagination was not robust enough to lay hold firmly on either a social crisis or a character. In none of the novels is there a vigorous resolution of any problem. Galsworthy tried hard to give this fault the look of a virtue. He eluded conclusions with the air of one being extremely judicial. Indeed, I think the reason for so many trilogies was that he was always a little timorously in flight from the necessity of coming to any conclusion whatsoever. It was easier for him, an expert craftsman, to write another book and another than to bring the work to any brisk and satisfying climax.

Of all his characters only one, Soames Forsyte, had real strength. The rest are either picturesque eccentrics, caricaturing the upper classes as obviously as Dickens did the lower, or emaciated, bloodless embodiments of the British virtues.

The whole design is as vague as these figures. Restless movement in Galsworthy's novels gives a false impression of drama. The truth is that each is fundamentally undramatic, because the novelist represents the conflict between man and institutions not as a struggle but as a pesky little war of attrition. We do not see a hero beaten down by society. We see merely a muddle-headed society and a nice, muddle-headed British chap coming to a draw.

There is still another fault. All his moral issues are forced and false. They seem to represent not so much "the troubles of our proud and angry dust" as the stubborn inflexibility of the British code trying desperately to keep dead issues alive. In each of the novels of this last trilogy Galsworthy presents an abstract problem of conduct. The three of them produce in me nothing but the successive stages of bewilderment, confusion, and indigation.

In *Maid in Waiting* we are asked to concentrate on the plight of a young Englishman who as leader of an expedition in South America has ordered a native flogged for maltreating horses. Later the natives mutiny against his authority and the same Indian is shot dead by the enterprising Hubert. He faces an investigation in England and society heatedly chooses up sides. In my myopic way I can see only one side. My view of Hubert is that he represents a peculiarly abominable type of bullying exploiter with a greater respect for horses than for men. But Galsworthy, humanitarian though he was, feels obliged to inject adrenalin into the dead issue of the white man's supremacy. His right to shoot natives must not be challenged.

In *Flowering Wilderness* we have the pleasing spectacle of a whole society baiting a sensible man for saving his neck. And in the last book, *Over the River*, the problem is this: Should an English gentlewoman leave the husband whom she has discovered to be a sadist? Again there is the edifying picture of a whole society conniving stupidly at the torment of an entirely innocent woman. This is perhaps the most lifeless of all Mr. Galsworthy's final crop of issues. Nevertheless his autopsy is thorough and detailed.

Perhaps in objecting to the validity of the Galsworthy view of human obligations, I expose myself as slack and decadent. But in his novels I see him constantly as the polite, regretful apologist for cruelty, reaction, and inertia. ❧

H. G. Wells

HERBERT GEORGE WELLS is far the most dynamic of all this familial group. The very antithesis of Bennett in his breadth of view, the antithesis equally of Galsworthy in his belligerent unwillingness to make any concession, Wells has used his talent as a writer to chasten society for its intellectual slackness, its flaccidity of will. Harassed in these latter days not merely by the years but by incurable physical disability, Wells has valiantly rejected the right to rest after his strenuous labors; he has gone on rebuking, ridiculing, and trying to reform us out of the stubborn childishness of our social philosophy.

His reforms, of course, have been always in the direction of liberalism. The themes have been the freeing of marriage from the rigidities of tribal custom; the freeing of education from its bondage to traditional trivialities, with the authority of modern science denied and derided; the freeing of the world spirit from its subservience to the meanness of a narrow nationalism and to the savagery of war.

Today Wells has lost the popular audience that once was his, not because what he has to say is out of date or even because his accent has the quaintness of another day, but simply because the larger audience has always regarded writers as entertainers and shamelessly confesses in its choices to a preference for novelty over any other quality.

But the position of Wells in the history of writing in our time is unshakable. He anticipated so much about the developing pattern of society that the commonalty of humankind has still to catch up with him.

A typical method with Wells has been to indicate, in fantasies of epic scope and superb violence, the direction in which human folly has been steering our planet. The fundamental purpose of these adventure tales has been to show us the beautiful utopian orderliness we might achieve if only we could bring ourselves to adopt sound Wellsian principles. At the age of sixty-seven, Uncle Herbert wrote the boldest tale of all. *The Shape of Things to Come* was a sort of Outline of the Future, a heroic fantasy, written as propaganda for heaven on earth, yet full of humor and sprightliness.

45

☞ Every time H. G. Wells publishes a book I think, "Now he's done it. The whole story of human folly has been reconstructed in his mind. There is nothing left to pigeonhole. It will be the end. He'll die of boredom."

But I am going to stop worrying about Mr. Wells. While he lives he will not be through exploring the devious passages of human life. And he will die expounding, exhorting. I should not be surprised if he were never to die at all, but simply be carried off one day in a cloud of ideas.

His ideas in his new book, *The Shape of Things to Come*, are, however, entirely concrete. He has imagined the world society of tomorrow in which there will be no individual nations, no profit economy; in which we shall all speak the same language (it will be English; isn't that convenient?); in which every man will live in the climate suitable to his physique and do the work suitable to his talents; in which all fundamental needs will be taken care of automatically; in which all labor will be beautiful and exciting. Do not despair, saying that these things will not come to pass in your time. Wells promises that the new order will be well under way by 1978, and he has graciously permitted all of us 105 years of life.

Many utopias, including one engineered by Bertrand Russell, have had much the same outline. Many of them, like Wells's, derive their authority from the will of the people, elaborately re-educated along scientific lines. But this book is unlike these others in that it undertakes to bridge the gap between then and now. Wells does not leap into a comfortable place in the next century and secure himself from challenge by becoming immersed in theory. Instead he patiently and with a great air of plausibility makes his way through all the years that lie immediately ahead. He imagines a succession of catastrophes which demoralize the world so completely that all links with the present system are broken. There is first the Sino-Japanese war, then a flurry of conflict between Japan and the United States, then a new European imbroglio begin-

ning with a contest over the Polish Corridor and finally involving the whole continent. None of these struggles has a
decisive conclusion. The contestants are simply worn out by
their own venom; after years of fighting, ennui triumphs over
malice.

Like a righteous Jehovah, Wells then sends a great pesti-
lence to the earth which all but wipes out our existing civilization. And so it comes about that the world in "the famished
1950's" is a desert once more. There is a steady progress backward, through provincialism, toward savagery. Wells has a
great deal of fun in this passage. He who has made so many
worlds for once plays the role of world destroyer and finds the
relaxation diverting.

All this is, of course, comparatively easy. But then he must
progress to the constructive phase. His resourcefulness never
wavers. With the world in ruins he proceeds to reshape it
nearer to his heart's desire. Renascence and regeneration come
about through the Air Dictatorship, which, having destroyed
the old grossnesses of attitude and bred into man a love of
equality to replace the old acquisitive and greedy passions,
abdicates and leaves the world to run itself according to the
noble pattern of philosophic anarchy.

The Shape of Things to Come inevitably suggests comparison with Bernard Shaw's *Back to Methuselah*, a cycle of plays
that attempted to cover much the same speculative ground.
Wells's book is more detailed. He has more space at his disposal. But it is also much richer imaginatively. And in the
final passage the way of life foretold really attracts the mind,
whereas that of Shaw repelled it. Wells has offered the first
tolerable utopia.

There is something completely irresistible about the strenu-
osity of Wells. So terrific is his mental abundance that he
invents a dozen imaginary scholars and under these several
pseudonyms offers theories about every aspect of human conduct. Nothing bores him; about nothing is he incurious. If a

terrier puppy were suddenly to become ennobled intellectually and the world of abstractions were suddenly opened up to him, he would act very much as Wells does.

To those who have accused him of being a superficial thinker he makes a pointed retort in his new book. Of H. G. Wells, the imaginary scholar Dr. Raven says in *The Shape of Things to Come:*

"You have defects that are almost gifts: a rapid but inexact memory for particulars, a quick grasp of proportions, and no patience with detail. You hurry on to wholes. . . . You get there. . . . You are a stripper, a damned impatient stripper. . . . It is really extraordinarily refreshing to spend . . . hours, stripping events in your company."

Wherein Mr. Wells writes a scented love letter to himself. Yet there is a something in his boast. He does get there, and it is fun to be a passenger on the trip. ‌ঌ

Few men could be trusted to conduct their own post-mortems. They would be sure to suppress the evidence of distressing or untidy degenerative diseases and turn in the report that death had been due to the breaking of a great and noble heart.

Wells, having been the world's leading disciple of candor all his days, was under a special obligation to be honest in his autobiography. He knew that his active life was over, that the rest would be mere review and summing up. It could not possibly be said of him that in the end he eluded his duty to tell the truth about his dismal beginnings, his perfervid middle years, and his scarcely less strenuous later ones. His *Experiment in Autobiography* is surely one of literature's great achievements of its kind.

ঌ All Mr. Wells's experiments have been on the great scale. He has created worlds, scrapped them, and made new ones with the creative enthusiasm of a very modern god with a liberal education. It was to be expected, then, that when he set about re-creating the world in which he himself has lived, the undertaking would be fast and bold. In his autobiography Mr. Wells has filled 707 large pages with "discussions and conclusions." They are the 707 pages of his tremendous literary output that interest me most.

No autobiography could fail to be profoundly engrossing if it were honest. Very few are. But this one is thoroughly honest, and if you insist on being shocked, shockingly honest. To me it seems a book of abounding good will. Life has treated H. G. Wells extremely well on the whole. He has been permitted to work at what he likes best to do. His work has been enormously profitable and it has also been admired. He has no personal grievances. There are no petty resentments to be exposed, no embarrassing rationalizations to cover lapses or failures. About the lapses he is heartily unregenerate, and all the failures are so long since past that they contain no longer any hint of bitterness. Patiently, with that scientific curiosity that has always characterized his methods, Mr. Wells reconstructs himself, and it is a very mellow, intelligent, companionable person that emerges.

His mellowness is not in the least concessive. He is not the sort of elderly man who, weary of battles and issues, decides that the world as it exists is a sweet and comfortable place. Wells is out of sympathy with his time in many important particulars. But his discussion of his dissatisfaction is all on the academic plane. He does not look forward to an immediate future when there will be no more clashes. His optimism takes the form of a belief in the new generation that is rising to take over the battle for human justice. The minds of the youthful leaders, he thinks, will be better trained and better disciplined. He seems quite ready to make over the work to his successors. Unlike most legators, he is not alarmed.

Bernard Shaw once said that no man could tell the truth about marriage unless he hated his wife. Wells seems to deny that. He had a first and a second wife, neither of whom he hated, but concerning his relations with whom he is astonishingly frank. The happy result of his forthrightness is that one has a real admiration for both women and an affectionate understanding of the man. The first marriage ended in divorce because it seemed to Wells that he must have a larger intellectual life than the first wife promised to give him. Yet he saw her frequently after they were separated and in his affluent later years took pride in providing for her comfort. She was, he says, his primary fixation.

With the second wife he had a long and agreeable companionship. The contract was unconventional and the indulgences it included will shock the stricter moralists. It seems to have satisfied the partners, however, which should be enough. That it was agreeable no one can doubt after reading the letters Wells wrote to his wife. They are full of private jokes and silliness of the sort that testifies, more eloquently than any afterthought could, to the charm of the intimacy. They are illustrated with crude, exuberant sketches brimming over with the spirit of spontaneous play.

It seems to have been Wells's principle of candor to set down nothing that could hurt the reputation of others and to expose only himself. He reveals a glimpse of his youthful self in a fit of hysterical weeping because he felt frustrated when denied a rather unreasonable request made of his divorced wife. Yet the manner in which the confession is made is so engagingly honest that understanding banishes any impulse toward reproach. . . .

Characteristic of the man is Wells's psychoanalytical report of himself. Curiosity and articulateness are the essential traits of H. G. Wells, and he must record everything that has ever interested him—the personalities he has encountered, the movements in which he has participated. The result is a copious outflow of issues and attitudes discussed in a discursive manner which nonetheless has order and definiteness.

In no memoirs have I discovered better character sketches

of writing men than Wells has set down. I see Bernard Shaw as an impecunious young man with a white face and a red beard generously helping a fellow journalist who was just beginning to get on to the tricks of his trade. Now, Wells comments, Shaw has a very red face and a very white beard, but he is the same Shaw. The estimate of Henry James seems to me discerning and just. I like Wells's description of the "lovely complication of veracity and disingenuousness" and the "curious intricate suavity of intimation" with which James could develop a point. Wells was in at the deaths of poor Stephen Crane and even poorer George Gissing and makes touching though quite unsentimental stories of their dreary ends. He is agreeably severe with the posturing Frank Harris. But generosity and appreciativeness are still the distinguishing marks of his intelligence, even though it refuses to budge from its own solid position in all matters of taste, morals, art, and social conscience. ह≥

In 1946 Wells still survives, having reached the age of eighty. Yet the octogenarian who did his own postmortem nearly a decade ago still speaks, if only occasionally, with the same saltiness of idiom and still rebukes society for holding back timorously from the loyalty it owes to the future. If his literary career really ended with the autobiography, his memory will not die soon. It will be, if not forever young, at least forever panting with indignation against stupidity and with devotion to the ideal of science.

George Bernard Shaw

IF WELLS has been the most dynamic of our mentors, George Bernard Shaw has been the most picturesque. Long ago he conceived a role for himself, that of the super-clown. Speaking with the immunity of pretended irresponsibility, he uttered truths about the relations of parents to children, of husbands to wives, of men toward professions, and of all human beings toward their world which would have seemed dull or impertinent or both had they been expressed with earnest, reformative zeal.

A certain middle-aged aptitude for buffoonery made Shaw, at forty, unique among the men of the theater into whose company he elbowed his way. He made a great show of irreverence not merely for the temple of the drama, but for all the beliefs that were being championed in it. Pinero and Jones had been doggedly writing and rewriting the well-made play until with much polishing it had become thin, frail, and transparent. There was, in truth, nothing to it at all, except a certain maudlin and mawkish concern for the "fallen woman."

Shaw could not write the well-made play when he first invaded the theater; he has made no attempt to learn to write it in all the half century of his uninterrupted activity as a dramatist. Each of his plays is a tract in dramatic form; the characters are all either mouthpieces of his preferences or embodiments of his aversions. But there were many able and industrious craftsmen who were willing to devote their small talents to the task of isolating, touching up, and framing a fragment of reality. Shaw's unique gift for setting off the firecrackers of ideas under the throne of stuffiness came to be greatly valued. He had something new to offer, a sort of practical joke that let tradition fall on its fatuous face, providing the irreverent, the speculative, and the experimental with a moment of unholy joy.

When Shaw first appeared he shocked criticism out of its bland complacency. His work fitted into no pigeonhole already neatly labeled and cozily stuffed with appropriate adjectives and scholarly references. In a mild state of the vapors critics went about asking each other, "Is he a charlatan? Is he a prophet?" But like any phenomenon, Shaw's gift became, in time, familiar if not wholly intelligible. We learned to steer by his inspired common sense as though it were a sort of North

Star of social judgment, an aloof but reliable guide toward reason and away from hysteria.

Shaw has always managed to make his kind of common sense attractive. But, fortunately for him and for his readers as well, there have been flaws in his gift of insight. Had it been unmarred he might easily have lost his hold upon the imagination of people who, knowing their own frailties, like to find frailties in their gods. Shaw has shown ludicrous limitations. His revolt against the authority of medical science, his espousal of cultist causes in matters like that of diet—these have assured us that Shaw, too, is human. He has spoken with the voice of prophecy, but, rich and sonorous though that voice is customarily, it is capable of falsetto breaks, slurrings, and an occasional inaccuracy of pitch, which have made his authority seem not too inexorable.

He, like H. G. Wells, has survived long past the time when a man becomes venerable and on into the age when he is likely to seem awesome. Yet he remains at the end exactly what he was in the beginning. This was what I took to be the striking thing about his latest (though one must not risk saying of Shaw, his last) published work, *Everybody's Political What's What.*

◆§ The amazing, the all but incredible, thing about Bernard Shaw is that now in his eighty-eighth year he is still able to delight, instruct, challenge, and infuriate us all at the same time in very nearly every sentence he writes.

This is precisely what his program has always been. He wants to delight us so that we will consent to listen to his exposition of ideas. He wants to instruct us because he is sure we desperately need instruction. He wants to challenge us out of the complacent acceptance of beliefs that may be lies and techniques of conducting social life that may be outmoded. And he wants to infuriate us so that the experience of reading one of his books or of seeing one of his plays won't pass off merely as a pleasant diversion but will force us to do some thinking of our own.

Today, though he is old enough to be Winston Churchill's father, he has lost none of his curiosity, none of his audacity, none of his ability to sting the mind. This distinction alone is enough to be cause for real gratitude on the part of those who respect fine intelligences. It is possible to go on living in a world that produces Adolf Hitlers only because it produces an occasional Bernard Shaw as well.

Shaw's latest book has been written to prove that in the world of tomorrow neither the democracy of Lincoln nor the dictatorship of Hitler will be regarded as satisfactory. In Shaw's view, government of the second type is not to be trusted because "great men," like Napoleon and Cromwell, often begin by being reformers but end by being despots.

Yet democracy is not adequate either. "I hope I have made it clear," Shaw writes with that air of patient reasonableness which the old devil knows will make his opponents yearn for a taste of his flesh, "that democracy thus defined [as government of the people, by the people, for the people] is romantic nonsense. The people have obstructed government often enough; they have revolted; but they have never really governed."

In his socialized state of tomorrow, government, he hopes, will be of the people, by the qualified, for the endless generations of mankind.

To Shaw one of the most ludicrously sentimental and pompous ideas our race has ever thought up is that "the voice of man is the voice of God." The voice of man, as many of his most engaging characters have been created to prove, is the voice of a babbler, parochial and full of prejudice, bigoted in the worst moments and sloppily indulgent in the best.

Shaw does not wish this creature ill. He refuses to see him bullied, exploited, and treated with brutal contempt, as Hitler has treated him. Indeed, he is determined that in the socialized world of tomorrow, "Mr. Everybody" shall have a far higher standard of living than he now enjoys, be better fed, housed, clothed, and educated than he now is, and be more secure in his enjoyment of these advantages.

But the Shavian code requires that he admit the worst about the limitations of the average human being. For his own good it is necessary that "Mr. Everybody" submit his carelessly formed, imperfectly disciplined will to "councils of tested qualified persons." These persons must, of course, be "subject to the sternest possible public criticism and to periodical (in pressing cases even summary) removal and replacement." But the aim still is to substitute for popular government, government by trained experts.

The argument is full of holes, of course. And in his irrepressible exuberance Shaw goes about knocking some of these so broad and gaping that no one could fail to see what they are.

For example, who are these "qualified persons"? Presumably they are highly trained men in political science and in the social sciences who, on the basis of their achievements, have a right to claim a measure of authority over those of us whose intelligences are untrained in these particular fields. Fine! But does Shaw himself accept the authority of such men? As he points out with blunt decisiveness, the economists, the bankers, the educators of our time have been creatures of ludicrous fallibility. These, of course, are fields in which anyone may, and must, have ideas. But in the field of the highly specialized sciences Shaw is no less certain of his heresies against authority. As an antivivisectionist and an opponent of vaccination he has set up his authority against that of the expert, the trained man, the "qualified" man, in a whirlwind of witty abuse. He has spent his life trying to demonstrate the necessity of having laymen check on what the rascals in various specialized fields are up to.

The fundamental logic of his position would lead anyone but Shaw himself back to the conviction that there is only one thing in which political man can safely believe all day, every day, and that is the essential wisdom of the race. And if you believe in the enveloping wisdom of the race, you must believe also that the only government in which it is safe to put one's trust is that of the people, by the people, and for the people.

Yet, though you may part with Shaw to come back to the very point from which he started out on an adventure in "heresy, eccentricity and innovation," it has been wonderful to go along for the ride. He is a brilliant man, a witty man, and fundamentally a great humanitarian, who says frivolous and sometimes even cruel things because he likes to be noticeable and also because he wants to remove the curse of sentimentality from his great fatherly love for a race of fools. ৡ঵

The four uncles were important, and the record of their work will continue to be important, because among them they summed up the intellectual life of a political democracy in our time. All of them except Galsworthy were self-made men quite as much as the great industrialists of the period were creatures of innate genius. They invented their own opportunities out of very nearly nothing at all and achieved domination in their world by virtue of their ability to make the fluidity of society carry them where they wished to go.

Having forced society to serve their private needs, none of the uncles persuaded himself to regard its ways as sacrosanct. Each meant to describe our world accurately and to criticize its ways soberly. Bennett and Galsworthy, however, represented the temperament that looks toward the past; Wells and Shaw, the temperament that looks toward the future. All are inevitable products of the freedom of political democracy.

Bennett's comments on the design of the British way of life tended to confirm his fortunate fellow countrymen in their satisfaction with the status quo. A world in which men could get on so mightily, in which a new man could earn a great deal of money, invest it in hotels, own yachts, collect good paintings, must be an excellent world.

Galsworthy was less sure that this was so. He was a highly cultivated man whose sensibilities made him aware of the plight of those upon whom the men of Napoleonic genius trod as they marched so picturesquely toward their goals. But he hadn't the slightest idea what he wished to see done about the faults of society. Nervous apprehension and blank misgiving were his distinguishing characteristics as a literary artist. He picked up issues, fumbled with them, displayed the British trait of keeping a stiff upper lip as he examined their cluttery surfaces, and then let them slip through his slack fingers. He, too, tended to confirm society in all its bad habits because his observations said in effect that change was difficult to achieve, that there was much to be said on both sides of every problem, and that after all . . . well, after all . . .

The concessiveness of Bennett and Galsworthy made them typical British conservatives. Belligerent determination to bring about change made Wells and Shaw the typical British liberals. Both were active proponents and supporters of advance guard ideas. Wells's fundamental conviction was that the soul of man could be altered into a more serviceable model by scientific processes. The individual was to become better educated, and what remained to be done toward making him less of a sluggish lump of prejudice and unimaginativeness was to be accomplished by improving his metabolism, removing him to a climate that suited his particular needs, and assigning him to a job for which science would discover that he had an aptitude.

The Fabian socialist, Shaw, has fought for the amelioration of the condition of man, as suggested in his *Everybody's Political What's What.* He, too, believed that more would remain to be done when full political justice had been achieved, and this was to be accomplished by regimentation of the mass of mankind under a benevolent leadership of the qualified.

If the records of our civilization were to be lost, everything except the writings of Bennett, Galsworthy, Wells, and Shaw, a scientist of some future time would be able to reconstruct all the significant aspects of the philosophy of the first four decades of our century from the novels, the plays, the journals, and the pamphlets left by the garrulous uncles.

It is also true, I think, that the novels and the plays could be destroyed without destroying these uncles. For into the minds of all of us who have lived through this period with them is written ineradicably the record of their thinking, in all its clear and in all its muzzy aspects.

Tenderly Tolls the Bell
for Three Soldiers

THEY were products of the midwestern tradition, these three soldiers; one of them lived his youth in St. Paul, the others theirs in the environs of Chicago. In their late teens or early twenties they closed their schoolbooks with a mixture of relief, impatience, resentment, and curiosity to go away to war. They did not like what they encountered in the midst of the military experience. They were, however, attracted by the freedom from parochialism they found in the European world.

Each in his different way was a glittering example of the psychology of the "sad young men" about whom F. Scott Fitzgerald wrote, of the despair-loving expatriates about whom Ernest Hemingway wrote, of the thwarted intellectuals about whom John Dos Passos wrote. They might have been the originals of the *Three Soldiers* of the title of Dos Passos' first important novel. They were the most conspicuous representatives of that "lost generation," fragments of which Gertrude Stein was forever stumbling upon in the byways of Paris.

The concept of a lost generation now seems an almost mawkishly sentimental one. Since 1918 another American generation has gone to war. It fought longer, harder, and in the face of a far more bitter challenge than did the generation of the First World War. Yet it has not become professionally "lost." Its psychoneurotics have been isolated from the healthy mass, which has survived with all its basic values whole and with perhaps a few worthy ones added as the gift of experience.

But there were extenuating circumstances to account for the intense self-consciousness of the lost generation. If cultures tend to pass through the cycle of birth, growth, and

decay as individuals do, then American culture was in its adolescence when the First World War began. Its representatives
had not been exposed to the shocks of conflict or to the discipline of comradeship as their French, English, and German
contemporaries had been. They were the products of a tradition that worshiped individual initiative, success, and a very
narrow interpretation of what constituted virtuous social behavior. Circumstances required them to learn a very great deal
in a very short time as they were rushed into a hastily impro-
vised and badly organized seminar of the human spirit. The
young men who had a similar experience a quarter of a century
later had something of cultural memory to draw upon. They
met the experience of war with much more of sobriety, sta-
bility, and maturity; they have, apparently, felt no inclination
at all to hide away in the dark alcoves of the mind and to
devote themselves to feeling lost.

The effort of these lost angels to find their way back to an
intelligible and endurable world can be traced out in their
books. Each took a different route; each wandered in ways that
seemed sometimes both hopeless and aimless. Yet the progress of all of them was marked by such brilliant qualities of
eagerness and dread that a very large American public followed
their movements with sympathy, curiosity, and absorption.
Fitzgerald, Hemingway, and Dos Passos burned all along the
way with fear and hope, with hatred and a never quite ex-
tinguished aspiration.

The drama of their association as representatives of aspects
of American culture was made the neater by the fact that
their personal association was intimate. Fitzgerald and Hemingway frequently linked their own names in considering the
problems of the creative mind; they had a kind of joint egotism based on the idea that they were the two most important
writers of their day. Dos Passos took a fraternal interest in the
crises of Fitzgerald's life and, toward the close of that crowded
chapter of human tragedy, an almost paternal attitude toward

the perplexities of a genius who was, even at the end of his life, an immature spirit.

Both as artists and as human beings these three men shared the problems of adjustment to the complexities of times that were out of joint. Among them they divided up the virtues and the limitations of Hamlet, and their several responses to the "cursed spite" of being obliged to try to remake their world are recorded in the most absorbing, original, and tragic documents of the literature of our time.

Scott Fitzgerald

FITZGERALD never found his way at all, but ended his life in the quicksands of half knowledge.

He seemed to have been born to all the good things that human society has in its gift. When he first appeared conspicuously before the public, he was, as an autobiographical character in *This Side of Paradise* remarked, "young, thank God, and beautiful, thank God. . . ." Yet he had little reason, in his last days, to address a beneficent fate. For though at forty-four he still seemed like a kind of faded photograph of a *jeune premier*, he was plagued toward the last by anxieties and doubts of peculiarly distressing kinds. His habit of juvenility, which was so attractive in the beginning, had betrayed him as it betrays all bright, spoiled children. The title of his second novel, *The Beautiful and Damned*, was tragically prophetic.

So also was the epigram which gave that book its theme: "The victor belongs to the spoils." Scott Fitzgerald was the victim of his successes. He devoted his career to describing a certain kind of society, and that society rewarded him with money, prestige, and personal adoration. The money he squandered; the prestige he whimsically brought to public ridicule; and from the personal adoration he contrived a succession of bitter personal tragedies.

It was the world of the very rich that Scott Fitzgerald undertook again and again to describe. He was at once dazzled by its glamour and disgusted by its cheapness. Whatever the privileges of that society were in the 20's would have seemed to be his by right of early association as well as by right of conquest. Yet, though the light of publicity always illuminated Fitzgerald's decorative person sympathetically, he never felt secure in his possession of that glittering stage devoted to the dramas of the very rich.

The kind of discomfort he felt is brilliantly and touchingly analyzed in his best book, *The Great Gatsby*. In the center of that story of the prohibition era stood a young bootlegger who, having achieved all else that money and power could give, yearned after the sense of being an initiated member of an inner circle of the elect. For him heaven on earth was represented by the green dock lights at the lake home of a princess of the sacred company, regarded by Gatsby as the well-born. Caught in a hurricane of melodrama, Gatsby dies, his hopes unrealized. He has never been anything more than a worried pilgrim toward Olympus, a trespasser whom no one has taken the trouble to send away.

Gatsby, Fitzgerald has said, was himself. But I think he did not truly understand the nature of his own sense of insecurity. He felt like a trespasser in that world of ennui, where demoralizing vices had to be invented to fill the empty hours, not because he was in any way unacceptable to the hereditary owners of it but simply because he himself did not feel at home in it. He knew, perhaps, that just as Tolstoy had rejected another glittering world to walk a difficult path in search of truths of broader significance, so he should have walked out of the Ritz to explore the highways leading nearer to the capitals of human experience.

Fitzgerald remained inside a tradition which essentially he despised. The tension of being caught, caged, turned in upon himself, grew more apparent with each book he wrote. The misery of his characters was duplicated in his private life by a wild determination to invent cruel and unusual punishments for himself. He was the most masochistic of writers, publishing to the world all the intimacies of his self-doubt.

"I have been but a poor care-taker of my talent," he once confessed. But even in that statement he seemed not quite to realize that he was the victim of his too easy success, not because he had been less than scrupulous in the development of the themes he chose, but because the themes themselves were too trivial fully to engage his talent. He was half blinded in his youth by the brilliance of the great world and he never quite managed to get the glitter out of his eyes.

Because it made so full and so touching a confession of this difficulty, *The Great Gatsby* delighted Scott Fitzgerald's contemporaries. They waited for it to be followed by another forward step, which never was taken. As a tremendous admirer of the earlier book, I was antagonized by what seemed to be the retrogressive tendency of *Tender Is the Night*, in which Fitzgerald explored the tragedies of the expatriates.

✍§ Re-enter, after many years, Scott Fitzgerald, leading by the hand a bewildered giant.

His new book is formidable in its bulk and intimidating in its attitudes. But since Mr. Fitzgerald himself is in a highly scientific frame of mind, it is appropriate to examine the medical definition of giantism in order to understand what he has produced. As the doctors in their grim, unfanciful way put it, giantism means a "development to abnormal size accompanied by various stigmata such as disproportionately large extremities or marked facial asymmetry and usually by constitutional weakness." That, I think, is an accurate clinical description of the giant in novel form that Fitzgerald brings us.

This is a big, sprawling, undisciplined, badly coordinated book. It is very far from being uninteresting. On almost every page one comes upon a passage of great literary brilliance, a little masterpiece of characterization, an extremely witty and cleverly recorded bit of dialogue. But the parts are not well integrated. It is not necessary to be an expert to observe the asymmetry and the disproportion. I think the constitutional weakness is also evident. The pituitary gland simply did not function normally. . . .

Tender Is the Night is a pathetic human story containing some of the elements of inevitable tragedy. But what alienates sympathy and finally interest is the fact that two people, trying to create a destiny for themselves out of unpromising emotional materials, should have chosen to live in so mad and chaotic a world.

The essential tragedy is that of Richard Diver, a doctor who sacrifices his individual integrity and his career to the protecting of a rich, psychopathic wife. The backgrounds are Paris, Zurich, and the towns of the Riviera. The incidental characters are the psychopathic wrecks of the sanitarium set and the decadent playboys of the cafés. The incidents include orgies of the peculiarly sinister sort invented by postgraduate adolescents—duels and race riots. The intellectual interest centers upon such topics as homosexuality, chronic alcoholism, and schizophrenia. There are three quite casual murders. Into this symphony of violence the motif of illicit love comes with the overtone of pastoral sweetness, and it is in that vein that Fitzgerald treats it. . . .

The book would have been better if a substantial man had failed under more nearly normal circumstances. It seems almost equally pointless to blame either fate or Dr. Diver for the failure of his life. Fate did not arrange the bizarre succession of catastrophes which *Tender Is the Night* records. It took an ingeniously misguided human intellect to do that. And from the beginning Dr. Diver is so obviously inadequate that one could just as reasonably reproach a scarecrow for not being equal to the emergency when birds, declining to be intimidated, defiantly fly into the field.

With fate and Dr. Diver acquitted there seems to be no indictment to return. And yet if none results out of all this social outlawry, the record seems more bewildering and pointless than ever. . . .

It is strange that after all these years Fitzgerald should have written such an immature book. It has all the faults from which he so triumphantly escaped in *The Great Gatsby*. That novel, too, had its tempestuous melodrama, its undisciplined characters. But Fitzgerald, standing aside, understood the pathos of the impulse that carried his central character stubbornly toward a quite unobtainable goal. The quality of compassion which he got into that admirable record was completely touching and persuasive.

I think he could have done it again in *Tender Is the Night* but for the fact that this time he was not willing to submit himself to the stern self-discipline which made him rewrite and rewrite *The Great Gatsby* many times until he had eliminated all its irrelevancies. Fitzgerald's chief fault is his facility. It makes him clutter his pages with a tremendous amount of amusing and entirely unimportant material which obscures the view of his theme. The night into which he has plunged is more murky than tender. ॐ

Just before the end of his life Fitzgerald escaped from his oppressive loyalty to the world of the lost generation, and in *The Last Tycoon* he came much closer to doing the work for which his gifts fitted him. But he died before the book could be completed. It was published in its fragmentary form together with notes and comments found attached to the manuscript. Even a sympathetic reviewer could but "look before and after and pine for what was not."

ॐ *The Last Tycoon* would, I think, have been a failure measured by the standard that Fitzgerald had set for himself. I see no evidence to make me believe that he could have adjusted its themes into a beautifully articulated piece of craftsmanship like *The Great Gatsby*. It would have sprawled like *Tender Is the Night*. It would have been a ramshackle vehicle for his great talent, packed with brilliance and also with many fussy souvenirs of the juvenility that he never quite threw off. The attitudes would not have been clarified, for obviously Fitzgerald saw no need to clarify them. For him the flash of insight was enough. He exacted no more of himself.

But even so, what a wide gap there was between him and the nearest contender for admiration in the middle ground of literary inspiration!

The story is about the making of films, but the background in Hollywood did not tempt Fitzgerald into writing another of these stereotyped kindergarten *Götterdämmerungs*. He wrote of the studios not because he wished to exploit their scandals or make cheap comedy of their minor figures but because he was fascinated by their art.

His central character, Monroe Stahr, is a motion picture producer, a man of high, though not solemn, seriousness, one of genuine creative imagination. It is his credo that the movies should take the folklore of the people and give it back to them enriched with bits of poetic insight. He repudiates sternly the obvious, the gross, the banal, and in a dozen ways he prods his directors and writers into taking the devious, hard, but rewarding, way toward truth.

The most triumphant bit of testimony Fitzgerald has to offer of Stahr's seriousness comes in a beautifully written scene (one that will startle other professional writers into a wistful, maddened envy of its absolute rightness). Stahr, walking on the beach at night, meets a Negro who has come out to read Emerson and pick up grunion fish. The two men talk about "pictures."

"I never go to the movies," the Negro says. "They's no profit. I never let my children go." And afterward Stahr feels the pinch of this rebuke. He broods about the earnest Negro and finds himself mentally scrapping four borderline films he had intended to make for the trade, while he puts back into his schedule a picture that he has previously renounced as too difficult.

No amount of analysis would have been as revealing and persuasive as this scene. There are many that do not fall far short of it. . . .

But much is very seriously wrong with the book. The narrative devices Fitzgerald forced upon himself are complicated and awkward; they underscore the artificiality of storytelling conventions. Frequently Fitzgerald's taste for fantasy gets out of hand. It is not fitted neatly into the essentially realistic design but stands out ludicrously like an intrusion of the Saroyan spirit.

The love affair is bad, laboriously uncontrived, and, as the book stands, curiously unrevelatory. And sometimes Fitzgerald, gifted stylist that he was, master of the flashing word of illumination, could write like a *True Confessions* tale teller.

The best and the worst of Fitzgerald's brilliant mind are clearly evident in his last work, and I have seldom had as engrossing an experience as that of trying to trace out the threads of fineness and of shoddy that gave his talent its curious, fascinating pattern. . . . ॐ

John Dos Passos

JOHN DOS PASSOS—born in the same year as Scott Fitzgerald, the product of a similar environment, and a bright young man at Harvard in the same period when Fitzgerald was a bright young man at Princeton—emerged into adult life with a completely unlike philosophy. His literary scene touched that of Scott Fitzgerald at some points, but his vantage ground of observation was very far removed from that on which the saddest of all the sad young men took his stand.

Many critics have considered Dos Passos to be the angriest of these young men. Having escaped from that sheltered inner circle of American society in which Fitzgerald was so miserably caged, Dos Passos tramped up and down the highways of our country, staring fixedly with his half-blind eyes into the faces of all the travelers, trying to discover the secret of each. He found little to admire in any of the varied types he introduced into his novels. The conclusion of the indictment drawn up against capitalistic society in the trilogy *U.S.A.* is that the lives of the majority of our citizens have been corrupted by the false values of our devotion to the religion of success. A further deduction made by some observers is that Dos Passos himself is a sort of long-winded Samuel Hall whose final comment on the life of our time is, "I hate you one and all, damn your eyes."

That, I think, is to confess to an inability to understand the psychology of detachment. Scott Fitzgerald is credited with having been a writer who appreciated all the delicate and assuaging powers of love, while Dos Passos is accused of being vindictive and spiteful in his treatment of the characters to whom he gave life. But Fitzgerald's love was really nothing more than a kind of muzzy loyalty toward the strange creatures with whom he was imprisoned. Caught on the inside of an unsatisfactory society, he sought the comfort of animal warmth from those who were caught with him.

Dissimilarly, Dos Passos ranged free, without commitment and without desire to apologize for the pictures he felt obliged to record. There is nothing so distressing, in the way of testimony against the human race, in any of the novels of Dos Passos as exists in many of the scenes of degradation in *Tender Is the Night.* The dismal news about human life contained in *U.S.A.* seems more wretched to some simply because it is recorded with the cool and complete impersonality of a police report.

It was something rather like a sociological survey, dealing with the effects of a political and economic system on various strata of society, that Dos Passos set out to write. That it was an ambitious and valuable project, carried through with brilliant effect, is not to be questioned by a reasonable analyst. To call the work of Dos Passos cold and mechanical is only to protest that one prefers a more lush and personal style. For the supposed coldness is merely the result of the author's refusal to cast a mellowing glow of pity over events which he wishes to have speak for themselves; and the supposed effect of being mechanical is instead the result of a deliberate attempt to capture the interest of the daily newspaper by bringing together, for purposes of contrast and completeness, the stories of many different kinds of people.

Too much literary criticism is devoted to a finicking display of dissatisfaction with a piece of writing for not being something it was never intended to be. The novels of Dos Passos at their best have been distinguished for the artfulness with which they expand the function of the reporter, broadening his field of vision, deepening his perception of the economic and political implications of events, and still leaving him a reporter, setting down what he has seen.

Dos Passos, of course, looked at a world that is passing. But at the moment when he made his observations they had great importance for others who were also trying to understand America.

The 42nd Parallel by John Dos Passos is a tremendous, exuberant, ironic novel. From its swift, yet detailed reporting of five lives, there emerges an essentially tragic significance.

Dos Passos' canvas is large, his method correspondingly bold and strenuous. Yet he is capable of the delicate and subtle effect also. His new book has dozens of qualities to excite admiration, but this must be confessed immediately: it is totally lacking in gentility. It is not nice. The author does not mean it to be.

What his title suggests he wishes to do, Dos Passos actually does with a great deal of success. He lets his eye round along the 42nd parallel of latitude that cuts the United States in two, and examines the specimens of life he finds living along it.

To be sure, he does not follow that imaginary line with unwavering devotion. He swerves a great deal, into California, Louisiana, New York, Mexico, even Europe. The 42nd parallel simply gives him several of his starting points for an explorative journey around the country. The findings he offers in the study of how Americans lived their lives during the thirty years that preceded the [First] World War.

The chief characters are five. There is Mac, the printer, who wanders from Chicago to the West Coast and becomes a radical with a loyalty to the I.W.W. that is his only mental interest. He makes a dull marriage, is threatened with the engulfing wave of middle-class respectability, runs away from it, and is left in Mexico, a thoroughly ineffectual but still devoted follower of the cause of revolution.

There is Janey, the nice girl from Washington, from whose position on the sidelines, as secretary to men of affairs, the official life of the nation is glimpsed. Through the veil of her sentimentality and conventionality, Dos Passos reveals many amusing ironies.

His most interesting character is J. Ward Moorehouse, the smart young man on the make, who cynically turns everything that happens to him to account and manages to rise spectacularly in the business world. When he is threatened with financial disaster, the war conveniently comes along, and posing as a loyal soldier doing his duty in a swivel chair at Washington, he turns that to account too.

Eleanor, whose father was in the stockyards at Chicago, represents America playing at estheticism. Her violent revulsion against the brutality that touched her early life gives her an idiotic passion for being nice. It is, of course, a spurious niceness, and Dos Passos makes it thoroughly irritating. ੈॐ

For good measure, Dos Passos creates a fifth character, Charley Anderson, out of Fargo, North Dakota, and the Twin Cities. Here the author offers a final crack on the jaw to the sentimental idea that America went to war in 1917 with the conscious and conscientious purpose of saving humanity. For Charley is the one figure of the novel who actually becomes a soldier, and his participation is represented as being neither idealistic nor adventuresome. It is simply the next step in a career of casual and meaningless vagabondage.

⋙ Two devices further illuminate the author's meanings. One, which he calls the newsreel, is extremely effective. He introduces it at intervals to show what is going on in the world at large at a particular moment of the narrative. It contains headlines from newspapers referring to political crises, social catastrophes, and casual human happenings. It contains also snatches of popular songs of the minute. The effect is to make the past suddenly real and sizzlingly actual.

The other device is less successful. Dos Passos calls it the camera eye. It follows the technique of the old silent movie, catching up here and there an irrelevant detail of the panorama to enrich interest. The fault of the trick is that though these passages often contain biting humor, their general significance is vague and elusive. The author overworks it too. The old movie employed these random shots sparingly as the action rolled up momentum. Dos Passos uses them to the end, and the reader is easily revenged on him by skipping them.

The style is the least "literary" style I have encountered in many months. That comment would make the author happy, for he doesn't want to be literary. He merely records with the swift, preoccupied concentration of a man rehearsing the events of his life. He even sets down, using no quotation marks, the typical slurrings and inaccuracies of speech. For *would* he writes '*ud*. His characters "kinder fall in love." This is, of course, not at all the method of introspection. None of the characters is completely aware of himself. The cleverness of the book is that it makes the psychological significance emerge clearly as an overtone of what is actually set down. It is brisk, brutal, and accurate reporting. ֶ֎

Dos Passos never found his way toward a satisfactory philosophy. Scurrying busily along on the periphery of the human experience, he was as lost as Fitzgerald, locked up in the household of the elect. Having made his analysis of the "nature of capitalist crisis" in *U.S.A.*, Dos Passos became restless and began looking about for new material, for new evidence of human folly, and possibly for something in which to believe actively. But he found himself still rejecting—first the American Communists, then the American Fascists.

֎ In *U.S.A.* John Dos Passos offered a picture of this country raising one kind of hell with itself, the kind that resulted at last in the stock market collapse. His concentration was upon the industrial riot and upon what happens when personal ambition is given reckless freedom from the restraint of principle.

Now he has begun a second series of novels in which he intends obviously to have a look at another kind of hell-raising. This time his concentration will be upon the wild dance of reckless men who have made the halls of government their playground. The first book in this second series, *Adventures of a Young Man*, had to do with a self-consciously righteous lad who became a Communist and lost his life in the Spanish war.

The second is called *Number One*, and it is devoted to a swift, dramatic survey of a potential Fascist movement in America. The two books are only very loosely related structurally, though it is clear that they are intended to be variations on the same theme, that of the folly of turning away from essential democratic principle toward any sweeping change. . . .

72

In *Number One* the reader is led behind the scenes to see just how the people are exploited by the shameless racketeers who elbow their way into government. The big shot of this fragrant little nosegay of types is Homer (Chuck) Crawford, first a representative and later a senator from a southern state. . . .

Behind the smoke screen of pretended concern for the people's rights, this vulgar and noisy dictator serves only himself. He juggles oil leases profitably; he buys a radio station to exploit his charms as an entertainer and to solidify the strength of his organization; and when his whole hierarchy is threatened with exposure, he slips away, leaving the one really faithful servant of the organization holding the now quite empty bag.

The picture of Chuck at play with his noisesome pals is brilliant. Sitting in hot hotel rooms in convention cities or in the private bungalows of expensive resort establishments, they make their deals. Through themselves they link venal judges to the actual underworld. And when their cozy little conferences are over, they paw torch singers, eat too much food, drink far too much, and then totter off to the masseur to be repaired for the next bout. And always they add further seasoning of corruption to their shame by pretending that all their acts are "clean as a hound's tooth." Never can they completely relax and admit restfully that they are just perfumed tramps. . . .

The trouble with the thesis novel is that while it may do very well with its villains, its hero always looks like a bit of a fool. Tyler Spotswood is no exception. What was he doing in that outfit? It is suggested that he is a man of brains, if not of flawless integrity. Yet he submits supinely to the humiliations offered him by Chuck and allows himself to be edged into a very bad spot indeed. Dos Passos gives us a Spotswood who is merely too busy, too drunk, and too ill to defend himself. He isn't really a character. He is just the adumbration of a stomach ulcer.

Of course, he exists in the book to be reformed in the end, to offer himself up as a sacrifice on the altar of principle. Dos Passos' point is that when a dictator rises to corrupt government, each of us is guilty for not being alert to the danger, for being too distracted, too indifferent, to strike him down. It's a good point. ह∾

Ernest Hemingway

ERNEST HEMINGWAY plunged into the foreground of the American literary scene with so pugnacious an air of dramatizing his own vitality that both the suspicious and the fastidious have been inclined to deny his pretensions to serious consideration as an author. In his early books it was clear that he was exploiting his own individuality, and in all his pantomime of muscle-rippling and shadow-boxing a naive exhibitionism was the most striking feature.

His every utterance, too, was characterized by a naive passion for the idiom of ruggedness. Like a very young boy who has just been initiated into manhood and who is not quite certain that his position is secure, Hemingway noisily paraded his interest in all kinds of sporting matters—piscatorial, taurian, and sexual.

He seemed determined to use literature for the purpose of advertising himself as a completely healthy male whose digestion was sound, whose metabolism offered a model of functioning, and whose general sense of well-being was greatly to be envied.

To be sure, he had the sane mind that belongs to a sound body, and that mind harbored certain resentments against the folly and viciousness of society. But in the early books this resentment did not run deep. Hemingway deliberately and consciously rejected the soft, narcissistic egotism that made the neurotics of the war generation regard themselves as lost. Indeed, in The Sun Also Rises he was careful to choose a

74

war victim whose wound was clearly, devastatingly, physical. What mental maiming the character suffered was a direct result of an injury that made it impossible for him to enjoy the euphoria which the typical Hemingway character has always experienced so abundantly. Hemingway interpreted the tragedy of war in his first novel in terms of the sufferings endured by a frustrated sexual athlete.

He continued to be a kind of glorification of the postgraduate 4-H lad in each of the next few books. (The four H's of the improving organization of young farmers are hands, head, heart, and health.) He was a somewhat garrulous and insistent celebrant of the joys of sex in *A Farewell to Arms.* In the critical discussions in *Death in the Afternoon,* he mixed the interests of sport with those of the more rugged aspects of the literary sensibilities. In *To Have and Have Not* sport and sex supported the slightly uncertain structure of a new social consciousness. But all the while Hemingway was still conspicuously healthy and manfully devoted to the somewhat primitive ethics of doing "what made him feel good afterward."

We live in so sophisticated a day that such blatant exuberance as Hemingway's seems to us suspect. The man who must be forever talking about his capacity for love is probably overcompensating, and the one who thumps his chest and calls attention to the marvel of its capacity for expansion no doubt has nervous inner promptings that all is not well in the empire of the body.

But the surprising, perhaps unique, thing about Hemingway seems now to be that he has always been quite as healthy as he has declared. There has been no weakening of his stamina, but rather a steady growth. There has been no sudden breakdown of his claim to euphoria in the midst of shattering external experiences, but rather a constantly expanding warmth of graciousness and mellowness. *For Whom the Bell Tolls* justified his essential belief in himself and reconciled his read-

75

ers to all the lapses from taste into tedium that had characterized earlier celebrations of his temperament.

His theme has always been man against war. But the earlier wars, actual or figurative, were ones into which his heroes had blundered, just for the hell of it, as they themselves would be sure to say, or which they did not understand. Robert Jordan's war in *For Whom the Bell Tolls* is one that he understands very well indeed. It is fought by a man of disciplined sensibility, for a completely altruistic and idealistic purpose.

Though Hemingway's most recent work was needed to justify his effort as an artist, his first novel spoke attractively and divertingly to his contemporaries because it had an original and audacious accent. This thin and largely uncritical comment of the young reviewer that once was I may serve to suggest what qualities in Hemingway's early work took the fancy of America. Recent graduates from college were looking for a literary tradition they could have all to themselves, one they need not share with the stuffy, censorious Victorians, the commonplace Edwardians, or the very nearly featureless Georgians.

⏤§ A novel that quotes from Gertrude Stein and the Bible on its flyleaf ought to be an extraordinary novel. Not, of course, because it is so impossible to imagine the two having any sentiments in common, but because it is a little startling that anyone who knows very much about Gertrude Stein should have also heard of the Bible.

The sentences quoted by Ernest Hemingway to suggest the theme of his first novel, *The Sun Also Rises*, are not in the least incompatible. Gertrude Stein said in conversation, "You are all a lost generation," and Ecclesiastes says, "Vanity of vanities . . . all is vanity. . . . One generation passeth and another generation cometh; but the earth abideth forever. The sun also riseth, and the sun goeth down, and hasteth to the place where he arose."

Miss Stein's lost generation and Mr. Hemingway's is the one which came out of the war, shocked and full of mockery for most of the things which had been believed before. Mr. Hemingway has chosen to write about the most unfortunate of the war's victims, and the tragedy of his story is not in the least minimized by the fact that his characters are not at all "like Patience on a monument smiling at grief." Rather they thumb their noses at grief and then go out to the nearest café and get drunk. . . .

Hemingway writes in the first person and he does not touch up the idiom of the people he is presenting. His characters salute each other as "gents." They say "those sort." "Swell" is their favorite adjective. . . .

The significant thing for anyone who interests himself in matters of style is that, perhaps in spite of, but more likely because of, this refusal to be literary, Hemingway achieves a very real literary distinction. Artfully and shrewdly he makes his effects, and they include, though he would grimace at being told so, not a little of the irony and pity about which he allows one of his characters to amuse himself.

This is not a story to be put into the hands of book lovers who say they do not see the necessity of writing about this and that aspect of the human tragedy; that there is enough unhappiness in the world without insisting upon it in books; that, after all, there are such things as music and flowers and happy laughter. Such readers would discover in *The Sun Also Rises* a sensationalism which it does not in the least contain. They would think it horrid and bitter and they would go about making themselves and a great many others miserable by complaining of present-day tendencies in fiction. To others this novel will seem a fine and touching examination of the futility and purposelessness which the war imposed on those marked for its malign attention. They will realize that Ernest Hemingway has suggested with finished art the desperate gallantry with which such men have had to arm themselves. ॐ

With *A Farewell to Arms* Hemingway established himself as dean of the tough-tender school of fiction, which presently had matriculants not only from every state in the union but from all the English-speaking countries, including Australia.

⋙ When he sat down to write this new novel, he undoubtedly told himself that it was time someone wrote the simple and sordid, tragic and touching truth about the war. Books had been written with elegance and books had been written with passion. He wanted to use his bluff, forthright, unadorned technique to tell what actually happened to men and women in the war, instead of what would have been theatrical and ethically improving if it had happened.

It was, of course, a fine idea. But unfortunately for Hemingway, an accident had entirely changed the face of the literary world before his book could get into print. The accident was the publication of *All Quiet on the Western Front*. The superlatives Hemingway might have had if *A Farewell to Arms* had preceded *All Quiet on the Western Front* he simply cannot have now. The adjectives *great* and *vivid* and *impressive* retreat just a little haughtily in the face of this book and leave words like *good* and *suggestive* and *dignified* standing their ground.

It is only, of course, in the approach to the subject of war as a human experience that there is any similarity between these books. Both authors are obviously bored and disgusted with the half-truths and evasions, the artificialities and manipulations which have made the previous war books seem trifling and frivolous even in the midst of their agonizings.

Hemingway like Remarque has refused contemptuously to heighten and exaggerate for literary effect. He means to reflect the war scene with literal accuracy. As in *All Quiet on the Western Front*, there is in the newer novel an unembarrassed and unself-conscious willingness to consider the grotesque and squalid impulse of the human animal at war. He has not been nonplused by the physical, nor is he morbidly concerned with it. The balance of values is sane and true.

But Remarque was able to blend into this treatment a vast and overwhelming sense of pity. He looked at the war through the eyes of a narrator who was acutely conscious of the world's folly in tearing itself to pieces. Hemingway has chosen instead a decent, intelligent, honest, comprehending person whose sensibility is on a distinctly lower and less interesting level. He has done what he intended to do, but what he intended was less important in the first place. . . . ❧

In his succeeding books Hemingway, never at a loss for words, was occasionally at a loss for a theme appropriate to fiction. At such times he indulged in curious extensions of the ego which exploited his audacity in snatches of criticism, fantasy, and nature lore. His audience followed him in these excursions with varying degrees of sympathy, not always sure that his work would be strong and enduring. His unsteady development introduced a sporting element into the effort to appraise his work, so that one felt like laying a bet on each book, hazarding a judgment in advance as to whether it would be one of the good ones or one of the bad ones.

❧ It is, however, no longer possible to make a guessing game of Hemingway's place in American literature. Now at forty-odd he has produced a novel of unquestionable importance. *For Whom the Bell Tolls* is not merely Hemingway's best book; it is one of the finest books written by an American in our time.

The scene is Spain; the theme is war. But to say so gives little idea of the universality of the book's interest or the high quality of the interpretive gift that it reveals. Hemingway has chosen a moment of tension when the spirit of man becomes quickened by a challenging crisis to an intensification of itself. Aware of the significance of its struggle, our human nature declares its character with dramatic emphasis. The contradictions are still there: the cruelty matched by tenderness, the cowardice by courage, the treachery by loyalty. But each is brilliantly defined in the light of a flaming disaster.

This long novel covers only four days in actual time. It begins with the appearance in the mountains of a young American intellectual who has gone to Spain to fight with the Loyalists. He is on a mission to blow up a bridge, which will be the signal for the attack on Segovia. There behind the Fascist lines he must seek the help of the guerrillas of the mountains—peasants, gypsies, women refugees from other battles—and among them he finds a microcosm of the Loyalist world in which all its attitudes, its loyalties, its fears, are vividly dramatized.

Each figure is strikingly individualized. Pablo, once the dominating leader of the guerrillas, has become their potential enemy because his peasant shrewdness predicts the collapse of the cause and his impulse is to take to safety. But there is still his admiration of personal courage to control his wavering faith. In the end it saves him from treachery. Pilar, woman of the earth, lover of its pleasures, helps to bully her man, Pablo, back into loyalty with her mystical awareness of the unimportance of personal failure. Anselmo, the gentle old man who cannot kill animals, kills men unwaveringly because it is necessary. Maria, pitiful victim of Fascist violence, finds herself healed of all the scars left upon her mind by the act of rape when the enveloping generosity of an honest love is offered by the young American. Robert Jordan himself, warm in blood but cool in head, becomes for the reader the interpreter of the struggle as he feels growing within him the "deep, sound, and selfless pride" of complete identification with these people and with the impulse that makes them fight.

The scope of the book, deliberately compressed in time for purposes of drama, is widened again by several retrospective glimpses of other scenes. Robert Jordan's reflections call into being the strange Russian intellectuals who direct the war from Madrid; Pilar remembers the slaughter of the Fascists when Loyalists take an embattled town; Maria describes the cruel perversity of the revenge when the Fascists have their turn at violence.

Hemingway, evidently determined to be innocent of any special pleading for the Loyalists, scrupulously reveals in the peasant temperament a curious, contradictory, and fascinating combination of elements. A droll formality in speech is balanced by a rugged gift for obscenity; a gift for idealistic self-sacrifice goes hand in hand with an inclination toward primitive savagery. Yet through the whole character of each there blows a gusty, invigorating love of life. The relations of such people toward one another and toward their cause produce that finest kind of drama in which sensibility, thought, and humor reveal themselves against the background of man's tragic plight.

All the Hemingway themes are restated here: the courage of which human nature is capable when it has managed to identify itself with a moral issue; the humor that is ever present in the story of the appetites; the tenderness that declares itself in honest passion. But of none of these things has he ever written so well as he does now. With a new maturity of insight and a new subtlety of emphasis, he communicates his admiration for the simple profundity of faith that moved and occasionally inspired the Loyalists. ᣠᴄ

The bell has tolled in all finality for only one of these three soldiers. Scott Fitzgerald is dead, but though the other two survive, it is probable that their best work is behind them. Dos Passos no longer seems greatly interested in the society at which he directed his bitter criticisms, and Hemingway is taking a very long time indeed to digest the experiences of the Second World War.

Fitzgerald, Dos Passos, and Hemingway were important interpreters of the life of our time because each was the embodiment of aspects of its doubts and searchings. Fitzgerald remained to the end a restless prisoner of a tradition that he could not love. John Dos Passos searched the structure of society thoroughly without finding values to which he could commit his mind and heart. Only Hemingway, concentrating in each of his books on a moment of conflict between man and his world, discovered at last a loyalty that could fully engage his vitality. It is, of course, a close identification with the people's struggle for freedom. Of all the conspicuous representatives of the lost generation, only he found a resting place, a sanctuary in which to set up a faith, within his own spirit.

"Very Important Personages"

ONE of the dramatic accelerations achieved by our American culture is that of the social cycle, as it whirls dizzily through its several traditional phases. In many American cities there are families that have managed to pass from pioneering exuberance to decadence in three generations. In the cities of the East, where people of the same family tradition have held leadership as arbiters of the elegances for two centuries or more, a patina of sophistication heavily encrusts the social code, giving it a look of antiquity far beyond its years. In the pageant of the ages our culture is still very young and new. But in our cities experts at "antiquing" have set up their booths to create a rigid snobbery "while you wait."

The novelists have seized eagerly upon the irony of what might be called, in a different figure, self-induced arthritis. In a literature which is already rich and varied they have studied the symptoms of premature senility in New York, Boston, and Philadelphia.

Edith Wharton was for many years the great figure of this literary tradition. No one has ever challenged her supremacy as a satiric interpreter of the mores of the elect in the city of New York. But from time to time candidates for honors of the same sort have shown themselves in other places—for example, writers like John Marquand and Struthers Burt.

There is a certain similarity in the approach of each to his material. The smiles that Mrs. Wharton, Mr. Marquand, and Mr. Burt have turned upon their communities are bland and knowing. Each of them is aware of the follies and pretensions of the "very important personages" who make up his cast of characters. These great ones, often lacking personal qualifications of any kind for living either a fruitful or a picturesque life, are able to live on terms of intimacy with ambassadors, to intimidate bishops, and to patronize publishers because of the prestige of their names. Mrs. Wharton, Mr. Marquand, and Mr. Burt are amused by the ingenious set of rules whereby these arbiters safeguard their uniquity. They are amused at the slyness with which the *arriviste* tries to break down the rules. They are highly diverted most of all by the way the man on the inside tries, in a moment of rebellion, to climb over the barrier himself and then, in a subsequent moment of panic, desperately scrambles back.

Yet, despite this brave show of ironic perception, all these satirists are under the spell of the great, glittering world they ridicule. Reverence lurks in the midst of their impudence, and each of them hopes, because he is himself a very important personage, to escape from the ostracism that his betrayal of the secrets of the inner circle might warrant. They are like people who contrive funny stories about the dull proceedings of the dull clubs to which they belong and yet who would not for an instant think of resigning from them for fear of losing the prestige the dull clubs were created to confer.

But this is a sprightly sort of weakness, one that everyone seems able to forgive, because out of it comes the usual by-product of sprightly weakness—a great deal of spicy and revealing gossip.

Edith Wharton

MRS. WHARTON was born in 1862 and published her first work of fiction in 1899. Most of her important work was done before the years covered by this exploration. Her most completely successful novel, *The Age of Innocence*, appeared in 1920. Then she said farewell to her talent at its best. The weapon of epigram became blunted in her hand and gleamed with a less highly polished hilt. After 1926 she wrote only a handful of novels and these, of which *Twilight Sleep* is a woeful example, offered merely unhappy caricatures of the suavity and competence that had once been hers. After many years of voluntary exile abroad, she no longer knew New York; her amusement at its ways had the curious ineptitude of comments made by a stranger. Writing fiction seemed to have become nothing but a bad habit, which, ironically, she was too well disciplined to be able to overcome.

There remained, however, the task of writing her delightful autobiography, in which she gave enough of her own story as a student of society to explain why in her late thirties, after a career as a social arbiter, she found herself yearning toward literature and like a figure in *The Age of Innocence* "bursting with the belated eloquence of the inarticulate."

When Mrs. Wharton died, one who had formerly been under the spell of her literary brilliance wrote this not very polite appraisal of her dwindling influence.

◆§ The close of a writing career like that of Edith Wharton cannot fail to seem to an observer of contemporary fiction both significant and saddening. There is a certain pathos to the end of anything, and with the death of Mrs. Wharton we have reached more than the end of a single human life. Finis has been written to an engrossing chapter in the history of the novel.

Mrs. Wharton's gifts were very great. She had an extraordinarily flexible and graceful style which so fascinated the young craftsman that if he once fell completely in thrall to her, it would take many years to escape the idea that nothing could be so desirable as to develop a talent for making epigrams as scintillant as hers or to achieve a satiric outlook as suave and cultivated.

There can be no doubt that she very greatly affected the novel in our time. Temperaments and talents amazingly unlike her own have bowed to her supremacy. Even Sinclair

Lewis reverently dedicated one of his novels to her. Scott Fitzgerald once, finding himself in a publisher's office at the same moment as Mrs. Wharton, literally prostrated himself at her feet. The older critics of the sedate publications reviewed her books with a solemnity that would have been proper in analytical minds among the children of Israel when they reviewed the first edition of the Ten Commandments.

Mrs. Wharton was a follower of Henry James. You may trace out the history of her discipleship by reading the letters which passed between them. James addressed his admirer first as "dear Mrs. Wharton" and ended by greeting her, with affectionate solicitude, as his "darling Edith." The artistic bond was probably never closer than when, in 1905, Mrs. Wharton brought out *The House of Mirth*, revealing at its best her feminine variation on James's absorption with the fine moral issue.

But there must have been from the beginning more sly insight than profound moral conviction to Mrs. Wharton's intelligence. The felicity of her style contained a subtle, satiric poison. It was directed in the early short stories at the pretensions of women and the muddle-headed rigidity of the social code. Perhaps it was her facility for writing in light vein that distracted her from more sober interests. Whatever the cause, she was betrayed in her later novels into the essentially trivial task of unmasking the vulgar idiocy of the smart world.

No such gift as Mrs. Wharton possessed for being deadly was required to destroy characters like those of *The Glimpses of the Moon* and *The Mother's Recompense*. Possibly she became aware that she was turning her cannon upon gnats, for with the strange perversity of one who knows that he is in the wrong, Mrs. Wharton increased the ferocity of her attack. In *Twilight Sleep*, for example, she introduced scenes of sensationalism and violence so far beyond what was needed to uncover tawdriness that they made her own efforts seem grotesquely tawdry.

The first brief accounts of her death identified Mrs. Wharton as the author of *Ethan Frome*. Only that one, the least characteristic, as it is certainly the best, among her novels, was mentioned. It would have distressed her to know that authorship of this novel would be regarded by critics as her principal claim to attention. In her autobiography she complained of the shadow it seemed to have cast over all her other work.

Yet she herself has explained its extraordinary difference from her other books. Having become a resident of France in the midst of her writing career, Mrs. Wharton wished to perfect her knowledge of the language. At the suggestion of her teacher she began to write out exercises in the borrowed tongue. Because she was a storyteller she decided to create something original. She selected a stark and simple tragedy of New England and told it without any of the epigrammatical flourishes that characterized her English style. It is a masterpiece of compression, directness, power. If Edith Wharton becomes known to future generations chiefly as its author, the critics of tomorrow will have a difficult time explaining to themselves how the same author happened to write *The Mother's Recompense*.

But Mrs. Wharton did have that moment of perfect inspiration. If circumstances had conspired to develop that aspect of her gift, she might have become something more than the brilliant social satirist whose obituary one writes today. We might be mourning one of the really great, instead of a successful and influential craftsman whose inspiration steadily diminished. ও

John P. Marquand

MRS. WHARTON always occupied the center of the circle of social satirists with a certain majestic pomp, a ceremonial sense of her importance. She was like a *grande dame* at the opera, wearing full regalia, complete with tiara and pearls.

Unlike her, John Marquand slipped quite unobtrusively into the box. He has had, ever since his first appearance in this fashionable company, a half-amused, half-rueful air of apologizing for being late.

Before he published *The Late George Apley*, Marquand was comfortably at home in a very different entertainment world. He was a valued author of popular fiction for the magazines. His polite melodramas of international intrigue found immediate favor with the public which likes to take its excitement in the homeopathic doses of the serials.

But an intimate knowledge of what he has called "the preposterous scene" of Boston prompted him to gather up his souvenirs in the casual, carelessly ordered form of his first satiric novel. A mild resentment, blended with an equal part of mild affection, made *The Late George Apley* agreeably stimulating. The theme, however, was flimsy and the veneer of satire was lightly applied. The book seemed to be a sort of Grand Rapids product. Mr. Marquand debased the function of the satirist by his superficiality, and recklessly threw away the satirist's power by making it too easy for those *The Late George Apley* was intended to embarrass to dismiss it as merely vulgar.

For his central character Marquand chose a prime minister of futility who reduced the functions of the *arbiter elegantiarum* to the utter boredom of board meetings and bird-watching. The comedy of Boston's parochialism dwindled into the idlest and pettiest of small talk. These futilitarians fluttered so lamely that it seemed hardly sporting to bring them down.

By the time he came to write *Wickford Point* Marquand had begun to realize that his serviceable knowledge of the tactics of the novel could be applied to the new type of narrative. Feeling no longer that he was trespassing upon the preserves of responsible writers, he built up a solid structure for his book and developed its architectural possibilities amply.

The theme was better too, for it touched upon the truth that a dead society does not lie indefinitely in an embalmed state, giving off an odor of drugs and roses, but begins to smell distressingly of decay.

⊷§ There is a curious parallel between *Wickford Point* and Scott Fitzgerald's *The Great Gatsby*. Both have as their central figures a group of decadent creatures who imagine themselves to belong to an aristocratic tradition and who take without giving, not so much because they are disgracefully conniving as because they have nothing to give. In each book a bemused young snob from Minnesota falls under the spell of these people, finding in the glitter of their beauty and the tinkle of their talk some fascinating fulfillment of his vague ideal of elegance. In his short novel Scott Fitzgerald drove his theme along to a climax of melodramatic tragedy. In his long book John Marquand plays with it always in the vein of comedy and leaves the situation exactly where it was in the beginning. But both versions have the overtone of desperation, and both, I think, will be remembered a long, long time by anyone who reads them carefully.

The Brills of Wickford Point are a New England family whose tradition of greatness goes back to the poet ancestor who clung to the coattails of the Transcendentalists. His mediocrity was wrapped up cozily in the reverence which everyone was taught to feel for the whole period. The Brills know that they are the best people. Though they never do anything, though their men in the present generation are silly and their women predatory, they have unlimited confidence in their social significance.

At Wickford Point they live more or less on the bounty of a cousin, Jim Calder, a successful writer of popular fiction. Sprung from a ruddier American tradition of sea captains and competent maiden aunts, Jim accepts his responsibility for the Brills partly because he finds their effrontery amusing, but chiefly because of a curious and tense infatuation that he feels for Bella Brill. He sees her in and out of scrapes, in and out of marriage to a close friend, experiencing a sardonic delight in the game of playing with an attraction to which he will not permit himself to succumb. Jim is an enormously attractive figure, vigorous and normal, capable of distracting himself with many interests, intellectual and amatory, but never quite freed from his obsession with the completely unmoral Bella.

The young man from Minnesota is Allen Southby, who has partially digested many cultures which attract him more than his own. He knows enough about England to dress like a figure from a Noel Coward comedy. He has swallowed Harvard whole and has become one of its pedagogical lights. And now he proposes to absorb New England. What he seems to be about to receive is Bella Brill, and Mr. Marquand's implied comment at the close of the book is that it serves him right.

If one were to look for an underlying philosophy in Mr. Marquand's exuberant satire, I think these generalizations might be identified: There has been in American culture something that is hard and rugged and direct. There is also something that is imitative, self-conscious, and phony. We have not always taken the trouble to be clear in our minds about which is which. From the second element springs a monstrous kind of decadence that has absurd, embarrassing, and dangerous manifestations. Mr. Marquand suggests, though only by implication, that when we talk fatuously about "the American dream," it would be just as well to realize that sometimes it is an erotic nightmare. . . . ?❧

The hopeful signs were misleading. Marquand's philosophy had no deep roots, and his effort at making an intellectual interpretation of the weakness of American society soon withered. With expert craftsmanship and much amusing, if quite pointless, incidental comedy, he began to tell over and over again the monotonous anecdote about a man who longed for escape from a handsomely appointed prison cell into a more rewarding way of life, but who found that he lacked the resolution and ruthlessness to break out.

◄§ It may be that *So Little Time* will be the most popular of all John Marquand's studies in the light complexities of American life. It is the mildest of his novels, lacking the satiric bite of *Wickford Point* or even the mild malice of *H. M. Pulham, Esquire.*

There are two narrative threads in *So Little Time.* Either might have made a full and satisfying novel. They might have been drawn together into a really brilliant job. But Marquand has muffed them both because he isn't really a novelist at all. He is a very clever performer, a man who can bring off an individual scene in a story triumphantly but who cannot make a succession of those scenes add up into anything very moving or very real.

The first of these threads is the one for which he wrote the book. It is the story of a man who fought as a flier in the First World War and who, twenty-five years later, wakes with a start to find himself the father of a young man who is hell-bent to become a flier in the Second. The father fears for the son, envies the son, feels a little that he is the son. It is a wonderful theme but Marquand can make almost nothing of it because there is no warmth, no richness, no depth to the relationship. It is all on the surface—high comedy, Broadway stuff, some nice little scenes, adroit little turns. But there is nothing that resembles real emotion, nothing that makes one sense the terrible intimacy of two people sharing, for a moment, the same mind, the same set of nerves.

The other narrative thread is even more inadequate. It is the story of the same man in his relationship with his wife. Somewhere in his young manhood, he feels, he took the wrong turning. His desertion of the nice, "homey" girl he had loved, ineptly, in his boyhood was a mistake. With her he might have been the person he was supposed to become. His wife has made him into something else, something glittering and artificial. He has lost everything, his talent, his joy of life, his curiosity. All because of that excellent woman, his wife.

Conventional as it is, this might have made a good story if Marquand had told it. But he hasn't. The youthful love affair is dramatized in the routine, competent Tarkington manner of polite burlesque. The relationship with the wife communicates no impression of a subtle, progressive demoralization. In moments of self-pity (a very smart, wisecracking self-pity, to be sure) the central character assures the reader that he might have had a very significant life if only things had been different. But Marquand actually shows him as nothing but an orderly and well-disciplined man on the make.

The best of the book is to be found in the sketches of the incidental characters. Here Marquand relaxes and turns out a succession of lively, superficial studies. His background is the world of the theater and books, and he has a splendid time kidding all the pretentious frauds that lurk in its alcoves. There will be malicious whoops of joy over his caricature of a foreign correspondent who is actually a wide-eyed yokel and who impresses the other yokels by murmuring significantly, "As Winston said . . . but don't get me started on that . . ." My own feeling is that this sketch is obvious, monotonous, and heavy-handed.

The trouble with Marquand is that his satiric detachment begins to seem chilly and meager. Some awareness of inadequacy must have troubled him as he wrote the book, for he went on adding chapter after chapter in a haphazard, formless sort of way until he had filled nearly six hundred pages, hoping all the while that some significance would presently emerge. There is no reason for the book's being so inordinately long. There is no reason for the floundering back and forth in time between the First World War and the Second, except that Marquand had no clear idea of where he was going and hoped accidentally to stumble on a design. He never finds the pattern really. The best he can do is to distract the reader by tossing at him from time to time quite brilliant, if entirely irrelevant, bits of satiric comedy. ॐ

Struthers Burt

LIKE Mrs. Wharton and Mr. Marquand, Struthers Burt is by temperament and training thoroughly cosmopolitan. He has wandered over a large part of the globe and has taken his characters of fiction with him on these "far behests." Deliberately rejecting the parochial notion that a man owes a monogamous devotion to one place, he has been the exuberant interpreter of a passion for two very different scenes: the community that centers around Philadelphia and the community that is as wide as Wyoming. Yet it is always to Philadelphia that Burt's mind returns in search of a base from which to take off on his philosophic flights of discovery.

The ambivalence of the American social satirists in their attitude toward the human comedy is more clearly evident in Mr. Burt's chatty and personal discourse than in the work of either Mrs. Wharton or Mr. Marquand. Philadelphia's most garrulous son loves his mother community for the venerability of her tradition; he feels also a mild repulsion, though never an open hostility, for the narrowness of that tradition. He has analyzed his mixture of amusement and irritation in the interpretive study called *Philadelphia: Holy Experiment.* His delight-and-despair over the curious confusion of values that characterizes the mind of Philadelphia is summed up in a revealing bit of gossip. Certain aristocrats, Mr. Burt suggests, are suspected of having lived out long lives of sin against the sanctity of the marriage contract, rather than face the punishment of being dropped from a Philadelphia club which denies membership to otherwise blameless citizens who have been divorced and remarried.

In his best novel, *Along These Streets*, Mr. Burt offers the idea that perhaps Philadelphia should not be blamed severely for its weaknesses. The times themselves are "out of joint," and ours is an age of mediocrity.

⋙ In a recent interview Struthers Burt, the novelist, declared ruefully that he couldn't for the life of him see any reason why people should read novels in times like these. Give him, for his somewhat austere money, things like *Berlin Diary*.

Well—to be surprisingly polite about so silly and fatuous a comment—I can think of a great many reasons why intelligent people should read Mr. Burt's new novel. None of the reasons, oddly enough, is the conviction that *Along These Streets* is a success as a piece of fiction. It isn't. Mr. Burt's central characters are inept people whose psychological probings lead them to such not very startling conclusions as that money isn't everything and that it is a good idea to marry the girl who appeals to your senses even if she is a bubble dancer in a night club.

It cannot be said truly that Mr. Burt has dredged up any profound conclusions out of the dark and disturbing welter of the human soul. But he skims along beautifully over the bright surface of the sophisticated mind. His talents are akin to those of the ballet dancer and the figure skater. The maneuvers don't get you anywhere in particular, but the Struthers Burt choreography cuts out of the mass of contemporary problems some interesting and amusing thought patterns. It is impossible not to admire the skill with which he does it.

It takes him 608 pages to put before the reader all his ideas about such diverse subjects as the relations of the sexes; the future of science; the future of religion; the state of civilization in Philadelphia; American intelligence as revealed in the Easterner, the Middlewesterner, the Far Westerner; snobbery in its various forms and manifestations; Hitler; the Republican party; liberalism; night clubs; and a great many other things that belong to what he calls the "fantastic charade" of human existence today.

The underlying theme is that though we live in a vulgar age we must continue to have faith in the destiny of man. All the thoughtful characters (many of them are intellectuals in one way or another—teachers, artists, scientists, speculative philosophers) keep coming back to the main issue. We are experiencing a revolution not of the proletariat, really, but just of the second-rate mentalities. The maladjusted, the inadequate have given life its design in a kind of morbid deification of mediocrity. But still the human race seems to be "the only reasonably interesting experiment nature has made" and mankind is "as yet too young to know anything or be anything." At least in America we are beginning to have an impulse to create a civilization of our own. "We have exactly the attitude of the European at the beginning of the Renaissance. They were a fine people then." And so, there is hope.

It has become the fashion with a great many young writers to pretend to have no ideas at all. Cold, uncompromising objectivity is their line, and its attractions are many. But in the end the pose of mindlessness becomes a bore. The copiousness of Struthers Burt's witty, provocative intellectuality comes as an enormous relief. Any man who has the impudence to demand your attention long enough to absorb 608 pages of his notions, prejudices, and prophecies, and who also has the tenacity to hold your attention to the end, must be a much more interesting creature than the average novelist.

There are some little chips of plot bobbing about on the surface of this tide of talk. Mr. Burt has come to regard narrative ingenuity with a contempt similar to that of another great talker, Bernard Shaw. Both are content to use hackneyed, even hammy tricks. Mr. Burt's story begins with an eccentric will which requires an heir, a young biochemist, to give up his job and live in Philadelphia. There the scientist encounters the old-fashioned snobs and the new-fashioned revolutionists. As in Christopher Morley's *Kitty Foyle*, part of the narrative interest has to do with the love felt by an aristocratic young man for a girl of the people. (Burt blandly tells it in duplicate, which does not make it twice as inter-esting.) Other literary influences can be identified. Mr. Burt kids Philadelphia as John Marquand has been kidding Boston. The atmosphere of intellectual speculation is a little like that which is so intoxicating in the works of Thomas Mann. One might even say that here *The Magic Mountain* has labored and brought forth *Kitty Foyle*.

But what is of essential interest is that Struthers Burt has written a long, readable novel which is gratifyingly unlike all the hard little books, the bitter little books, and the confused, lyrical big books that our young men have been writing. ক্ষ

We have not reached the end of this tradition in American writing. Indeed, we appear to be just at the beginning of a new phase of the discussion, in fiction form, of the sharp conflict between contrasted social values in the urban arena. Henry James, who was, if not father, at least uncle to all the American writers who have undertaken serious critical exami-nations of society, found his native community too young, too undercivilized, to interest him deeply or to nourish his dra-matic imagination. He took as his theme the impact of Euro-pean culture upon Americans who wished to broaden their outlook. But his literary nieces and nephews have found no dearth of interest and no lack of complexity in the ethical clashes that are characteristic of their own scene.

No longer is the theme of social unrest offered to readers of novels as a crisis that is characteristic only of the large cities. Writers in much smaller communities are beginning to dis-cover restive minor heroes, full of eloquent protest against the arthritic lethargy of those who consider themselves heredi-tary possessors of an ill-defined authority. The ambivalence of Mrs. Wharton's preoccupation with New York appears again in such writers as Josephine Pinckney, whose analysis of the city of Charleston in *Three o'Clock Dinner* offers evidence that the genre has gained, rather than lost, importance in the midst of the storm of social change.

None of these observers believes that rigor mortis has settled upon American social institutions. But as the reports concerning the health of the nation continue to come in from Fargo, North Dakota, Butte, Montana, and Tulsa, Oklahoma, we shall begin, perhaps, to get a clear clinical picture of our weaknesses, along with some suggestions for treatment that may give us renewed vigor.

Forever Panting and Forever Young

Wʜᴇɴ a way of life is new, the writers who rise up to describe its character and celebrate its excellences tend to dramatize in their own temperaments the youth of the society they love. Today this is most noticeable in the Russian men of letters, whose passion for the USSR is expressed often with the egocentric earnestness of adolescence.

In his novel *Days and Nights* Konstantine Simonov has given full and exuberant utterance to this self-love. He writes as though there were no one in all Russia who is older than twenty-nine, at the very most. Though the background of the book is the battle against the invading Nazis, its vital young men and women feel no fear at all except that they may die before they have satisfied all the various kinds of hunger for experience that gnaw at their hearts. Pride in the innocence of Russia's unsullied youth animates every page.

The nonfiction analysts of contemporary Russian society, among its own members, are quite as unrestrained in the delight they take in their own accomplishments. They consider the superiorities of their way of life to be so completely self-evident that there is no possible reason for withholding the acknowledgment of these facts. Everything in Russia is the biggest, the broadest, the best designed, the most hopeful for the future. In their present mood of juvenile delight with themselves, the Russian writers seem to be, like the figures on Keats's Grecian urn, "forever panting and forever young."

This should remind us of ourselves as we were a century ago or less. The similarity should make us unwilling to criticize. Now we are an old society as societies go in our age of dramatic change. With our revolution far behind us we have become widely experienced in the practice of democracy, well-versed in the disappointments as well as in the satisfactions of our way of life. Yet everyone who was literate and intellectually explorative in the days before the depression can remember when we had a large company of writers who sounded very much as the Russian writers sound today. We, too, have had our celebrators of the life of our time, writers whose chief contribution has seemed to be the ecstasy of the "forever panting and forever young."

America's most recent pair of adolescent geniuses, Thomas Wolfe and William Saroyan, have expressed so many doubts and implied so many dissatisfactions with our way of life that they may seem not to belong to the category of juvenile enthusiasts. Compared with the gleeful Russians of the moment, Wolfe and Saroyan have been sober, searching, and orderly critics of our society.

But it is the ecstasy glowing inextinguishably in both of them that draws them back into the company of lyrical celebrants. Thomas Wolfe was precisely like the young men and women in Simonov's novel; he was the intellectualization of a great and unappeasable hunger. The only apprehension that could shadow his mind for long was that of dying before he had felt all there was to feel, seen all there was to see, learned all there was to learn, and celebrated, in appropriate organ-like rumbles of rhetoric, his own particular kind of religious worship. Wolfe was a young priest of life in almost exactly the same way that the young Russian writers are priests in the worship of their country.

Saroyan, though his ideas are few and vapory as compared with the churning current of them that poured out of the mind of Wolfe, has been noticeable, nonetheless, for the same quality of ecstasy.

If it is true that our culture has progressed to the point where it must leave self-congratulation to the Russians and engage in a more mature examination of the values by which we live; if it is true that in literature as in life ecstasy is something that can be appropriately associated only with the beginnings of expression and that sober and discriminating insight should characterize a culture's later years, then Wolfe and Saroyan are significant as the last representatives of a passing phase of America's development. Each offered a portrait of the artist as a perennial adolescent.

Thomas Wolfe

IT IS quite impossible to dissociate the personal history of Thomas Wolfe from his work. It was the absorbing task of his whole life to write his autobiography. He wrote it first in the two novels, *Look Homeward, Angel* and *Of Time and the River*, calling himself Eugene Gant. Then he wrote it all over again in another pair of novels, *The Web and the Rock* and *You Can't Go Home Again*, calling himself George Webber. In between these major efforts he produced volumes of short stories which read like, and probably were, shavings from the novels, which publishers dreaded to see grow out of the capacious limits of a thousand pages. He also wrote such highly personal footnotes to his own career as *The Story of a Novel*, in which he tells of his home town's bitter first reaction against his work. (One salty old lady wrote to him that "although she had never believed in lynch law, she would do nothing to prevent a mob from dragging his 'big overgrown karkus' across the square.") When he died at thirty-seven, it was found that he had written enough letters to his mother to fill another sizable volume, and these contained still another intimate record of his spiritual and material progress.

It might be said that he spent his life crying "Wolfe! Wolfe!" and whether or not he did it once, twice, or several times too often is wholly a matter of personal opinion. For the first cry was almost exactly like the last. There was no growth and very little change in his philosophy or outlook.

Indeed, after the appearance of the first book, which seemed

so compelling in its fresh, tireless exuberance, it became increasingly evident that Wolfe had no philosophy at all. My
own interest dwindled as I found that I was expected to follow
this copious writer again and again through the dark and
tortuous passages of a boy's mind.

Thomas Wolfe was, as his later books forced his first admirers to admit, an egocentric monster, tenderly concerned
with his own sensibilities, yet capable of blighting cruelty in
his relations with others. Empathy frequently prompted him
to search out the secret that moved the mind of another, but
when he had found it, a characteristic adolescent impulse inspired him to expose, with gleeful spite, the pitiful weakness
he had discovered. His chief requirement of experience was
that it should feed his own insatiable need. His recurring cry
of "Oh lost! forever lost!" was really nothing but the adolescent's characteristic incantation of wonder and self-pity and
fear.

Yet in its early expression, as in *Of Time and the River*,
the cry had a certain urgency and freshness that seemed impressive.

⮑§ In *The Autobiography of Alice B. Toklas* Gertrude Stein
said of Glenway Wescott: "Some syrup there; but it won't
pour." She could not have said that of Thomas Wolfe. There
is plenty of syrup in his new book, and good heavens, with
what copiousness it pours! Every ten pages or so one comes
upon a different manifestation of the author's vitality. It shows
itself in yearning, lyrical poetry; in impudent, witty char-
acterizations; in long, exultant discussions of food; in striking
passages of criticism; in silly, affected, almost effeminate dips
into sentimentality; in an avid curiosity about every way of
life; in a tireless concern with tricks of speech and vocabulary.
What Thomas Wolfe has observed Thomas Wolfe must interpret. And he must take as much time in interpreting it as
he likes.

There is almost no effort to pretend that *Of Time and the*

River is anything but an autobiography. Eugene Gant's experiences follow too closely the experiences of Thomas Wolfe. The physical events of the story are few and comparatively unimportant, but they directly parallel those of the author's life: the boyhood in a southern town, the postgraduate years at Harvard, the return to his mother's house, the period of teaching in New York, the flight into exile in England, the European journey, the return to America.

It makes the examination of Wolfe's book easier and more rewarding simply to admit that he is writing about himself and his inner life exactly as Proust did in *Remembrance of Things Past*. The similarity between the impulse of Proust and the impulse of Wolfe is so great that one marvels at the completeness of all other differences between them. The basic difference is that Wolfe's sensibilities are wholly normal. His response to people, places, pictures, books, and food is that of a man whose appetite for understanding is simply insatiable.

This is his description of Eugene Gant's monstrous desire to see and be and do: "He would get up in the middle of the night to scrawl down insane catalogues of all that he had seen and done: the number of books he had read, the number of miles he had traveled. . . . And at one moment he would gloat and chuckle over these stupendous lists like a miser gloating over his hoard, only to groan bitterly with despair the next moment and to beat his head against the wall as he remembered the overwhelming amount of all he had not seen or done or known."

It is important to remember about Thomas Wolfe that when you stand beside him he seems to be seven feet tall, to weigh two hundred pounds, and to have atop his broad shoulders a child's touching, eager face. I wonder if it is too fantastic to suggest that Thomas Wolfe has somehow come to contain within himself the genius of our time. He is still young and vigorous; he is shrewd and curious and naive; he is a poet; he is a man whose keen eye penetrates through sham;

he is a great, blundering, egocentric lout of a boy. He is all
these things at once and there is no denying that anyone who
can be so much is important. As Eugene Gant's great friend,
Francis Starwick, says of him, "There is a great river of energy
in you and it keeps bursting over and breaking loose. You
could not hold it back if you tried."

I apply that to Thomas Wolfe, as he means us to understand we are entitled to do. He is a river of energy, plunging
through mysterious dark caverns, rippling pleasantly under
the sun, leaping from high places, recklessly spending its
power, creating power—a terrific elemental force.

The narrative does not count at all. The individual scenes
do, because each communicates something to Eugene Gant
which Thomas Wolfe gives back to the reader. The relationship of Eugene to his strange Boston uncle is full of drama.
The devastating analysis of Professor Hatcher, the elegant,
shallow teacher of drama at Harvard, who actually taught boys
to be only dilettantes wooing triviality, is a brilliant achievement. Eugene's bitter beginnings to many friendships, like
the one with his Jewish student, Abraham Jones, are packed
solid with good psychological observation. Thomas Wolfe can
turn any literary trick that anyone in our time has tried. He
goes in for melodrama, social satire, sentimental comedy
(pretty bad and momentarily alienating). He cannot walk
through the lobby of a hotel without having to overhear and
record every conversation and the curious accent of every
speaker.

Wolfe's virtuosity is very great. But it does not show itself
merely in the power of his effects. He has his fineness too.
He makes telling phrases: "the wretched kind of hatred that
comes from intolerable pity without love"; a "good grotesque
old empress of confusion"; "trying to suck sweetness out of
paving brick." I pick these at random. But the one that seems
to me most accurately to express his own mood is "ecstatic
and insatiable glee." Even when he broods and yearns and

feels that all is "lost, oh lost," there is in him still an ecstatic and insatiable appetite for life. ౽౿

By the time he published the volume of stories *From Death to Morning* I had begun to wonder how long the reading public would be patient with Thomas Wolfe as he performed his protean act, playing the dual role of high priest of the cult of ecstasy and garrulous occupant of the confessional booth.

౿ঙ The question is: How long can Thomas Wolfe go on being simply Thomas Wolfe? So far in the two thousand pages, more or less, that he has written we have had a series of experiments in autobiography. He makes very little effort to conceal what he is about. In *Of Time and the River* he sometimes forgot to write of Eugene Gant and wrote "I." It matters so little that his proofreaders did not even catch the mistake.

In this volume of stories it is the same thing. It is Thomas Wolfe who dines in a penthouse near the East River in New York and gives his posturing host a lecture on loneliness. It is Thomas Wolfe who broods about death in Brooklyn. It is Thomas Wolfe who describes the strange world of a man who is very tall, as he himself is.

He is the "nutty guy" who baffles an unimaginative companion by prowling about in the remote corners of greater New York, guided by a map to places the names of which sound romantic. It is he who sees the circus setting up its tents; he who makes encounters with many sorts of men and women and, with a kind of volcanic sensitivity, feels qualities of being "lost" and "ruined." While he is quivering over these unfortunates, it is still his own highly personal emotion that matters to him and that he seeks to make important to the reader. Surely few writers in the whole history of literature have so abundantly exploited themselves.

It is true that he deserves to be exploited far more than most. Everything about Thomas Wolfe is on the heroic scale, on the scale of his six feet, six inches. His curiosity is tremendous, his energy gigantic, his senses powerfully acute. He knows how to communicate the heightened quality of all his emotions. Taste has a richer flavor when it has been rolled under his tongue; sight a greater vividness seen through his eyes. His brightness is brighter, his strangeness stranger, his darkness of a more utter impenetrability.

And yet the question remains unanswered whether it is enough for a creative writer to be able to dissect himself and offer in each new piece of work a sizable section.

The element of autobiography is very strong in any work of fiction. Somewhere Somerset Maugham has made the confession, to which any honest craftsman would subscribe, that every central figure in a story is the author in disguise. A discerning reader can verify the truth of the statement for himself. The conscientious John Galsworthy appears in all his novels; cultivated, worldly, liberal-minded, sensitive, and slightly bemused. The strenuous "Red" Lewis is in Doc Kennicott, George Babbitt, Elmer Gantry, Martin Arrowsmith, and Doremus Jessup.

But Galsworthy and Lewis always have gone to a great deal of pains to vary the disguise. The world of a creative artist should be large and he should roam through it to the farthest limits. When he has identified himself with a new scene, a new set of characters, he must still draw vitality and passion from within himself. But that is quite a different process from remaining within the limitations of one's personal self, exploiting constantly the fervors and perturbations of the inmost soul.

Thomas Wolfe seems to have accepted the boundaries of his own temperament as those that must always limit him. That seems to me unwise. For though the temperament is large and stocked with many provocative interests, it is not as large as the world. The creative artist should be satisfied with nothing less than the whole world.

Wolfe is a giant, but he is a giant in chains.

There are many extraordinary passages in *From Death to Morning*, passages of great beauty, of wild humor and genuine pathos. The scene in which a careless riveter working on a building receives the red-hot steel not in his bucket but in his body, and falls with his clothes in flames, is an unforgettable bit of description. Wolfe's sense, after the accident, of being two-dimensional, of looking out on a flat world in which nothing curves, except the despairing scream of the victim, is received by the reader with an almost unbearable sharpness. Yet in the same sketch, "Death the Proud Brother," he reveals his worst trick. When he begins to add adjective to adjective in an effort to pound out an effect, the hammering becomes monotonous, almost soporific. All meaning is beaten out of the passage.

"Poor, shabby, servile, fawning, snarling, and corrupted cipher, poor, meager, cringing, contriving, cunning, drearily hopeful, and dutifully subservient little atom of the million-footed city. Poor, dismal, ugly, sterile, shabby little man . . ." All those words, the glut of which help Mr. Wolfe to write novels nine hundred pages long!

Thomas Wolfe is a very powerful and provocative writer. Despite his mannerisms and his lack of a point of view, he is able still to fix one's attention upon what he has to say. But will he be able to do it forever? I wonder. Perhaps we lesser men, lacking his capacity for emotion, will find presently that we have learned all we care to know about him. ⤷

But the doubts of the critical could do nothing to deter Wolfe from the orgy of self-revelation which proved so exhausting to everyone but himself. The most he was willing to do, by way of making a concession to critical taste, was to give himself a new name in his last two novels. Eugene Gant became George Webber, a shorter man, with a different background and a different set of idiosyncrasies, but the suffering, hungering heart remained the same, that of Thomas Wolfe.

It was Wolfe's misfortune that he did not grow more mature from book to book. The individuality that seemed so striking in the first and that was still of more than average interest in the second had become altogether too familiar in the third. Although he had poured out his yearnings without reserve and with overpowering effect in two books, there was still nothing on his mind except the absorbing interest of doing it all over again. Wolfe's stature as a man and as a writer did not seem nearly so great at the end of his career as it had at the beginning.

⁂ And now finis is written to the career of Thomas Wolfe. Out of the brief but intense tumult of his spirit came four novels, a volume of sketches, and another volume of critical comment, which will have to be re-examined and reappraised by anyone who wishes to interpret the writing of our time.

The importance of his work lies in the fact that he made so complete and for the most part so honest a revelation of what went on in the mind and heart of one man living under the conditions of our present-day world. He was certainly not a great creative artist. Only a reader as naive as Wolfe himself could possibly regard him as a thinker. Until he approached the writing of this last book he made scarcely any effort to generalize on his themes. He simply wanted to encompass the copiousness of himself and make permanent the record of his driving needs.

It was rather fatuous of him, in the first place, to assume that he had the right to set down at such length and with such a prophetic air his not at all remarkable observations on the education and development of a sensitive young man. But because he persisted in his task with such vehement determination, because he approached it from many angles and with an exhaustive thoroughness, the body of his work becomes a kind of heroic monument to one of the popular impulses of American writing. Thomas Wolfe was the yearning, demanding, hungry young man par excellence. . . .

So Wolfe's career ended with a question still unanswered. Who was this giant who cast his shadow over America for a decade? Was he not the attractive, unreliable—even dangerous—embodiment of all restless, assertive immaturity? I think so. ᕦᕤ

The posthumous publication of *Thomas Wolfe's Letters to His Mother* offered the literary critic and historian a final opportunity to achieve insight into the mind of the writer.

ᕤ "I know this now," Thomas Wolfe wrote to his mother when he was a young man in his teens, "I am inevitable."

It is interesting that he should have had an intuitive, anticipatory glimpse of the fact that he was to be unique among American writers of his time. But his comment does not indicate that he understood himself well then or at any later time. In 1921 he thought that a career as a playwright was inevitable for him. Actually no effort could have been more inappropriate to a man who needed nine hundred pages in which to turn around and who had no notion of compression or of economy of means.

The letters are not in themselves distinguished. They are the work of a young man who within the shell of his egotism felt pitifully vulnerable and insecure. An obsession with money runs through these pages. His tuition at Harvard has not been paid. He needs more socks. Can his mother let him have a hundred dollars a month on which to live abroad? It will be impossible for him to economize because he is traveling with some wealthy people and must live by their standards. All the while he worries about being a taker. Yet when he accepts a teaching job, he hopes fervently that something will turn up so that he can slip out of the arrangement into a more com-

fortable one. More comfortable ones were constantly being
arranged for him.

Later the obsession turned to a flood tide of comments on
royalties, lecture fees, hopes for magazine profits.

With schoolboy naiveté Tom tells "Dear Mama" about the
"wealthy ladies" whom he has met in Paris and in New York.
Despite the protestation of the editor of these letters that
Wolfe did not share his mother's love of great names, it seems
evident that both the wealth and the ladylikeness of these
acquaintances dazzled him.

But for the most part the letters are about that glittering
inevitability of fame toward which he makes his faltering but
determined way. "I get lots of praise," he wrote to his mother
from Chapel Hill. "There is no one like me, and I shall conquer," he chirps a few years later. "Fools will call this conceit,
but let them say what they will—they are fools."

It was not at all clear to him, in those early years, what he
proposed to conquer. He did not wish passionately to say something bold and free, something that would change people's
minds, alter the outlook of a country's thinking. He simply
had to be on a platform in a well-lighted place saying something, anything, that would make him noticeable, constantly
noticeable, unique among all other exhibits of noticeable
people.

Thomas Wolfe was devoted to his mother and she to him.
This volume of letters addressed to "Dear Mama" explains
the closeness of the bond that Wolfe felt with the past, with
the village of his childhood, with the neighbors about whom
his mother, who was herself a novelist manqué, had told her
rambling stories, with the problem of whether or not you can
go home again. In her talks with the editor of this volume
(recorded verbatim in the introduction) Mrs. Wolfe tells
such astonishing facts about the beginnings of her famous son
as that she nursed him until he was three and a half years old
and that every day she curled the beautiful brown hair which

hung to his shoulders until he had begun to go to school. "He being the baby," she said, "I kept him a baby."

That was why he wrote the books that are his curious monument. They are the tributes of Tom Wolfe to Tom Wolfe. There he stands against the background of Asheville, scowling at fools and grasping at fame, a symbolic figure representing youthful urgency.

It is disappointing, but hardly surprising, to find that the Thomas Wolfe who revealed himself in all his unguarded innocence to his mother was such an overgrown boy. He lacked completely that selfless humility which is so touching in many of the finest creative spirits. Genius, of course, has often been petulant and demanding; it has often been bitter and dismayed. But there are a surprising number of instances in which it has shown itself to be patient and unprotesting as long as it was permitted to be the medium through which the creative impulse expressed itself. But that was not Thomas Wolfe's way.

Yet he said things about himself that were true. There was no one like him. His work stands as a monument to the adolescent as genius. ᘓᗉ

William Saroyan

THE clue to the secret of what goes on in William Saroyan's conscientiously elfin intelligence is to be found in one of his less well-known works, the play *Jim Dandy*. The scene is a public library in San Francisco, one of those extraordinarily serviceable institutions which can be counted upon to supply such props as a piano, a clarinet, and a little red wagon whenever the sweetly unreasonable Saroyan requires them. One of the librarians observes with the dreamy intensity of all the gentle people who drift in and out of his plays, "We are not seeking truth. We've tried that and now we want something better."

The something better than truth for which William Saroyan is looking is quite simply love, that genial, unselective, un-critical sentiment that falls, like rain from heaven, on the just and the unjust. Saroyan's moonstruck passion for the human race is certainly the most immature attitude that has ever sup-ported a literary career through a decade of almost uninter-rupted success.

William Saroyan was born in Fresno, California, of Arme-nian parents, less than forty years ago. He published his first book, *The Daring Young Man on the Flying Trapeze*, when he was twenty-six, and since then he has become the author of books sponsored by the glossiest of the clubs, films starring the most deeply treasured of Hollywood's stars, plays presented under the most sober, fastidious, and responsible of auspices. He has won distinguished prizes and has been the pet of exact-ing critics.

Though he was scarcely to be classified as an infant prodigy when he began his career, he has plunged through every phase of its surprising development with the fresh-faced audacity and disarming egocentric enthusiasm of a perennial adolescent.

His philosophy amounts to no more than this: that people are beautiful; that the most foolish among them must be cherished if only for the lovely, inept yearnings in them; that society jostles them idly and indifferently, underscoring their weaknesses with so little concern for justice that Saroyan must equalize the matter by underscoring their virtues with a com-parable lack of concern for justice.

Saroyan himself is a little like a character in a comic strip who deliberately hits himself over the head so that he can see stars. His dazed quest for something better than truth has resulted in his creating delightfully unexpected effects both on the printed page and in the theater. Occasionally, when a completely sympathetic hand has been put to his work, as was the case in the production of the play *The Time of Your Life*, an evening of pure enchantment results. The more characteristic effect of his juvenile juggling with ideas is a confused, mixed pleasure.

The collection of sketches called, after one of their number, *The Daring Young Man on the Flying Trapeze* is still the best revelation of his curious talent that Saroyan has offered.

❧ You might suppose that a story called *The Daring Young Man on the Flying Trapeze* would be tricky, super-smart, or simply exhibitionistic. Its reference to a currently popular ballad suggests that perhaps we have to do with a very young man who is desperately determined to call attention to himself. But the story to which Saroyan has given that name has none of these characteristics. It is, instead, a curiously appealing small sketch of a young man who is ill from hunger. For a long time he has had no work and his only nourishment has been from black coffee. He tries to find a job and fails. He tries to write in the YMCA and grows dizzy from exhaustion. He drinks a great deal of water, trying to feel nourished. He goes to the public library and reads until he becomes dizzy again. The phrases about the flying trapeze go through his mind as the vertigo of hunger seizes him. That is all; but good heavens—it's enough!

Better than any other sketch in the volume I like the one called "Seventy Thousand Assyrians." Its small event—physical happenings are very rare in these pages—is the meeting of Saroyan the Armenian with Theodore Badal the Assyrian, to whom the young writer goes to have his hair cut. As sons of men who came out of the East, there is a special bond between them. So they talk of the life from which they have sprung, a life which had once its own nobility and dignity but which is dying. Badal says that in all the world there are only seventy thousand Assyrians. "And the Arabs are killing us. They killed seventy of us in an uprising last month. There was a small paragraph about it in the paper. Seventy of us destroyed. . . . There is no hope. We are trying to forget Assyria."

To Saroyan this constitutes the whole drama of human struggle, persistence, failure. "I am thinking," he concludes his sketch, "of Theodore Badal, himself seventy thousand Assyrians and seventy million Assyrians, himself Assyrania, and man, standing in a barber shop in San Francisco, in 1933, and being, still, himself, the whole race."

These sketches are the work of a man who has suffered continuously while they were being written. A sense of futility and failure broods over them. Saroyan fears that they will never be read, that he might just as well not have got his typewriter out of hock. The feeling of writing for an indifferent audience oppresses him and makes him insist over and over again on the philosophic principles that uphold him. His philosophy is frequently naive and sometimes banal. In the writer it amounts to a determination to produce nothing that would be acceptable to the *Saturday Evening Post*. In the man it is reducible to the Rousseauvian doctrine that man is good and the institutions he has created are bad. Saroyan shouts his battle cries over and over again. But his defiance is touching because it is entirely right-minded. Even the rather juvenile statement and the persistent repetition cannot rob it of dignity.

Most of the time he writes with a kind of childlike beauty, a new awareness of the possibilities of words that, for me, definitely enriches language. "Night came and he sent his sadness into his sleep, weeping softly there without shedding tears." There is a spontaneous art in the arrangement of those words and sounds that gives to a simple old experience a fresh meaning and a sharper poignancy. . . . ঽ

Borrowing a title from the uncompromising Balzac to go along with the fragment of philosophy carelessly snatched up from Rousseau, Saroyan produced *The Human Comedy* shortly before the war thrust its great hiatus into his career.

⏎§ The truth about Saroyan's first full-length novel is just the same old truth that has always had to be pointed out concerning him and his work. He is a gentle and beguiling creature whose fresh, humorous exuberance can, under the happiest circumstances, be turned into pure enchantment.

But because innocence is his gentle racket, Saroyan has never developed the slightest trace of a critical faculty. He cannot distinguish between the best and the worst in his work; between poetic compassion and moony, indulgent sentimentality; between dramatic inspiration and mere tricky improvisation. . . .

The Human Comedy sounds best when it is read aloud by someone who reads well. Under such fortunate circumstances, one is likely to say of its view of the world, "Well, it isn't true, but it ought to be."

But later there comes to the mind a more profound protest against the world of Saroyan. It is too flawless a world and there are no dissonances in its song. The enemy is far away and vague. His threats can be exorcised by murmuring incantations about how wonderful people are, how beautiful, and how sweetly fragrant of innocent desire are even their mistakes.

Everyone behaves in *The Human Comedy* under the enchantment of graciousness. A whiskey-soaked old man understands a child's heart with the most delicately attuned intuitions. A young man when he is held up at the point of a gun by a wild-eyed youngster hands over all his money, not because he is frightened but because he understands the youngster's deep, spiritual needs.

Mothers, schoolteachers, contemplative grocers all read neat little homilies about the living of this life. Saroyan, sometimes accused of having no ideas, bursts with sententiousness, now, like a wall-motto factory.

The individual bits are what make the book so often striking and touching: Ulysses Macauley waving at a Negro on a freight train and suddenly knowing ecstasy . . . a melancholy man looking at his dissatisfied little boy and thinking in a kind of panic, "Be happy! Be happy! I am unhappy, but you must be happy." . . . a little boy watching a mechanical man in a drugstore window and being all at once tragically and frighteningly aware of what it is to live and to die.

These are the moments of illumination to which Saroyan brings something that lies outside the power of any writer who is not touched with genius and for which it is always necessary to forgive him his excessive tenderness, his sometime laborious improvisations, and his not infrequent flashes of juvenility. ॐ

A Local Habitation

I<small>F A</small> critic of American writing were required, at the point of a gun, to say what manifestation of the creative impulse has seemed to him the most significant of the past two decades, he would answer, just a little sulkily, that it was probably the development of the school of literary interpretation called regionalism.

His reluctance to commit himself even to that extent would be due to a fear that he might be suspected of joining a cult. A school of writing, if it becomes too closely organized and self-conscious, is likely to gather unto itself some of the more intense features of a religion. Its adherents become fanatics, regarding those who choose to remain outside its discipline as renegades from the faith. A detached analyst finds himself quite unwilling to say that simply because the type of writing called regionalism is good, it is necessarily the best. Some of his closest friends, this impartial critic will stubbornly insist, are cosmopolitans.

For many years past, wherever two or three writers were gathered together, outside Boston, New York, or Philadelphia, an eager and often acrid discussion of regionalism has been likely to ensue. The esthete will object to the whole idea on the principle that literature does not concern itself with what happens to the family of a grocer living at the corner of Pine and Maple streets in Topeka, Kansas, but rather with "a bouquet of jonquils in a silver vase." Another type of observer whose mind is moved only by the delirious uncertainties of "the universal theme" will feel that he has clinched the case for the prosecution by asking, "Was Dostoevski a regionalist?" Even writers who have been called regionalists will deny hotly that they are any such manner of creature, feeling that to submit to such pigeonholing would be to narrow their field and dwarf their interests.

All such objections are based on a misapprehension about what regionalism can and should accomplish. The impulse of the best interpreters of the school is not sluggishly to reject the universal theme, but rather to display it to most dramatic advantage in a setting of particular interest. The effort of the regionalist is to

> . . . give to airy nothing
> A local habitation and a name . . .

The grocery store in Topeka, the farmhouse in the Red River Valley of Minnesota, the town meeting hall of a village in Vermont—these are simply the backgrounds against which the conscientious regionalist attempts to display the drama of some universal theme, man against himself, man against the temper of the times, man against the world.

Many things have happened during the past twenty years to bring to a kind of crisis the effort to describe the actual conditions under which the citizens of the United States live their lives in the various alcoves of our society. They all have to do with America's rediscovery of itself.

During the early years of the present century American artists tended to be impressed to a stultifying degree by the idea that our literary tradition was derivative and imitative. They had lost what the much earlier writers of the New England group possessed, an awareness that their own time and place were of preoccupying interest. What might be called the Henry James complex became widespread and all the bright young men thought of themselves as Europeans in exile. The culture from which they sprang seemed to them so parochial and meager that it could be made dramatic only by showing it in conflict with the rich tradition of the Old World. The expatriates who flocked to Paris after the First World

War were typical of the group of interpreters upon whom we had to depend for our literary record of the life of the century.

It was the threat of a second world war that changed many minds. Not only did the unsettled conditions of Europe (and the loss of a favorable exchange rate) send the artists home; the impending collapse of one world made inquiring minds begin to engage in speculation about what might have been happening in a world that seemed to be more or less whole.

The men and women who became the interpreters of American life in the 1920's and 1930's were not, to be sure, the expatriates who had come back to our soil chastened and repentent. The men who returned from Paris—Hemingway, Fitzgerald, and Bromfield—did not become regionalists dedicated to the celebration of the ways of life lived along the highways of America. But finis had been written to one chapter of American letters, and a new group of writers came forward to start the next chapter on a fair white page.

When they began to examine the life of America as it is actually being lived under contemporary conditions, these interpreters found that it was by no means as whole or as innocent of any kind of blame as it had been made to appear. Writers for the popular magazines had invented a beguiling legend about our land. Its point was that anyone having his proper share of American energy could count upon achieving a dazzling triumph in whatever work he adopted. The great American success story was told over and over again, with minor variations and in a modest variety of settings. Patrons of the slick-paper publications, the lending libraries, the stage, and the screen had their minds edified to the point of utter ennui by these dreary repetitions of a childish myth.

Flattering as this pretense was to American ambition and to the American ego, the legend began, in the years of the depression, to lose its hold upon the imagination of the public. Let us hope that its stereotyped generalizations and its monotony would eventually have palled even if its lie had not finally brought it into disrepute.

Sober-minded men and women, undertaking an orderly reappraisal of life in the United States, saw that the sharecroppers of the South were not successful; that the dwellers on the cutover lands of Minnesota did not climb from strength to strength, straight into penthouse apartments; that the crackers of Florida and the Spanish Americans of New Mexico did not share in the limitless abundance of the "American way."

Inspired by no desire to be iconoclastic, but merely by an impulse to describe the life of America in all its infinite variety—from sybaritic luxury to the most squalid need, from fastidious nurturing to utter neglect, from a high degree of civilization to abysmal ignorance and misery—the men and women who called themselves regionalists began to pour out their findings.

Erskine Caldwell

ONE of the earliest to arrive with the bad news was Erskine Caldwell. His debut was so surprising as to leave public and critics alike completely bewildered about his intentions. Reviewers of the first of his books to receive wide attention, *Tobacco Road*, insisted upon regarding him as a kind of low comedian. The most perceptive among them professed to find a wild hilarity in his description of the rough-and-tumble existence lived by the undernourished, subhuman creatures on the nearly obliterated bypaths of Georgia.

The reason that Caldwell's curious gift was so completely misunderstood was that he chose to write his first books with an air of detachment which leaves the gross discrepancy between the social values of normal people and those of his characters suspended in midair, outlined against no background of judgment or even of comment. The people of

Tobacco Road, not inhibited by training of any kind, follow the simplest impulses of hunger and desire like primitives. Yet they are rather worse than savages, for, having been negligently shuffled out of the American tradition, they lack even the modifying and corrective influence of primitive mores. They live in a vacuum. All this seemed so odd to readers that they were moved by it only to laughter.

But it was certainly far from being Caldwell's intention that they should laugh. His own fabulous history has touched the life of the underprivileged at nearly every turn, and he himself is deeply concerned over its problems. In the course of his early years, after being tugged into many an unlikely setting as the child of a Methodist minister who went where his work took him, Erskine Caldwell served as seaman on board a vessel running guns to Cuban revolutionists, professional football player, salesman of Alabama lots that were three feet under water, bodyguard for a Chinaman, cotton-picker, millhand, hack-driver, stagehand in a burlesque theater, cook, and waiter.

Having been for so long a time quite unprotected by social conventions, Caldwell became unconcerned with conventions of any kind, including those of literature. The result was that his early work read like a kind of cross between a social worker's case report and an adventure story told by a naive but exuberant beginner.

Tobacco Road was nonetheless an important and a serious book.

⇥§ Erskine Caldwell is a new American realist to whom we are going to listen very attentively during the next few years. His early book called *American Earth* created a new and surprising literary mold. It was a volume of sketches in which the author demonstrated clearly that he possessed the shrewdness and the detachment for telling harsh and horrible little truths about certain aspects of the American scene.

His first novel is in the same mood. But it has as much

more power as a novel should have. *Tobacco Road* is a grimly fascinating study of the degraded conditions under which the poor whites of Georgia live out their meaningless, pitiable, and altogether distressing existence.

Jeeter Lester is one of those utterly forlorn creatures who may perhaps be aptly described as disinherited by nature. He lives on the ungracious land from which all the men and women in whom ambition and protest have not quite died out have long since fled. He has lost any desire to compete and even the will to survive is sluggish in him.

He lives with his wife, mother, son, and daughter on the ruins of his farm, slowly starving to death. Every virtue that we claim for human nature has sickened and died within him and he has sunk far, far below the animal level. He has lost even the impulse to find food for himself and his family. His torpor is complete, and consciousness survives in him only as a warped, perverted, and absurd burlesque of human intelligence. His vague mental retrogression is somehow more distressing than madness.

At first it is difficult to believe the picture. From its explicit portraiture the imagination of the well-fed and comparatively secure reader retreats into incredulity. But gradually one becomes aware that no one could have made up such horrors. Not even a man of letters could be so morbid as to plague us with despair like this unless he had the justification of telling the truth.

In the first scene the Lesters are revealed in all their hopelessness. Jeeter's son-in-law, Lov Bensey, has come to complain about his wife. Pearl will not behave as a wife should. She will not talk. Even when Lov tries such disciplinary measures as throwing rocks at her, she only runs away. He cannot think what is wrong. He wants advice and help.

But Jeeter and his family are not thinking very concentratedly of Pearl. They have seen that Lov has a bag of winter turnips on his back. On that they fix their attention. When

Ellie May Lester, whose one flaw as an example of feminine loveliness is her cleft lip, distracts Lov into a flirtation, Jeeter catches up the bag of turnips and runs into the woods. There he gorges happily until his son Dude descends upon him to claim a share in the booty.

But much worse is to follow. A woman preacher, Bessie, visits the Lester home to pray their sins away. She casts her eyes upon Dude, the sixteen-year-old boy, and straightway decides that God means him to become a preacher too. So she marries him. The boy is lethargic and unconcerned until Bessie promises to buy him an automobile. This distressing little romance has its complete fulfillment for Dude when he drives the car down Tobacco Road, releasing all his inner soul by honking the horn incessantly.

The appalling episodes pile up. Dude runs into a truck. The Negro driver is thrown into the street and his skull crushed. The Lesters decide that probably he is dead and drive unconcernedly on. In a terrific family battle over whether Jeeter is to be allowed to ride in the car, a break comes between Dude and his parents. He backs the car out of the yard, running over the grandmother as he goes. No one pays the slightest attention. Several hours later Jeeter examines the body, decides that though she isn't yet dead she soon will be, and goes to dig a grave.

Later still in the same eventful day Jeeter has one of his rare impulses to assert himself. He will farm his land once more. The first step is to burn the sedge. He sets fire to it and retires to bed. The fire envelops everything in the neighborhood, including the hut in which Jeeter and his wife lie asleep.

The next day Dude and Bessie come to survey the ruins. And presently as they drive away Dude is saying, "I reckon I'll get me a mule somewhere and some seed cotton and guano, and grow me a crop of cotton this year. It feels to me like it's going to be a good year for cotton. Maybe I'll grow me a bale to the acre, like pa was always talking about doing."

The hideous story of Jeeter is to be repeated all over again. All this is told by Erskine Caldwell with complete objective detachment. It is as though Mr. Caldwell took the reader by the hand, led him to the scene of these dreadful happenings, commanded "Look! Listen!" and then retired to let the onlooker draw all his conclusions for himself. From beginning to end he makes no comment, no interpretation. He resists every temptation to point a sociological moral.

Obviously Caldwell does not consider the plight of Jeeter Lester to be inevitable. It is his literary slyness to force a sense of responsibility upon the reader by seeming to take none himself. It is a triumphantly successful method.

We are blandly unconscious in America of the squalor that exists in hidden corners. *Tobacco Road* should be read aloud to everyone who has ever made a glib, ignorant generalization about the high standard of life in the United States. ઠ

When Caldwell's collection of short stories, *Kneel to the Rising Sun*, appeared, the fact that he wrote as a conscious social reformer became so apparent that only a few die-hard esthetes remained determined to deny it.

ઠ The story that gives its name to the new collection of Erskine Caldwell's studies of the good life in Georgia is one of the most painful and impressive I have ever read. With the extraordinary economy of means that characterizes the best of Caldwell's work, he packs into this tale all the wretchedness of the share-cropper's existence, all the piteousness of the Negro's plight, and all the insensate brutality of the South's new tyrant, the landlord.

Lonnie, the share-cropper, is entirely dependent for food upon the caprice of Mr. Arch. He and his wife and his father are slowly starving to death on the short rations allowed them. But Mr. Arch maintains a sort of merry detachment, employing his leisure in the torture of dogs. Desperate at last, the father tries to satisfy himself with the slops given to Mr. Arch's hogs. He falls into the pen and is horribly destroyed by the boars.

With the help of Clem, the Negro, Lonnie tries to pull his father out. Their human dismay is met only with inhuman cunning by Mr. Arch, who tries to drive them away. The action of the Negro in defending himself from physical blows is interpreted as insurrection and the vigilantes are called out to track Clem down and shoot him. Only Lonnie knows the hiding place. Threatened by Mr. Arch with the loss of his pitiful social superiority as a white man and threatened also with the loss of his meager livelihood, Lonnie betrays his friend. . . .

It is ridiculous to believe that Caldwell writes this kind of story because he has a morbid obsession with the unpleasant. It is even more ridiculous to believe that he sets these things down in a misguided spirit of fun. He is as sincerely a reformer as the author of *Uncle Tom's Cabin*. He sees no reason why we should be let off knowing the truth about the degraded and horrible conditions under which we permit fellow Americans to live. He would like to use his influence to bring about a change in the institutions which allow one group to prey ruthlessly upon another, the tyrants themselves becoming brutalized in the process. It is strange that he could have been so misunderstood. I attribute that misunderstanding to an obstinate determination not to believe what he has to tell. ❧

For a period in the late 30's and early 40's Erskine Caldwell turned his attention away from the American scene. He went as a war correspondent through the East and into Russia. The experience was not rewarding for a man who had spent so much of his life as interpreter of a scene quite different. His nonfiction study of life with the Red army and a novel about the Nazi domination of a Russian village were completely uncharacteristic works which seemed to exaggerate Caldwell's literary faults and suppress his literary virtues. But in *Tragic*

Ground he returned to the native scene and brought *Tobacco Road* down to date.

◄§ In his new book Caldwell seems determined to declare himself as a reformer. He has not modified his style of writing. He still has an air of being at once uncritical and uncompromising in his objective dramatization of shocking occurrences. But his title tacitly confesses to a critical point of view. And this time he has permitted himself the luxury of creating one symbolic figure to act as his spokesman. What Caldwell wishes to say in this and in each of his other books is something quite simple. It is that only a fatuous fool can shut his eyes to the threatening existence of Tobacco Road. Men of good will cannot and dare not reject responsibility for the dismal failure even of their least worthy fellow countrymen.

Spence Douthit, the central figure of *Tragic Ground*, is own brother to the Jeeter Lester of *Tobacco Road*. He is the bland, unworried victim of his own utter incapacity for living. He drinks his days away while his wife degenerates into a sick shrew and his daughter into a juvenile delinquent. He is a coward and a lout, yet his worthlessness is wrapped up in an air of sweet, kindly indulgence that makes it impossible to abuse him as vicious. He is, as everyone discovers sooner or later, just "that doggone Douthit" with whom nothing can be done.

His significance lies simply in the fact that he represents a type of misfit brought to noticeability by war conditions. Douthit has been uprooted from his backwoods home by employment agents and carried off to a boom town to work in a powder plant at what seems to him a fabulous wage. But very soon the plant closes and Douthit, with nothing to show for his moment of affluence, moves into a particularly dismal offshoot of Tobacco Road, a community called Poor Boy.

There, with his venomous neighbor, Chet Mitchell, and his dolorous friend, Floyd Sharp, he declines into complete hopelessness and helplessness. The thirteen-year-old girls of the community learn the first bleak lessons of concupiscence while their fathers look the other way and distract themselves by losing the little money they can lay their hands on in sordid night clubs and crooked crap games.

The only departure from this routine comes when the alert and sparkling social worker arrives to put things straight. She goes on at eloquent length about "the complex pattern of modern life" and the intricate problems of adjustment. But she creates an inexpensive diversion for the community when one woman mistakes her intention in offering money to her husband and drives her off with missiles and profanity.

It seems to me impossible to miss the significance of *Tragic Ground*. The Douthits are incurable. By removing them from one congested area to another slightly less congested, one does not remove the danger to the health of society which their apathy and inadequacy represent. The only hope is that we may learn to be sufficiently concerned about our own good to seek out and correct the conditions that produce Douthits. &

Erskine Caldwell bears the same sort of relationship to the art of fiction that a primitive like Rousseau bears to the art of painting. His intentions have been sober and his naive style has been in complete sympathy with his material. His sense of drama is vivid; his observations have been acute and significant. His whole purpose in writing of the contemporary scene was summed up in the title he gave to a pictorial survey for which he supplied the text, *Say, Is This the U.S.A.?* And his purpose has been a sufficient one. He is a useful writer who has contributed more to the understanding of our times than many a laboriously artful and conscientiously trivial scrivener.

Marjorie Kinnan Rawlings

MARJORIE KINNAN RAWLINGS might well be called the adopted sister of regionalism. She is not native to Florida, though she has dramatized many aspects of its life admirably in her novels *South Moon Under*, *Golden Apples*, and *The Yearling*. Born in Washington, D.C., and educated at the University of Wisconsin, she had "shopped about" for a setting rather widely before she chose an orange grove in Florida as the place in which she felt at home. Perhaps she has been able to analyze the quality of life at Cross Creek the better for the fact that she came to it a stranger and had slowly to edge her way into the sympathies of its inhabitants.

To say that Marjorie Rawlings writes about the crackers of Florida with feminine sympathy is not to say that she writes with sentimental yearning. Her voice is a steady, well-modulated one into which there never creeps any sobbing intonation. She is shrewd and humorous and acutely discerning; she can even be cruel when her nerves have been rasped by pretension. On one or two occasions her pen has prodded at false pride with a relentless passion for vengeance. But her characteristic mood is that of gracious and receptive sympathy, which discovers in a primitive and apparently uncomplicated way of life its own subtleties, its own delicate distinctions in the field of morality, its own complexities of impulse.

The striking difference between the approach of Marjorie Rawlings and that of Erskine Caldwell is that she chooses to identify herself closely with the life of Cross Creek, while he looks on at the domestic crises of Tobacco Road from a slightly distant vantage point. Marjorie Rawlings has moved into the cracker's shanty as a trusted neighbor and friend; Erskine Caldwell looks in at the window of Jeeter Lester's ruin of a house without entering. Tact, I think, has prompted each of them to make these different kinds of approach. Marjorie Rawlings does not wish to dissociate herself from the life of her kind; Erskine Caldwell does not wish to appear to spy on misery or to gossip about his neighbors, and therefore he escapes into a mood of scientific detachment. Her feminine values prompt Marjorie Rawlings to participate; his masculine values persuade Erskine Caldwell that it is best to be impersonal.

The pleasure that Marjorie Rawlings' style can give to the mind and ear is, of course, far greater than any at Erskine Caldwell's command. All the dramatic interest of Cross Creek's rowdiness has been filtered through a cultivated mind. This action does not screen out the irony, the unconscious bawdry, or the pity; it merely eliminates the gross shocks. Marjorie Rawlings shapes her narratives neatly, and into their design she fits all manner of revealing observations about the essential character of life among people who, like those of Erskine Caldwell's stories, have been jostled out of the march of what eulogists call "democratic progress."

In *Cross Creek*, Marjorie Rawlings' autobiographical account of life in her community, she has supplied such a good introduction to her work that it seems well to consider it first.

⋙ If our civilization were to be thoroughly wiped out in the manner imagined by H. G. Wells in *The Shape of Things to Come*, and then if Marjorie Kinnan Rawlings' *Cross Creek* were suddenly to be rediscovered, social historians would have a puzzling time of it trying to reconstruct the sort of life lived in the twentieth century on this continent.

Not that Mrs. Rawlings hasn't been explicit in this account of the society in which she lives; not that she hasn't painted a fascinating picture full of absorbing detail. She has. But it would seem very strange that Americans of the great machine age should have led so meager an existence. It would seem strange, also, that they should have had miserably inadequate shelters and too little food; that they should have resisted education, feared inoculation, hugged their ignorance and their parochial pride.

The virtues of the Cross Creek way of life would puzzle the social historian no less. It is Christian in a homely and uncomplicated way that we have long since given up expecting to find in sophisticated worlds. There is no prejudice of whites against Negroes, no fear of Negroes for whites. There is a casual sharing of resources, a sense of community responsibility. When Mr. Tubble "comes up missing" and his neighbors suspect that he may have gone off somewhere with a gallon jug, they drop everything to go and look for him before harm can come to his sodden, irritating, but somehow precious carcass. When Mrs. Rawlings' Negro helper fails to turn up on a Sunday morning, her friend Moe, happening by, forgets his private interests to do the chores for her. Mrs. Rawlings makes return payment in kind by canceling all her personal responsibilities in order to get Moe's sick child under proper medical care, ruining her best city clothes in the process.

It does not sound very much like mechanized, standardized, overstimulated America. To read *Cross Creek* is like taking a bypath away from reality to come upon a wonderland of sights and sounds, full of lush natural beauty, peopled with impoverished but gallant and uncomplaining poets. Mrs. Rawlings has written a kind of humorous song in praise of obscurity, an idyl of the undemanding.

There is nothing sentimental about this approach to a study of a curious social phenomenon. Marjorie Rawlings went to Florida, not to exploit the quaint natives in fiction, but to manage an orange grove and to try to make a living from it. She had a hard time of it at first. The royalties of her first books, *South Moon Under* and *Golden Apples*, merely satisfied old debts and got her started. With the incredible wealth put into her hand by the magazine editor who bought "Jacob's Ladder" she indulged in the luxury of a bathroom. All that while she was living the life of the place, liking it for the same reasons that Tom Glisson and old Aunt Martha Mickens liked it. She belonged to the place because she liked the eagles and the magnolia trees and the moss-hung jungle.

As soon as they were sure she belonged, the five white families and the two Negro ones began to reveal themselves to her. They invited her to "pound parties" to which every guest brought a pound of this or that, preferably a sizable cake. One

of them once took her an antique piece of furniture, real
Floridiana, explaining that it should be hers because she "lived
nice . . . been layin' up all these years for the right person."
The children revealed their natural poetry to her. A little boy
happily put a toad into her hand, saying, "Look at the little ol'
hoppy-toad. He's got eyes jus' like our baby."

They lived together in amity: the ageless Negro woman
Geechee, blind in one eye from an ancient battle, who went
on heroic drunks and yet was capable of the deepest and most
touching loyalty; Mr. Swilley, who was looking for a rich
widow and who thought Mrs. Rawlings might be the one, so
that he was forever hopping fences to fascinate her with his
prowess; Tim, who refused to let his wife do Mrs. Rawlings'
laundry, saying,

"A white woman don't ask another white woman to do her
washing for her, nor to carry her slops. 'Course in time o'
sickness or trouble or sich as that a woman does ary thing she
can for another and they's no talk o' pay."

Mrs. Rawlings writes of this scene and of its people with
an affection that is obviously sincere and deep. . . . For the
beauty of Cross Creek she has a sensitive appreciation; for its
people she has a dramatic, highly personal sympathy. Toward
nothing in the way of life is she patronizing. *Cross Creek* is
as vivid as any of her novels and wider in its range over the
whole scene of the curious corner of America of which she is
the literary discoverer. ૐ

The book that reveals Marjorie Rawlings' feminine perception of her world at its most gracious is *The Yearling*. Besides
being an admirable example of how regionalism can set the
universal theme against a background of unique interest, it is
one of the most perceptive studies of family life that the copious literature based on that theme has yet brought out of our
culture.

The reason why the work of Mrs. Rawlings makes a peculiar appeal is that it has, besides very genuine literary distinction,
the enormous advantage of being like the work of absolutely
no one else. She first discovered to readers the curious fascination of the "hammock" country in Florida. Now within the
special province of social study that she has made her own, she
has found another novelty. The Yearling is the analysis of a
twelve-year-old boy's relationship to his world: the physical
world, the social world, the world of emotion.

Deeply embedded in a story which is full of vivid action
and event lies a sensitive perception of what it is to live in the
child's realm, to feel a child's curiosity and zest; and then to
perceive the tragedy of human life through a child's eyes and
say farewell to childhood.

The sentimentality into which another writer might have
been trapped is avoided quite without effort. Through most
of its pages the book is concerned with very objective matters:
with hunting and fishing and planting crops; with the effort
to force a living from capricious land and with the effort to
have a modest amount of pleasure in moments of relaxation.

But beneath the surface the interest of the relationship between the boy Jody and his father, Penny Baxter, runs ever
more searchingly into the profound places of human emotion.

The father is an undernourished, underprivileged, under-
sized man who has compensated for the insufficiency of his
life by becoming a genius at hunting. The boy has a natural
taste for all the things in which the father takes satisfaction.
Their alliance is close. It takes the form of an amiable program
of noncooperation with Ma, a hard-working, likable creature
who cannot share their interests. She complains vigorously of
the way "you fellers" go wandering about the woods together,
neglecting immediate family duties. Each protest seems only
to strengthen the understanding between man and boy. They
continue to have great adventures like the stalking of "Old
Slewfoot" the bear.

Tragedy enters the boy's life when Jody's pet fawn begins to be an insupportable nuisance to Ma. She endures all kinds of minor trials, but when Flag destroys a whole season's crop, the boy is ordered to shoot the animal. Even Penny supports Ma's decision. Because Jody is unable to carry out her instructions, Ma shoots Flag herself. The boy's world comes tumbling about his shoulders. Not only has he lost Flag; he has lost faith too. For the first time his father has betrayed their shared ideals. Jody runs away.

After a period of starving on the road there is nothing for him to do but return home. Then for the first time the father expresses his touching, valiant philosophy.

"You figgered I went back on you," he says. "Now there's a thing ever' man has got to know. . . . 'Twan't only me. . . . Boy, life goes back on you. . . . You've seed how things goes in the world o' men. You've knowed men to be low-down and mean. You've seed ol' Death at his tricks. You've messed around with ol' Starvation. Ever' man wants life to be a fine thing, and a easy. 'Tis fine, boy, powerful fine, but 'taint easy. Life knocks a man down and he gits up and it knocks him down agin. I've been uneasy all my life."

There is no more robust writer in America today than Marjorie Rawlings. She has gusto and dramatic instinct and humor and insight. Her characters are full-blooded. Even the vicious, brawling Forresters, who work all the mischief which afflicts the neighborhood, are presented with amiable relish. When these thumping, lusty men are wakened in the night by a "varmint," they turn the incident into a major engagement with life. Like angry gods they storm about the cabin in the naked splendor of their wrath; and loath to return to bed after such a contest, they sit down before dawn for a "frolic," playing their fiddles and guitars and mouth-organs and drums.

To whatever incident she turns her hand, Mrs. Rawlings writes with unforced exuberance. The sheer physical excitement of many of her scenes challenges the literary hardihood of Hemingway at his best. She is completely mature as an artist. Every passage in her new book deftly and vigorously serves three purposes: that of immediate, dramatic interest, that of advancing the narrative, that of deepening and enriching character. ❧

John Steinbeck

JOHN STEINBECK combines the masculine objectivity of Erskine Caldwell with the feminine intuition of Marjorie Rawlings. This psychological flexibility makes him, at his best, regionalism's most adept son. It also makes him, at his worst, regionalism's worst enemy.

Like many another fine artist, Steinbeck has a kind of enriching bisexuality. He could not have created the magnificent Ma of *The Grapes of Wrath* had he not possessed an extraordinary ability to identify himself with the problems and preoccupations of women. His sense of the significance of the family unit is something that is ordinarily found clearly and passionately defined only in the novels of women.

Yet the scope of his work as a whole, its richness of incident, and its control of the strategy of a large enterprise are the assets of the masculine mind. So is another asset that is always present, an awareness of the pleasure of sheer animal activity, an unrepentent zest for the expression of physical vitality.

Out of this rich blend of traits Steinbeck has produced books of striking variety. In *The Red Pony* he has created one of the most believable children in all contemporary literature, a small boy as sensitive, sturdy, and appealing as Jody in Marjorie Rawlings' *The Yearling*. He has escaped from the confines of regionalism to write in *The Moon Is Down*, with an insight still largely unappreciated, of the plight of a people living helplessly under conquerors whom they despise.

Steinbeck's combination of masculine-feminine perceptions has sharpened his curiosity and broadened his view of the whole human enterprise. It has given him a harmonious style in which the counterpoint of action and insight enriches every theme.

This is clearly apparent in *The Grapes of Wrath*, which is also the most completely characteristic of the regional novels because of its concern with human dignity.

⋙ This is from every standpoint a fine and moving book. The central figures are those homeless wanderers who trail vaguely up and down the state of California, looking for work, finding it seldom, creating nothing out of their lives but an economic problem. It is not easy to know what to do with them and nothing approaching a satisfactory solution has been found. Steinbeck has set himself the task of looking closely into their private lives to make us see the pity and the terror of their plight.

They reach California from many starting points. The family upon which this book concentrates its attention has lived on the poor soil of Oklahoma, knowing the meagerness of the life it offers but feeling a close identification with it nonetheless, because fathers and grandfathers have lived there before them. The Joads have been share-croppers in cotton until the company for which father, mother, grandfather, and children all work decides that the tenants' share is just the margin of profit it cannot afford to lose. Machines begin to do the work of men. The tractors lumber through the dooryards and finally shatter the tenants' flimsy houses.

So they take to the road. Every one of them has heard of the gracious way of life that the grape-pickers and the orange-pickers lead in California. The Joads sell everything for which there is a price and set out in a secondhand truck. Sickness and death ride with them and their little company dwindles as they go. But it is still too large. For every job available in the vineyards and the orchards there are three hungry applicants. Wages go down, the price of food goes up. An entire family working from morning to night cannot earn enough to buy a proper meal.

And off they start again, looking for a safer haven which only their innocence can persuade them to believe exists. Steinbeck leaves the Joad family still in the midst of a flight for which there seems to be no end except that of utter exhaustion and death.

Steinbeck makes no effort to present his people as anything other than they are: ignorant, used to squalor, submissive and violent by turns. The eldest son, Tom, has been in jail for a killing which was the climax to a meaningless drunken quarrel. Al, his brother, is a restless young creature entirely without sense of direction. Grandpa is an impenitent old rascal in whose unbroken spirit the family takes a naive pride. Ma is the dominating figure, the embodiment of the homely wisdom of the race, whose duty it is to try to hold the family together, though she constantly catches glimpses of its dreary destiny.

The thing that crystallizes a reader's understanding of the Joads and their companions in flight is the sense of closeness which they feel for one another. It is not enough, Ma Joad has decided in the end, to devote oneself to husband, sons, and daughter; all the stricken must be absorbed into her family. In a final scene which is at once shocking and beautiful, that attitude is effectively stated. It has been the theme throughout the book, dramatized in a scanty meal shared, in a gradual extension of a sense of obligation toward the group.

It is the small incidents of daily life that concern Steinbeck throughout the novel. A car breaks down and everyone forgets his private interests to see that it is put in shape once more for the journey toward the promised land. Grandpa dies and is buried. The daughter's husband becomes discouraged and drifts off. The family is momentarily happy in a government camp, exulting in the magical luxury of modern plumbing. Steinbeck fills his big book with copious notes on a way of life.

Every other chapter of the book deals, not explicitly with the Joad family, but with the group to which they belong. These passages are like the choruses in Greek drama which enlarge and generalize upon the theme. They are done with complete simplicity of style. Steinbeck speaks directly and without affectation each time he assumes this role of interpreter. But the quiet intensity of his feeling takes on the moving accent of poetry.

A symbolic figure further helps to interpret the theme. He is Casy the preacher, whose private doubts concerning his usefulness have driven him from his wilderness pulpit. He can see no duty but to identify himself closely with the people among whom he lives and to shoulder their problems when he can. In the end his life is sacrificed to this service.

Very shrewdly, very skillfully, Steinbeck has kept the desolation of his material from snuffing out liveliness. The book is full of glancing wit. It illuminates character and touches even misery with a momentary brightness. The largeness of his gift may, in fact, be measured by the breadth of his emotional range. His insight perceives all those qualities of gallantry which make human life dignified and touching even in the midst of degradation. ૱

No blend of opposites can be quite perfect, and sometimes Steinbeck's masculine toughness is betrayed by his feminine tenderness. This tendency of one part of his nature to undermine the authority of the other was revealed in the sentimental illogic that marred the effectiveness of his novel and play Of Mice and Men. There was no sufficient reason why the resolute George, who could have "lived so nice," should be tied to subhuman Lonny, except that the sentimental mind of Steinbeck found the union dramatic. There is something corrupt about a love of wastefulness, and it was wasteful to have a potentially useful citizen turned into something like an outlaw because of a sense of responsibility for an antisocial creature who would have been far better off under the impersonal protection of an institution. Certain unfortunate women woo martyrdom of the kind suffered by George because they manage to idealize passivity. A man who submits to an utterly meaningless martyrdom merely seems ridiculously soft.

In *Cannery Row* the betrayal of the shrewd and humorous Steinbeck by the grotesquely soft Steinbeck became complete. Its idealization of negativism into some vague sort of supermundane divinity of tenderness resulted in as feeble a caricature of values as a clever man has ever permitted himself to write. It seemed to me to be also a sort of handbook of what the young regionalist should not do.

◦§ Cannery Row occupies a position in literary geography that is close to Tortilla Flat. Both Steinbeck neighborhoods are peopled by big-hearted eccentrics, vagrants who spend their days and nights planning and executing the quaintest of brawls, deliriously imaginative painters who don't paint, and, of course, a large supernumerary cast of gentle prostitutes.

Sometimes literal-minded readers complain that the novelists whom critics admire seem never to concern themselves with normal people, but spend their entire time in fascinated examination of the periphery of human experience. What these readers have difficulty in understanding is that one can learn more about the problems of society from the study of the behavior of the antisocial member than from the respectful examination of the plodding conformist.

Steinbeck, like Faulkner, Caldwell, and most of the other major American writers of our time, has fixed his attention on the striking circumstance and the unusual character produced by the conditions of our present-day world. His major efforts have been concerned with the plight of society's rejected children, like the tragic Okies of *The Grapes of Wrath*. In his minor vein he still follows the fortunes and misfortunes of the maladjusted, putting emphasis upon the low comedy of their waywardness. In *Cannery Row* he chronicles chiefly the charms of the subnormal. . . .

John Steinbeck seems to me to stand before his public, at this moment, as a perfect example of the writer who has been too successful. Because his work has been so extravagantly admired, he himself has come to admire it even more enthusiastically. He has lost his critical faculty, and everything that he writes is for him unchallengeably good because it came from his hand. Only a man living under the spell of his own reputation could have written and allowed to go to the printer the three-page introduction to his new book. It is from first to last a masterpiece of embarrassing ineptitude. Its mixture of bland, flaccid tenderness and earnest, hard-working buffoonery sets up in the reader a mood of hostility even before the story has been begun.

There are a great many engaging and disarming episodes in Steinbeck's new book. It would be easy and pleasant to write indulgently of these absurd happenings and of the author's talent for sweetness and light. Steinbeck himself might go so far as to say that his gift is that of plucking the fragrant rose of graciousness away from the thorn of lawlessness.

But I, for one, find myself quite completely alienated by such a specimen of the tough-tender school of American letters. If one is to write a *Beggar's Opera* then let it be with the hearty reversal of all values in which John Gay so triumphantly indulged. Let the pimps be the heroes and the pickpockets the admirable men of action. What I object to is the half-hearted style of antisocial comedy in which the vices, the weaknesses, the maudlin concessions to mindlessness become, under the treatment of irony, unbearably cute.

Really to enjoy *Cannery Row* one would have to be willing to nod one's head in fond agreement with Steinbeck's implication that utter inertia is the most blissful state of man and that only in the condition of blind staggers does divine inspiration come. Notions like these send me screaming toward the protective arms of bourgeois respectability. But I get only halfway because bourgeois respectability is not really sympathetic to anyone who fears boredom. So Steinbeck drives me into exile and leaves me feeling very much like the boll weevil of Carl Sandburg's song-bag, looking for a home. ঙ্ক

Steinbeck remains, midway in his career, a variable artist who has made unhappy concessions in his best works and risen to moments of unique excellence in his worst. Perhaps the very fact that he still gropes, and often bungles, will keep him interested in his own talent long after other contemporary writers have lost any impulse to use their better integrated skills. That has been known to happen.

The impulse of regionalism to relate the story of the progress of man to the immediate conditions of a particular man's time and place gave more contemporary writers their cue for action than any other impulse of the century. There have been regionalists in every conspicuous center and every obscure corner of America. Mary Ellen Chase in *Windswept*, Gladys Hasty Carroll in *As the Earth Turns*, and Rachel Field in *Time Out of Mind* have celebrated the local genius of Maine. Glenway Wescott, who later became one of the most complex of cosmopolitans, began by being an interpreter of Wisconsin in books like *The Grandmothers*. Archie Binns in *The Laurels Are Cut Down* has touched on various aspects of the special social and economic problems of the Pacific Northwest. Doubling back in this literary grand tour, ones comes upon Robert Bright, revealing with distinguished courtesy the tragedy of the Spanish American of New Mexico in *The Life and Death of Little Jo.*

But obviously one would need another book in which to cover all the ground, even at the pace which the indefatigable American tourist permits himself in his tours of the country.

At his least orderly and responsible, the regionalist may be nothing better than a propagandist for the local chamber of commerce, chanting the innocent delights of parochialism. At his most prejudiced, he often confuses issues mischievously, as some southern regionalists have done in discussing the relations of the races. At his most frivolous, he merely gathers together oddments of village gossip. But at his best, he has done a great deal to make the face of America a really familiar face.

Aunts from Virginia

VIRGINIA, once the all but unassailable stronghold of the South's lavender-and-old-lace tradition, has in our time made honorable amends for its fatuity of the past by producing two writers of distinction whose intelligences were shrewd and sharp and who took no nonsense from the code of the cavaliers. Willa Cather and Ellen Glasgow were American literature's aristocratic, but at least partially emancipated, aunts from Virginia.

One writes of them in the past tense because Ellen Glasgow has lately died and Willa Cather seems to have said farewell to her writing career. But their contributions to the tradition of our time were important and will continue to be admired by another generation or two among all who value a formal, reticent, and disciplined literary style.

For me the spurious refinement of the best remembered phase of the southern romantic tradition of letters has been represented, with appalling and ineradicable clarity, by a love scene from one of Thomas Nelson Page's stories in which a young man woos a girl by telling her how he has "kept himself pure for her." If any such gruesome young prig ever existed, to indulge in so vulgar and humorless an offense against delicacy, decency, and the rudimentary rules of reticence, one's only hope can be that his young woman rejected him firmly and finally before he could propagate his kind.

Against this false niceness, which is so much more nauseatingly improper than any healthy impropriety could be, these two Virginia writers took their stalwart stand. They cleaned house of many tawdry souvenirs of the past.

Yet, though they worked, like good housewives of their art,

to eliminate a great deal of rubbish from the furnishings of the novel, neither of them wished to change it from its classic design. They were rather like people who have lived with dignity and self-respect in very old houses. The spacious rooms were kept as they had been in the splendid days of a more leisurely era. The old hangings were dry-cleaned and replaced because their owners had taste enough to realize that the materials were superior to the machine-made product of our time. The old family portraits still hung on the wall. Only the sentimental Victorian intrusions were eliminated—the sculptured clasping hands, the pallid little girls in marble with every button on the high shoes faithfully reproduced. There were discreet improvements in matters of lighting and general comfort. But the house of the novel, as Willa Cather and Ellen Glasgow chose to live in it, stood on slightly "removed ground." The excellence of its lines guaranteed a permanent attraction for the eye. The solidity with which it was constructed guaranteed that it would survive longer than many modish, but jerry-built, structures.

The Cather and the Glasgow novels are monuments to the classic tradition. Neither chic nor odd, they do not express in their form anything of the spirit of our time. This judgment would not displease Miss Cather or Miss Glasgow. Both wished to be artists in cool command of their craft. Advertisement through eccentricity never made the slightest appeal to either.

There is, however, a difficulty with detachment of this kind. Inevitably it denies to the artist the special interest that goes out to newsworthy creatures like Fitzgerald, who dramatized youth, and Hemingway, who dramatized manliness, in novels that throbbed with the excitement of the moment. It is not merely the publicity department of the publisher's office that is concerned with this matter of newsworthiness. A whole generation of readers spontaneously gravitates toward the man or woman who identifies himself with the battle of the hour and who defends certain popular convictions with attractive clamor.

Even critics, who should be cool and detached too, and who should be dedicated to the task of surveying the whole scene of literary activity with impartial and temperately appraising gaze, are likely to respond in urchin glee to the sound of melodrama in the next block. If John Dos Passos sets fire to his house of the novel and the sirens scream as the apparatus of the fire department goes rolling by, the critic, too, is likely to come pelting down out of his ivory tower and go in hot pursuit of the fire truck. The candle-lit houses of these Virginia *grandes dames* do not detain them as they pass.

Willa Cather and Ellen Glasgow were alike in their virtues and in their faults. Both possessed minds of a high degree of cultivation. They were discerning and unsentimental. The style of each, considered simply as a product of self-conscious art, is much more satisfying than that of most of our contemporary writers in England and America. There is fastidiousness to the workmanship of each line, skill in the design, even a kind of glitter to the whole effect.

But in the end neither of them proves to be distinctive enough in the presentation of thought or of emotion to vie successfully with the people of more strenuous, if less correctly disciplined, talents. The *femmes savantes* of England, though they do not compare favorably with Willa Cather and Ellen Glasgow as stylists, nonetheless challenge one's respect, almost one's awe, by their readiness to undertake the complete renovation of human society in each of their novels. No institution is so fortified against change that these literary amazons will not assail it, and no theory of world affairs is so cumbersome that they will not try to cram it into the narrow confines of a novel. Set beside these eager and ardent creatures, Willa Cather and Ellen Glasgow must seem like polite and passive products of another world.

Certain observers who never have become perfectly reconciled to the spirit of our time believe that it is our paranoid ailment to demand that every work of fiction shall be a dramatization of a cause or a statement of a philosophy. May novels not be, they plead wistfully, what the novels of Willa Cather and Ellen Glasgow have been—shrewd, civilized comments on the sometimes pleasant, sometimes painful, always circuitous and puzzling way human life has taken in certain places and at certain times in our century?

It is certainly true that novels may offer passive comments on scenes and people, with never a theory of economic reform casting its shadow over the narrative. The authors of such books are in no danger of violence from thoughtful people. One is even grateful to them for their wit, their taste, and their discernment. But it is not too stern a thing to say that in the summing up they seem to add little to one's apprehension of the human plight. Willa Cather and Ellen Glasgow have tended to look backward too wistfully, to let skepticism debilitate emotion too sluggishly, in brief, to put too arbitrary and old-fashioned a discipline on their material.

Willa Cather

WILLA CATHER was removed from Winchester, Virginia, where she was born, and taken at the age of eight or nine to Nebraska. Yet it was to her native state that her fancy returned in the end, and her most recently published work, *Sapphira and the Slave Girl*, resolved her literary conflicts by giving her back, at the same time, the past and the region for which she had yearned always.

In her youth and in her middle years Willa Cather experimented with a variety of materials, though never with any bold innovations in form. *My Antonia* is a beautiful and often moving re-creation of the pioneer days of Nebraska. The stories in the volume *Youth and the Bright Medusa* reflect the worldly atmosphere that absorbed her talents when she was a critic of music and an associate editor of a mildly radical monthly magazine. There is a patina of sophistication to some of these skillful exercises in the field of high comedy that might surprise readers who know only Willa Cather's later work, in which her always detached style became even more severely impersonal.

The list of Willa Cather's novels includes only one that is an out-and-out failure. Her story of the First World War, *One of Ours*, showed the same straining after effects of sentiment, which essentially she despised, that made Edith Wharton's book of the same period, *A Son at the Front*, more than a little embarrassing to read. *One of Ours* was really Willa Cather's last attempt to write of our own time and its crises. Her curious duplex novel, *The Professor's House*, was only in part a comment on the contemporary scene. The feeling for antiquity lay all over its pages. *A Lost Lady*, too, offered a backward glance at a society in which the reader was invited to feel passively at home.

The other-worldiness of *Death Comes for the Archbishop* and *Shadows on the Rock* is immediately apparent to anyone who follows Willa Cather in her retreat from today. But it was in her novel of pre-Civil War days, *Sapphira and the Slave Girl*, that Willa Cather finally found refuge. Her talent had led her at last to a place of complete intellectual security, from which the human scene could be viewed without any danger of getting the dust of battle in one's nostrils.

◄§ It may a little relieve your mind to know that Willa Cather has not gone all the way back to ancient Egypt for the material of her new novel. Somehow the queer, old-fashioned title gave one the slightly anxious feeling that her retreat from the present had now become complete, and that she was writing about a high priestess of an Oriental cult and the slave girl who helped her at the pagan altar.

Instead, she is writing a story of the years just before the Civil War, when the tensions of the time were stirring in minds of strong, stubborn people and also in the minds of generous people of vision. This growing sense of the wrongness of owning human beings was presently to lead to war; but Miss Cather, eluding the great, gross conflict as she always wishes to do, has concentrated upon a crisis in a household of Virginia, where the seeds of dissension are already subtly and secretly at work, destroying the relationships within a family group.

Sapphira Colbert is the mistress of an estate in Virginia. She has dominated its life until invalidism overtakes her in her late maturity. But even in her dependence upon others and upon her wheelchair, she does not renounce the impulses of a stubborn will. Her marriage to Henry Colbert had been a puzzle at the time she made it, for her husband was her inferior in the estimate of the social arbiters. It has ceased to be a relationship of any importance by the year 1856, when the story begins. Henry Colbert devotes himself to his mill, while Sapphira in her wheelchair keeps to her house and its immediate circle of interests.

But differences of philosophy have driven a wedge between two branches of the family. Henry's growing sympathy with the plight of the slaves is shared by his large-minded daughter, Rachel. But opposing their will is that of Sapphira, defender of the old entrenched privileges, representative of a fatuous philosophy of caste.

Her grim determination to keep what is hers and to punish anyone who would undermine authority takes the form of a terrible hatred for the slave girl Nancy, child of Till, the parlor maid, and a painter who had visited the estate to do portraits of its master and mistress. When Henry Colbert refuses to sell Nancy, Sapphira's hatred becomes an obsession from which she cannot be turned aside. The course this passion takes gives its design to the novel.

It has been Miss Cather's way in all her recent work to view her material from a discreet distance, so that none of its violences may have an unpleasant impact on the nerves or senses. This method has the obvious advantage of giving an air of elegance to everything she writes. Even when she is concerned with willful people and with the effects of their cruelty, the author remains aloof.

But an approach so disciplined and discreet has its disadvantages, too. Chief among them is that of making the whole drama seem to be one in which it would be somehow improper to invest our own emotions, as we are invited, even required, to invest them in the drama of Hemingway's *For Whom the Bell Tolls*. We nod our heads in admiration of the art of an urbane storyteller, but the tale itself never takes on importance for us because Miss Cather's mannerly style seems almost to rebuke, as vulgarly impetuous, any effort to involve ourselves in it.

She is better off with the intimate, small touches that never fail to give her work distinction. As poet, Miss Cather offers many charming pictures of the scene. As observer and critic, she enriches her pages with humorous characterization and provocative comment. But as novelist, in this long-awaited work of a greatly accomplished American artist, she is a disappointment.

Willa Cather is one of the sacred figures of American writing. It is lese majesty to criticize her openly. Reviewers, therefore, bring out only the most discreet clichés in commenting on her work. One of these clichés is that she has a "flawless technique."

Nothing could be more absurd. There are many admirable things about Willa Cather's work, but technical facility is not one. She has never really mastered the craft of the novel. About her book *The Professor's House* she is said to have made the strange comment that its two inadequately linked stories were presented as one because she had been thinking about two different novels, neither of which seemed to be quite long enough, so she put them together.

The same innocent disregard for unity of effect is responsible for strange intrusions in each of Willa Cather's novels. Despite the distinction of her style and the multitude of her gifts, Willa Cather remains one of those troublesome writers who is neither great enough to transcend the rules nor patient enough to learn them. ૐ

Ellen Glasgow

BOTH as a person and as an artist Ellen Glasgow attracted one's great admiration. In each of these roles she took the long, hard, winding road toward such fulfillment as she had, and in each she played with the slightly imperious, but nonetheless attractive, authority of an individual who had refused steadfastly to attempt to become anything she could not feel herself honestly to be.

As a well-born girl in the tradition-ridden city of Richmond she met strong opposition to the plan of embarking upon a literary career. Her experience may be summed up in the story of a young woman in another society of the same period who took to writing poetry. When this vagary was reported to a matron who regarded herself as an arbiter of the elegances, the lady arched her eyebrows and commented, "Indeed! She seemed such a nice girl!" Ellen Glasgow had seemed "such a nice girl" to Richmond. But despite its disapproval she went her own way resolutely.

As an artist she had to struggle desperately for her identity. Editors were forever telling her what sort of book to write. Though she produced many kinds she never allowed herself to be lured out of her own role to grasp at wide popularity by aping the success of others.

What she wanted to do, and did, was to write shrewdly and candidly about the Virginia that spread out before her doorstep and on over the hills to the border. She did not limit herself to one style. In *Barren Ground* she wrote with an unremitting grimness of the plight of the underprivileged, yet without the professional reformer's preconceived notions about the causes and cures of poverty. The novel *In This Our Life* fitted sufficiently well into the pattern of criticism of contemporary manners and morals to be made into a film in Hollywood. But Ellen Glasgow's real absorption was with the aristocratic class of her own society, and her typical method was to chasten what she loved with a discriminating wit. This was the satiric approach to her material in *The Sheltered Life* and in *They Stooped to Folly.*

It is the métier of the writer to get at the heart of a psychological secret. Many an author cannot resist the temptation to practice on himself. As a critic he explores his own works, determined to discover the special kinds of intuition that helped him to find his way through the jungle of his literary material.

In *A Certain Measure* Ellen Glasgow evaluated not only the novels of which she was author but also the succession of impulses that prompted her to write them. The book was by way of being an obituary, for Miss Glasgow knew well that it was her last word to her public. And a curiously just and truthful obituary it was, defining the limits of her art, listing her assets and, by implication at least, her liabilities as well.

&⸱§ Anyone who has ever permitted himself the delicious indiscretion of writing fiction must have been asked many times by infatuated but timorous beginners, "How do you start to write a novel?" In *A Certain Measure* Ellen Glasgow tells, in brilliant and illuminating detail, how she came to embark upon each of the novels which make up the report of her life, the lives of her neighbors, and the lives of their ancestors in the state of Virginia.

These discursive essays on literature and life were written first as prefaces to various reprints of Ellen Glasgow's books.

They have been gathered together into a readable volume which belongs on that still far from crowded shelf devoted to the consideration of fiction as an art. Put it next to Mrs. Wharton's *The Writing of Fiction* and compare its witty, yet essentially sober, judgments with those in the prefaces of Henry James.

The enthralled beginner in writing may find stimulation in Ellen Glasgow's story of how one of her novels came, firm and whole, into her mind when she recalled a story told to her in childhood by a "romantic lady" with "slightly mottled and invincibly smiling features." Another novel took shape all in an instant when, walking with a friend, she passed by "a woman of later middle age who looked at us with eyes of a faded flower-like blue and the smile of a wistful Madonna" and her companion murmured, "How lovely she must once have been!"

This talk of the springboards from which imagination takes off on its adventures is pleasant. It may nudge the fearful into the audacity needed to make a start. But Ellen Glasgow has much more important things to say about her craft: how, for example, she came to reject the nostalgic southern tradition which devoted itself to a "mournful literature of commemoration"; how she undertook to bring to the writing of fiction a needed "blood and irony"; how she tried to feel her way all around the life she knew, expressing her discoveries now in grim realistic novels of the poor and disinherited, now in comedies exposing the pomposity of romantic notions of social life; how, in brief, she taught herself to be an artist, making her way along the lonely path the conscientious must walk.

The difficulties she faced as an artist were aggravated by her family traditions. When her early books appeared, though they now seem to their author like highly romantic exercises, they were regarded by many, even among the genteel reviewers of the day, as observations which were quite improper on the tongue of a well-brought-up young girl.

She had to struggle for her identity at the beginning and even in the middle of her career. There were always people about, and some of them were publishers, urging her to write "an optimistic novel of the Far West" or something in the vein of Henry James. Despite these shocks and the others which came to her when she found that writing men, gathered together, talked not of technique and themes but of the prices paid by the magazines, Ellen Glasgow persisted stubbornly in regarding fiction as an art. In her own contributions to it she reworked her raw material three times before offering it to public view.

These essays have two levels of interest. On the first there is that of a craftsman's discussion of ways and means of creating effects. Every intelligent artist is fascinated by the problems of technique because they are ones which he has had to solve, in solitude and pain, before he could get his work done. It is not Miss Glasgow's task to give fully illuminating lectures on the point of view, on the drama of the interior of the mind, on the relation of character to environment, or on the obligation to make style suggest the temper and the pace of the story. But she does cast light, from her individual experience, on all these matters and she analyzes her effects with insight.

The book may be read as autobiography, describing not personal pleasures and crises, but the growth of an attitude and the gradual development of the hardihood that makes it possible to survive for forty years an an artist.

Or it may be read simply as a shrewd and humorous woman's comment on the life of our time. Ellen Glasgow, sixty when she wrote most of these prefaces but feeling younger, she says, than she did in her youth, is full of opinions on a variety of matters, all related to literature but having a wider application than can be found for them in the studio. Her South, she finds, is beginning to "coquet with alien ideas." It loves "noise, numbers, size, quantity"; its "ambition is to be more Western than the West and more American than the whole of America." This she obviously regrets, for it tends to spread vulgarity and produces the "barbaric fallacy" represented for her by the books of Erskine Caldwell and William Faulkner.

She has many quarrels and she states them with epigrammatic wit. One is with the cult of youth, wielding the weapons of the new sciences. "Pompous illiteracy," she writes, "escaped from some Freudian cage is in the saddle and the voice of the amateur is the voice of authority."

Many a reader will wish to argue with Ellen Glasgow on every page. He may think her an opinionated and imperious person. But he will admire the sharpness of mind out of which these attitudes spring and the wit with which they are expressed. ঔ

Willa Cather's and Ellen Glasgow's renovation of the old-fashioned novel produced many charming and impressive effects. But neither went so far toward complete modernization as to install central heating. Their rooms, beautiful as they were and filled as they were with evidences of cultivation and taste, remained chilly and a trifle forbidding.

Further, no very striking bulletins about "this, our life" were issued out of these strongholds of dignity and formality. Despite Miss Cather's concern with fine moral issues, despite the "blood and irony" that Miss Glasgow attempted to introduce into her satire, the summing up offered little in the way of an ordered philosophy. The voice of the illiterate and the voice of the amateur, which Miss Glasgow so fastidiously despised, really had much more to tell us.

It is quite possible that both these distinguished women from Virginia will be admired more by future generations than they have been by their contemporaries. Their cool detachment alienated those whom the questions of our troubled age had made eager for guidance. But when Willa Cather and Ellen Glasgow are re-read a hundred years hence, and their talents are reappraised, they will be valued, one is sure, for the gift that sensitive readers of our own time always have admired in them. Each had full command of a flexible, graceful style. Each, with an art very like that of the expert jeweler, could set her delicate perceptions, her shrewd intuitions, and her witty observations in a prose design of the greatest refinement and elegance.

The Catastrophe of Competence

THE bland satisfaction taken by nonartists in the thought of the sufferings of artists is one of the constant features of the tension between two worlds. Writers themselves do not share the enthusiasm, which has been expressed not infrequently by critical observers, for starvation as the diet best designed to nourish poetic imagination and dramatic intuition. The unheated attic room which has so great a romantic appeal for the sensitive and suggestible soul who does not have to live in it; the long period of apprenticeship which seems so obviously rewarding to the man who has never had to wait for anything; the isolation so heartily commended as the neighborhood of wisdom by people who have never spent fifteen consecutive minutes alone in their lives—these are all attractions of the literary life which men of letters would be quite willing to forgo.

Lord Dunsany once wrote to a young admirer: "I think that our poets in England are seldom or never neglected, but we have one almost absolute rule, that to be appreciated they must be dead. This is why the appreciation of my work which at different times has come to me from America has meant so very much to me, apart even from the pleasure that one has in the sheer generosity of it, for without it I should have worked without any appreciation at all, and to work at an art without any answer whatever from mankind is to have with one always the feelings of one that pulls a bell-rope to which there is no bell or that tries to gather taxes from a quite penniless man or that sings in a nightmare to a crowded hall but surrounded by a vacuum that no sound can traverse."

Perhaps there is a bleak sort of reciprocity in these literary matters. For if English poets can count upon getting attention only from the American audience, it has been true in many a conspicuous instance, all the way down our history from Walt Whitman to Robert Frost, that American poets have long been denied recognition except that coming to them from England. This mutuality of lack of interest and disbelief in the talents of our fellow countrymen seems to be part of a joint Anglo-American program for making quite sure that artists suffer as much as is good for them.

And yet there can be little doubt that some few men and women of marked literary talent are permitted by circumstance to walk too broad and easy a highway toward the prestige, the appreciation, and the economic security that every writer would like to gain. They find early in their careers that they are able to snatch out of the top drawers of their minds literary costumes that please the eye of the great public. In these fine circus bangles they parade conspicuously and win loud applause. It is all very intoxicating and gratifying.

But sometimes, when the parade is over for the moment and they are quite alone, they look wistfully at those lower drawers of their intelligences and wonder what is in them. Sometimes they timorously pull out a less spectacular literary wear; sometimes they even put on these coats of mail, these haircloth shirts, and venture out onto the highway again. But usually, after many years of polite exhibitionism, such performers find that they cannot wear sober dress with poise or an air of authority. They are uncomfortable out of motley, and the public that has loved them before is bewildered and annoyed by the new masquerade. So the popular artist goes home, snatches off the haircloth shirt, stuffs it away in the lowest, least accessible drawer, and turns the key. Who wants to put on such out-of-date garments anyway? they ask themselves angrily. "Motley's the only wear."

This problem of the very able writer who allows his talent to become garish and vulgar is closely related to the problem of the mass production of entertainment. The habits of the American reading public are such that, while all but a very few books sell only by the thousands or less, the magazines sell by the millions. This demand for stories, or parts of stories in serial form, which can be digested with as little conscious effort as is required to digest a beefsteak or a raspberry parfait comes chiefly from people with a negative set of literary values. They say that they "read to be amused"; that "there is enough sorrow in life without seeking more of it in fiction"; that the man or woman who undertakes to analyze a sober theme is doing so merely to satisfy the perversity of his own morbid mind; that for their part they read only "clean" stories with a "wholesome" tone in which they can decently hope to find "not a word out of the way from beginning to end."

It would be grossly unfair to suggest that all magazines truckle at all times to the smug and superficial preferences of such Philistines and Pharisees. A few American magazines never surrender to the bullying authority of the mass mind and each of the others occasionally overcomes its timorousness to publish a wholly admirable piece of fiction that has somehow taken its editor's fancy.

Yet it would not be unfair to say that the great majority of the work published year in and year out by the publications that owe their existence to the indulgence of a large public is strictly limited in its view of the human scene, in the degree to which it feels free to challenge existing mores, in the emphasis it can allow itself to put upon serious themes. Magazine fiction is designed to flatter the prejudices of suburbia and to confirm its citizens in the conviction that their values are the best ever conceived by the mind of man. Such fiction is victimized by so many confusions of ethics and so many rigidities of convention that it is bound to be at its best superficial and at its worst essentially immoral.

Two groups of writers present themselves at the desks of editors to satisfy the demand created by that powerful eco-

nomic unit, the American magazine. In the first are the graduates of suburbia's school of ethics, who themselves believe in
its standardized chaos of the spirit. To glorify triviality by
dressing it up in a costume by Hattie Carnegie is a labor of
love completely sympathetic to their kind of subservient snobbery. They are propagandists for all that is negative and meaningless in our society.

To the second group belong that handful of able writers
who happen to have too much adaptability for their own good
and the good of standards in American fiction. Because their
creative gifts are of a high order they find it easy to canalize
their energies in any direction they may choose. Rewards offered by the magazines are great and tempting, and, with the
conviction that they can turn away from temptation at any
time they decide to do so, these lively intelligences direct their
vitality into the narrow courses designed by the engineers of
formula fiction. Because in the beginning they are people of
distinguished quality of mind and spirit, they do an attractive
job of satisfying the rudimentary requirements of the magazine story.

Yet, from the standpoint of the detached critical observer,
the enormous competence of writers like Edna Ferber and
Louis Bromfield is, both for them and for the standards of
contemporary fiction, a sort of natural catastrophe. It over-
whelms even their remarkable capacity for resistance and reduces them in the end to the intellectual level of the meagerly
gifted folk who limp along beside them in the big parade.
A man who has told himself that presently, when he has earned
enough to own and operate a nice little house in the country,
he will turn away from temptation, wakes at last to find that
he no longer has the desire to turn away from temptation.
Like his less competent confreres he can no longer write anything but flattering little love letters to suburbia.

This judgment may sound severe, but it is less severe than
that which in his secret mind the man who has betrayed his

competence brings against himself. Criticism says merely that it is unfortunate for gifted people to allow their talents to dwindle into facile triviality. What the victim of a too adaptable competence says to himself must be infinitely worse, for he develops the attitude of hostile self-defense that betrays the suffering mind. He talks back, in terms of angry, personal defiance, to his critics. What is the harm in being a public entertainer? he demands. Is it not obviously a thousand times better to reach a public of two million than a public of two thousand? Is it not mere jealousy that makes people who contribute to the magazines rarely or not at all complain of those who have life tenure to places in any or all of them?

Granted there is little harm even in the most time-serving of entertainers, and anyone who is fair-minded will admit that the applause and the rewards that lie in the gift of the mass public must be very sweet indeed. But this concession cannot set aside the judgment that for an artist to write on a level that lies far below his capacity, simply because it is easy and profitable for him to do so, is a kind of sin against the creative life.

Edna Ferber

EDNA FERBER is an enormously gifted person. She is also a thoughtful analyst of human experience. This aspect of her intelligence she has seldom revealed in her fiction, which habitually takes a firm, possessive hold upon a heroine and leads her resolutely through a series of highly contrived incidents in a standardized siege against the citadel of success. Ironically, it is in Miss Ferber's autobiography, A Peculiar Treasure, that she fully reveals her talent for offering a detached and impersonal comment on the mixture of perils and pleasures in human life. Here she has made a carefully critical examination of the assets she brought to the task of writing fiction and of the high-handed use she has made of them.

◆§ "What there is to see, I'll see," was Edna Ferber's battle cry almost from the moment she was born. As a little Jewish girl she saw what there was to see in Ottumwa, Iowa, and that was plenty. It included a lynching performed at a street corner of the tough mining town in broad daylight. As a girl reporter in Appleton, Wisconsin, and in Milwaukee she saw what there was to see. And that was plenty, too, because her assignments included everything from covering murder trials to interviewing "Fighting Bob" La Follette.

As a prima donna in the world of popular letters, she saw everything in New York, Berlin, and Paris because she had not lost her curiosity and knew that everything noted with the novelist's insatiable appetite for detail might eventually come in handy in a book.

She has told all this in her autobiography, A Peculiar Treasure, her richest, most honest, and most searching story.

When a popular, competent craftsman turns his back upon the long years of constructing stories to satisfy the magazine audience and decides at last to tell about himself, he almost always writes a good book. All the experience of disciplining his material stands him in good stead. The dramatic instinct for finding the word, the phrase, the happening that will reveal character and light up the significance of a way of life has matured. But there is no longer any need to be sly and cunning in bringing the tale to a right conclusion. The pattern of the life exists. It has justified itself. All that is required is to chip away deftly what is irrelevant or repetitious and let the truth be shown. That is what Edna Ferber has done in this admirable autobiography.

In a curious way A Peculiar Treasure follows the formula of Edna Ferber's novels. It is a success story. As in So Big and Show Boat, the central character begins her life in obscurity, struggles resolutely, battles down the succession of emergencies that intervene between herself and triumph, and winds up at last in a Park Avenue penthouse.

But the difference between Edna Ferber's own story and that of the characters she has created in fiction is that nothing in her upward climb seems fortuitous or contrived. Her triumph can be completely understood when the whole record is given with candor and courage.

Miss Ferber has been tremendously successful with her audience because she had qualities which, however imperfectly she revealed them in her early work, sprang out of self-respect. She had a proper reverence for her Jewish background, for the Hungarian forebears who she could still remember had been men of substance and achievement even when the bitter loafers in an Iowa town flung the word *sheeny* at her. She had a proper confidence in her ability to make use of the opportunities offered by the prewar America into which she had been born.

Two other habits of mind brought her success in her middle twenties. One was the fact that she used the material of her own world in her fiction. She saw her mother, a sad, high-hearted woman, turn in and run the family store when her husband's sight began to fail. Out of that experience she created, with the large help of intuition, the first American businesswoman in fiction, the triumphant Emma McChesney, whom Theodore Roosevelt liked so well that he undertook to advise the author about what the course of the character's subsequent life should be. To American readers, Emma McChesney seemed like a brilliant new creation simply because Edna Ferber had the good sense not to take her characters off the hand-me-down shelf. Today, looking back over what she has written, Edna Ferber is able to see that what she did with her material was often tricky, sentimental, and unworthy of the fine urgency of the first creative impulse. But she profited nonetheless by that original desire to write honestly about American life.

The second thing that helped her was her dramatic flair. The little girl in Appleton won prizes for declamation. The mature woman says that she is still a frustrated Bernhardt because she has never been on the stage. But the harnessed lightning of insight which makes a play move is in the best of her stories.

Yes, this is a good book, revealing and humorous. But what is for me the most interesting part is the brilliant record of the early years spent in a difficult milieu, each trial of which was faced with a gay resolution.

As a Jew Miss Ferber is concerned, eloquently and with the greatest dignity, over the plight of her fellow people in other lands.

"All my life," she says in conclusion, "I have lived, walked, talked, worked as I wished. I should refuse to live in a world in which I could no longer say this. . . . It has been my privilege . . . to have been a human being on the planet Earth; and to have been an American, a writer, a Jew. A lovely life I have found it, and thank you, sir." ⁊∾

Louis Bromfield

WHEN Louis Bromfield made his debut as a novelist, he seemed destined to become one of the able craftsmen of the second order of excellence who make up the great company of respectable writers in any tradition. His themes were sober, his attitude toward society critical and discerning.

In the group of four related books—*The Green Bay Tree, Possession, Early Autumn,* and *A Good Woman*—he offered a study of a parochial, midwestern community the several aspects of which were highlighted by an unfailing sense of drama and a certain shrewdness of intuition. The first of these novels was the most original and the last the least so. *The Green Bay Tree* dealt with the impact upon a censorious and essentially jealous world of a woman with the glitter of worldliness upon her brow and the subtle, pervasive hint of decadence in her individuality. Even Mr. Bromfield's keenest admirers must have been disturbed by the suggestion that he was succumbing to the lure of the cliché when in *A Good Woman* he took up a theme that happened in that season to be extremely fashionable. His central figure in that novel was a woman who hid a destructive passion of selfish possessiveness behind a mask of universal benignity. She mothered and smothered a son into futility just as the other pious frauds of the year had done.

Nonetheless, Bromfield's tetralogy was accepted gratefully as a rather impressive monument to the ambition, energy, and originality of a useful new talent.

But Bromfield was determined to be something more important than a sober and dignified novelist of the second order. He set out to demonstrate that he was able, by dint of much wandering over the face of the world, always with a typewriter in his luggage, to make himself a luridly spectacular, aggressively tawdry, affirmatively vulgar novelist of the fourth class.

He lost nothing of his craftsmanship in doing so. Indeed, his ability to produce a readable and arresting page grew from novel to novel. He marshaled events with the competence of a seasoned campaigner. Like a latter-day Arnold Bennett he kept his literary pot boiling at a white heat, bringing up out of its depths tasty tidbits about India, Paris, New Orleans in the time of the Civil War, the American West in its formative years—anything and everything that seemed at the moment to be marketable. *Wild Is the River* sufficiently represents the whole lot.

 I find something almost admirable about the wholehearted enthusiasm with which Louis Bromfield has lent his great talent to the building up of a huge romantic cliché. There is nothing about his narrative that is not faked and phony. His characters are the familiar ones of dramatic stock: rugged, amoral he-man, *femme fatale*, sultry French courtesan, eccentric New England spinster. Everything goes into the heady brew Mr. Bromfield is stirring up: voodoo charms, sadism, wily intrigue. The climaxes of duels, beatings, burnings, and plagues come at set intervals when they are needed to pick up the narrative. A beginning writer could learn a great deal by studying Bromfield's methods, because he never leaves off being the ardent storyteller who is putting his heart into the effort.

Yes, despite Mr. Bromfield's attractive energy and glittering competence, his new book remains trivial, trite, and insincere.

The action of *Wild Is the River* (and a generous lot of it there is) takes place during the Civil War when New Orleans has been taken by the Union army and its proud inhabitants are being humiliated daily by soldiers and carpetbaggers collaborating on plunder. The curious cosmopolitan society of this southern city is no match for northern ruthlessness and vulgarity. Its people are driven from their homes, the women bullied, and the men punished on trumped-up charges. The soft way of life—created by climate, setting, history—caves in before the hard greed of men who are strangers to graciousness of any kind.

Obviously a serious novelist could have found in this material a "motive and a cue for passion"—a passion of moral indignation. But Bromfield has muffed the cue in the midst of the tempestuous brawl he has imagined. Wisdom has spoken to him in the night and prompted him to declare that he meant his book to prove no thesis, but merely "to present the people and the city . . . as they were during the occupation." This, I think, is a clever afterthought. For surely so very shrewd a man as Louis Bromfield knows better than to think that his garish pageant of the major and minor vices bears any real resemblance to the picture of a tragic city struggling to restore its dignity after a crumpling defeat.

No, he merely meant to stir up a noisy doings, and certainly he has succeeded. . . .

I shall not blame the hundreds of thousands of readers who

will walk straight into Mr. Bromfield's trap and sit down to make a hearty and satisfying meal of his elaborately served cheese. All of his book is readable; its zest is infectious; its audacities are tempting. It just isn't a serious novel. ॐ

In all the repertory of refined sadism there is no cruelty greater than that of nagging at men and women to satisfy elevated standards which they never professed to admire or wished to serve. But Edna Ferber, in *A Peculiar Treasure*, and Louis Bromfield, in certain brief passages of *Pleasant Valley*, have written with discernment and charm. The standards that satisfy them in fiction are so far below the level of their own best accomplishments that it is not unfair to accuse them of a kind of apostasy.

Obituary for the Human Race

A curious intellectual fatality has hung over the
talents of two of England's most skillful men of letters, putting a bleak and oppressive shadow upon the undeniable brilliance of their gifts. Though they share little else as artists,
as men of ideas, or as interpreters of the contemporary social
scene, Aldous Huxley and W. Somerset Maugham have in
common a tragic weakness which devitalizes the philosophy
of each, making it seem whimsical and negative. Neither of
them is able to feel any hope for the future of mankind. Both
have spent the past two decades writing, bit by bit, obituaries
for the human race, naming over, with a kind of ghoulish
satisfaction that betrays them often into lurid venom, the
faults that have pushed us all toward an unlovely death.

Satirists have long been fascinated by the grim pleasure of
contemplating, in the form of fantasy, a possible end to the
highly unsatisfactory experiment of human life upon our globe.
Almost always one senses in such writers a passionate grief
over the loss of the familiar, even though they feel obliged
to denounce with the greatest bitterness of spirit the grotesque
moral inadequacies of this untidy habit of living. The very
urgency of their protests indicates that they do not really believe what they are saying. Even while they assume the dual
role of judge and executioner, they hope against hope that
their sweeping denunciations will be taken as mere threats
and that the race, awakened at last to its danger, will shake
off sluggishness to assume the virtues it has lacked.

This is not at all the tone of the work of Huxley or of
Maugham. Having lived for most of their lives as men of the
world, they are concerned with the realities of the contempo-

rary scene. Their imaginations do not send them on far flights, seeing the race in a moment of extremity. They do not present the picture of an entire people being prodded into oblivion by avenging angels. What they describe is the death scene of a mortal who has never been offered an opportunity to reform. In his last hours he lives exactly the same futile, charmless, and debased existence he has always lived.

The preoccupations of man, as he appears in the novels of Huxley and Maugham, are snobbery, petty persecution, and the more offhand manifestations of the sexual impulse. He goes down to his death with no grandeur in his fall. He merely piddles along toward the abyss, unaware that it lies open before him. He gossips as he goes, seeming to suffer from a particularly virulent form of diseased chattiness. The talk is different in the books of Huxley from that in the books of Maugham. In the first there is a steady flow of bogus philosophy; in the latter, an equally fluent outpouring of drawing-room comedy chatter. But the babble is almost entirely meaningless in both, for as Huxley and Maugham record these outpourings, they are intended to indicate merely how trifling and bemused is the human mind.

There is another similarity between these two writers in their latter-day development. Each, after making his rejection of the human race complete, has found himself becalmed in limbo. Neither quite likes that situation. Each has begun in recent years to grope his way myopically toward some faith that may prove to be higher and finer than the one he has renounced. Huxley would find it impossible to recant his negative philosophy, and Maugham would find it a socially inept thing to do. Huxley, therefore, has tried to satisfy himself by finding a religion. His restless intelligence has searched the writings of the Eastern philosophers, seeking some extra-worldly commitment of the spirit that will leave man out of account and still offer him individual salvation. Maugham, having a much less vigorous and exacting intelligence, has become languidly interested in the psychology of sainthood. Without exploring Eastern philosophy himself, he creates characters who explore it. He gives himself a vicarious sense of engaging in a spiritual adventure by watching these creatures of his imagination as they reject the human experience and settle down permanently in the environs of that state of somnolent and divine irresponsibility which is so warmly admired by Eastern thinkers.

Aldous Huxley

JUST at the moment when the century came of age, Aldous Huxley began to delight the intellectuals of England and America who had recently escaped from adolescence and come into possession of some of the rights of maturity. With deft audacity he discussed many of the matters that occupied their minds. "Now this man is a wit," wrote Scott Fitzgerald with an air of enchanted surprise in the opening paragraph of a review of *Crome Yellow*. Fitzgerald seemed tacitly to be saluting across the Atlantic a confrere in the task of analyzing the love life of the postgraduate prom-trotter.

Huxley's possession of a great name inevitably impressed everyone who in a college course in English literature had read the essay "A Piece of Chalk," written by his grandfather, Thomas Henry Huxley. It was thought that since young Aldous came of a long line of distinguished scientists and men of letters, he must certainly mean more than he actually set down when he satirized dalliance with belles-lettres and dalliance in love. To be sure, many other young writers did exactly the same thing, but none of them bore a great name.

The elegantly and artfully sadistic stories of *Antic Hay* had an inescapable attraction for the postwar generation. One recognized the essential cruelty of such a short story as "Nuns at Luncheon," but its very hardness had a gemlike perfection that dazzled and delighted the exploring eye of youth. Huxley's work became a sort of touchstone by which one young person tested the intelligence of another to determine whether or not the new acquaintance possessed a mind sufficiently rocky with what was called realism to be worth mining.

As the list of his books grew longer, Aldous Huxley became more deft, more chatty, more disturbing. Following him along the periphery of ideas in *Those Barren Leaves*, a sympathetic reader had the impression that at any moment the way would lead down into the profundities of philosophic truth. *Brave New World* offered the wittiest and most audacious of all the satires on the idea of supplying man with a scientifically improved milieu while requiring him to manage with the same old, unimproved intelligence. *Point Counter Point* offered the ultimate improvement upon the style and technique of *Crome Yellow*, with all the qualities of merciless grace glittering as never before.

Reviewers began to classify Aldous Huxley as an exponent of the mature delights of the philosophic novel. And still it was not at all clear what his ideas were supposed to be. In *Point Counter Point* the artistic world impinged upon the great world of society just as it had in *Crome Yellow*, and the same routine of betrayals and suicides tended to show how little store man sets by his own life. Aldous Huxley seemed to be particularly obsessed by a determination to expose the grotesque indignity man suffers as victim of his amorous passions. The subject of love was never far from his mind, but its culminating act was represented always as one of squalid or ridiculous impetuosity. Huxley went to melodramatic lengths to dramatize the bestial unworthiness of a meeting which the poets of all ages have done their best to glorify as the most illuminating and refining in all the human repertory of experience.

Aldous Huxley's youthful admirers began, as they progressed deep into their thirties, to have doubts about how long they could continue to follow him with pleasure or confidence. It is not at all strange, since he had been attempting through all those years to record certain typical experiences of his generation, that he himself began to have doubts about the path he had been following. The first novel which revealed a new interest, the quest for a faith, was *Eyeless in Gaza*.

⊷§ The diary of Anthony Beavis, the central character of the novel, contains at the close of one of its passages of abstract speculation this query: "How to combine belief that the world is to a great extent illusory with belief that it is none the less essential to improve the illusion? How to be simultaneously dispassionate and not indifferent, serene like an old man and active like a young one?"

Thus Huxley states the dilemma of the intellectual, not only for his character but for himself and his generation. He does not offer any of the answers with which zealous reformers have made us familiar. Yet it is a startling conversion toward which Huxley leads his character, who is exactly the same sort of brilliant cynic about whom he has been writing for twenty years. Anthony Beavis the scholar, who rejects love in favor of irresponsible sensuality, who rejects life in favor of the opportunity to observe the follies of life with amused detachment, is at last persuaded that human experience is not a tremendous practical joke but something having profound significance. The unity of life which can be scientifically demonstrated is the fact on which he builds his faith. Life is one, in the midst of separations, divisions, and destructions. What is important to Anthony Beavis in the end is the compassion that helps to put down the separating fears and aversions, that helps to reveal the identity of life. . . .

All the more militant reformers, hot for the principles of one cause or another, are likely to find this solution of human problems a little inadequate and this faith a little thin. A religion that bases its appeal upon the reiteration of formulas— all is unity, all is peace—seems rather ill designed to appeal to the complicated intellect. When Huxley mounts the platform and begins crying "Peace, peace" like Father Divine of Harlem, the men and women who have sat in his audience, fascinated and beguiled until now, are likely to retire in embarrassment and confusion.

The Huxley formula for compassion is one that permits a great deal of latitude to a man of wit. At least in his present transition stage from worldliness to patient faith in the sublime destiny of the race, Huxley still indulges in a good deal of adroit and clever malice. His book is peopled with men and women whose lives have been ruined by the fact that they have gone the wrong way about finding love. . . . And as these debauched egocentrics act upon one another, cruel scenes in which their weaknesses are ruthlessly exposed follow in brilliant, engrossing, and quite continuously distressing succession. . . .

As an evangelist, Huxley still leaves much to be desired. It would be ever so satisfactory if he had offered a faith to which one could wholeheartedly subscribe. Instead he has bravely failed at what is probably impossible. ❧

It is easy to see, in retrospect, that *Eyeless in Gaza* covered the first stage of Aldous Huxley's journey away from earth and all its interests. In it he called upon man to reject the concerns that tend to separate human beings one from another, and to seek a unifying peace. The worthlessness of much of human experience was heavily stressed, but there was still a trace of hope for the race if it would only learn to understand that its experience is simply a dream. Huxley's project was to create a more refined dream by encouraging a kind of premature senility. In that project all men of insight and delicate feeling were urged to participate.

But when he began the novel called *After Many a Summer Dies the Swan*, Huxley had become discouraged about the prospects for even that degree of participation. Human experience seemed to him more degraded than ever. He was ready to accept a new religion, the chief attraction of which was that it rejected the values of earth entirely.

◂§ Reading the novels of Aldous Huxley is just a little like going on a tremendous spree. One has a thoroughly good time at the moment and only afterward remembers to be censorious.

This is all very ungrateful. One has even the uncomfortable feeling that anything said against Huxley smacks of hypocrisy. The generation which has grown old along with him has been greatly in his debt for entertainment, for stimulation, for instruction in a wide variety of matters. His version of the philosophic novel has blended the interests of science, social comedy, and intellectual speculation, and done all that with a rare amount of skill.

And nowadays Huxley takes himself seriously as idealist and reformer. He recommends the most correct attitudes. In his new novel he is taking the first steps toward the construction of a new religion which will renounce materialism and strip from the soul all those burdens of personal desire and individual impulse that keep us from being aware of the unity which all beings will find in eternity. (Well, something like that. It is not easy to epitomize a mysticism so new and, if I may be impolite about it, vapory.)

Yet there seems to be something cockeyed about the man's mind. In the course of instructing the reader in the superb obligation of consciousness to destroy itself in the interest of something higher, wider, and handsomer, Huxley titillates consciousness with tales of refined bawdry, scandal, and violence. What is more annoying, because it is essentially so unfair, is that he undertakes to reduce the romantic ideals of human love and humanitarianism to utter absurdity by displaying before us gross forms of love and inept, immature forms of humanitarianism.

The excuse for doing this is that he is a satirist. In a passage of curious narcissism—which cannot be unconscious, because whatever else he may or may not be, Mr. Huxley is never naive—he preens himself a little brazenly. All ordinary literature, he suggests, is a degrading nuisance because it gives an elevated tone to essentially squalid themes like those of *Othello* and *Wuthering Heights*.

His mouthpiece of the moment continues to reflect that good satire is "much more deeply truthful and of course much more profitable than a good tragedy." The trouble, Huxley suggests, is that few good satires exist because few satirists are "prepared to carry their criticism of human values far enough."

But Huxley is prepared to go very far indeed. In fact he is prepared to cut all the old values from under our feet to make us, in the full cry of panic, accept his new ones. That, I suppose, makes him the greatest satirist of all time.

The narrative framework of *After Many a Summer Dies the Swan* has several major supports. There is the interest which Jeremy Pordage brings in, that of an extremely erudite Englishman's amused view of the idiocy of life in California. There is the gross drama of greed and fear represented by Jo Stoyte, who has grown rich enough in the course of his exploitation of the people to build himself a castle, complete with moat and improved by many modern bathrooms, in one of which hangs an El Greco. Mr. Stoyte does not want to lose his mistress and he does not want to die. For Huxley this painful creature of his fancy is the embodiment of a philosophy based on preoccupation with personal desire, and he succeeds in knocking it over as you could destroy a straw man. Enlivening the passages of scandal is the gleeful cynicism of Dr. Obispo, who seduces Jo Stoyte's delectable moron mistress and gets a completely innocent young man shot on suspicion of being the girl's lover. And wandering about as the author's mouthpiece whenever he feels an essay coming on, is the brilliant Mr. Propter, who really outlines Huxley's new religion for him. . . .

Hardly a page of this book fails to contain a provocative, teasing idea, a flash of wit, a bit of sly comedy. And so whether or not you believe in either Huxley's rococo hell on earth or the sightless, soundless wonder of his new heaven, you will read it, I predict, with a stimulating blend of pique, fascination, rage, sorrow, disapproval, and unholy joy. ఔ

If any doubt remained that Aldous Huxley wishes, now that he has reached the serenity of middle age, to reject the world, its evil ways, and its distracting responsibilities, that doubt has been dispelled by his anthology of the writings of the mystics, called *The Perennial Philosophy*. Quoting liberally from Lao-tzu, St. John of the Cross, Jean Pierre Camus, Buddha, and the authors of the Upanishads, he brings forth, out of "right rapture," his own statement of faith. This is, in brief, that men of saintly spirit—the "first-hand exponents of the Perennial Philosophy," who alone among the analysts of other-worldly experience "knew what they were talking about"—have always been concerned with "the one, divine Reality substantial to the manifold world of things and lives and minds." The nature of this Reality, Aldous Huxley warns the uninitiated, "is such that it cannot be directly and immediately apprehended except by those who have chosen to fulfil certain conditions, making themselves loving, pure in heart, and poor in spirit."

The spiritual experiences of the illuminati have ever been the subject of rude and mocking irreverence on the part of gross, earthbound men. Aldous Huxley must expect to receive his share of such impious jeers, for of all the men of subtle, complex mentality who have lived and written in our time, he has been himself the most rude and mocking.

Now that he has established himself in such an equivalent of the saint's wilderness sanctuary as California has to offer, his claims to having fulfilled the conditions that make a man "loving, pure in heart, and poor in spirit" are sure to be examined with great curiosity. In his recent novels he has had a great deal to say about love and compassion, but he has never demonstrated in the intimacy of his relations with his characters that he feels even a hint of either sentiment. His way of suggesting purity of heart has been to degrade human experience by rolling his tongue over every bit of evidence he can invent to the effect that man is lacking in dignity. By way of offering proof that he has become "poor in spirit," he continues to be sniffishly unconcerned with the problems of human life and snobbish toward all those whose mentalities do not yield to the cloudy charm of his mystical incantations.

Huxley feels that men who make a faith of their belief in the dignity of man and the importance of his destiny delude themselves with false and evanescent values. In precisely the same way, the hard-minded are sure to believe that Huxley has deluded himself into rejecting the world and rushing into the embrace of eternity with a very nearly unbearable preciosity of spirit. His witty, spiteful novels, with their poisonous emphasis on all that is mean and negative in human emotion, are unlikely to make converts to his faith.

The snobbish hauteur with which Huxley glances back toward earth is not in the least ingratiating. Those who have been more and more alienated by each of his novels in turn and who feel a distinct distaste for the softness of attitude that he reveals in *The Perennial Philosophy*, are bound to suspect that the kind of other-worldliness he now champions is not the gift of insight but merely the compensation he has offered himself for a set of weaknesses of character and twists of temperament and impulse that have made it impossible for him to believe in the dignity of man.

Somerset Maugham

SOMERSET MAUGHAM has been one of the most influential, as well as one of the most popular, writers of our time. He

will be remembered for two works in particular, the novel
Of Human Bondage and the story "Miss Thompson," from
which John Colton and Clemence Randolph made the play
Rain. To have been the inspiration of a play the name of which
still glitters from time to time on the marquees of urban
theaters, and to have written the novel most prized in each
succeeding generation by the "sad young men" assures Somerset Maugham a memory that will endure at least as long as the
temper of our times.

What is virtually a cult exists among the youthful intelli-
gentsia who worship the craftsmanship displayed by Maugham
in his perennially popular early novel. The young men admire
it with a respect verging upon reverence, and though the reverence is extravagant, the respect is not.

Of Human Bondage is the archetype of the autobiographical
novel about the education of a sensitive young man which
every sensitive young man must write before he can write
anything else. Somerset Maugham has been candid about the
fact that it is, in part, his own story. When an overzealous
devotee asks him why he does not write another such book,
he answers with a shrug, "Because I have had only one life."

More deft in its style, more secure in its knowledge of the
tactics of the novel, more searching and explorative in its
spirit than any of the recent novels modeled on its design,
Of Human Bondage is still the pure example of the school
of writing it has inspired. Some of its early passages were obviously modeled upon those in *The Way of All Flesh* dealing
with distaste for avuncular authority. Some of the last chapters may seem contrived, spurious, and superfluous pendants
to the body of the novel. But that body, dealing with the life
of a medical student in the London slums and with the distressing amorous experiences of a tormented human creature,
is engrossingly anatomized.

If Somerset Maugham were writing *Of Human Bondage*

today, now that he has become, as he has said, "quite an old party," he would be, I think, more candid or more shrewd or both in his analysis of the maladjustment suffered by his central character, Philip. Today's psychoanalysts would be able to offer a guess or two about why a young man of this type should allow himself to become obsessed with a girl whom he cannot respect and from whom he can receive no rewarding intimacy.

Even in those early days Somerset Maugham had the beginnings of that attitude which has become his unaltering pose today. He is now, and was even then, the detached observer who recorded no more than he saw and refused to probe under surfaces which were, to him, sufficiently interesting in themselves. And so he never tried to make clear the reason why Philip wished to make a relationship of complete surrender and trust between man and woman seem both unattainable and unattractive.

On the basis of the evidence which Maugham has actually offered it is possible to say only that the story of Philip and Mildred, like so many of the tormented stories told by Aldous Huxley, is by design tawdry and unlovely. It means to indicate that the human race is doomed and damned for its unfastidiousness.

As Somerset Maugham's devoted following grew in numbers year by year, he found a great variety of ways of being entertaining. As a man of cultivation and curiosity he enjoyed travel. Studies like his *Don Fernando*, which resulted from the encounters with men, letters, and art on foreign soil, leaped smartly onto the best-seller lists. It was even possible for him to make literary criticism attractive to the large audience. But his greatest success was in the theater. Through two decades he adorned the tradition of drawing-room comedy with plays suitable as vehicles for the smartest stars of the London and New York stages. Maugham's plays—*Our Betters* and *The Circle*, for instance—were elegant and insouciant and just audacious enough to flatter the worldly with the hint that their weaknesses, though naughty, were after all very chic.

It would be too much to say of Maugham that he has occupied the place of Oscar Wilde in the theater of our time. He has seldom attempted to achieve the *mot d'esprit* of which Wilde was master. His assets as a dramatist were facility and suavity. He had, if not a silken skill with dialogue, at least a rayon proficiency. But he stood on the threshold of the Oscar Wilde world and held that door open for a new generation of playwrights, including Frederick Lonsdale, Noel Coward, and Ivor Novello. The fact that these men proved to be intruders was not Maugham's fault. Nor is it his fault that when his popularity ran out, the tradition of drawing-room comedy in England seemed to be about to perish completely.

There is nothing more gratifying to a department store owner, or to a writer, than to have his wares liked. Somerset Maugham came more and more to resemble a merchandiser of smart examples of a great variety of goods. People came to his market as often as he opened its doors. Little by little he began to think of himself exclusively as a tradesman. It was first a business necessity, then a defense against those who kept asking him to do harder literary chores than he cared to perform, and finally a becomingly nonchalant and somewhat insolent pose.

Maugham the merchandiser became increasingly interested in narrative models that blended sensationalism with a serene, detached, and irresponsible disdain for humankind. This direction of his later period declared itself perhaps most clearly in the volume of short stories called *The Mixture As Before.*

◄§ Somerset Maugham is an entertainer. He doesn't want to be anyone's inspiration, or tutor, or intellectual duenna. His shrewd, hard intelligence has given him doubts so fundamental that he rejects the responsibility of being teacher or even guide. There is nothing left for him except to observe and to record interestingly what he sees.

The *London Times* tried toploftily to rebuke him in a review of a recent volume for falling into an unambitious routine. Here, the critic said, is "the mixture as before." Mr. Maugham, unrepentant about his methods, adopted the phrase and has given it as title to the new book. He offers the mixture as before and you can take it or not as you like.

We get an intimate glimpse into Mr. Maugham's state of mind particularly in one story of the present volume. "A Man With a Conscience" is written in the first person. The author speaks out about his findings much as he does in *Don Fernando* and *The Summing Up*. He has been in a French penal colony and has talked with many prisoners about their histories. None of them seems to him to have any of the moral values which writers continually assume are the common property of all human beings. The murderers have murdered solely for convenience. They experience no torments of remorse, no unbearable pity for their victims.

Among them Maugham found only one man of delicate conscience. Like the others, he felt no regret for having bashed in the head of his silly wife. What had tormented him and what had led indirectly to the murder was the fact that he had once lied about a dear friend in order to remove him from the society of the girl with whom both were in love. Having married that girl and found her insensitive and morally gross, it seemed to him almost like a penance to kill her.

Maugham does not have to apologize for what is certain to seem like a warped moral outlook. If he were making up a story, he says, he would put in nothing so violent and upsetting. He is merely recording facts about human psychology as he has uncovered them.

He has, however, his own notions about the inevitability of punishment for selfish or antisocial behavior. "The Lotus Eater" is the account of how a youngish Englishman fell in love with the gracious life of Capri and decided to make it his own by spending all his savings upon an annuity which would see him through twenty-five years of ease. That span would carry him to the age of sixty, at which time he might well be dead. He felt sure that even if he did not die conveniently he could end his life when the leisure he had purchased ran out. So he lived a contented, useless existence during his prolonged vacation from duty.

But time and the annuity run out. The lotus eater faces the act of self-destruction to which he is morally committed, and he funks it. Ease has sapped his hardihood and he puts off his suicide. Living on under the rebuke of his own conscience, he collapses into dependence, into insanity. Guilt for having failed to accept his share of human responsibility has overtaken him and poetic justice has been meted out to him in a peculiarly ruthless way.

It is no ordinary world of men and women into which Maugham introduces us. Nor is it a pleasant one. It is peopled with creatures like the ones presented in "Gigolo and Gigolette," who sit night after night in a Riviera place of entertainment hoping to witness the death of the frail girl who dives from a high tower into a shallow pool alight with flaming oil. At once pathetic and appalling is the loving husband of this frightened girl, who urges her to take this risk twice nightly that they may not have to return to the precarious existence they lived before this turn was invented.

Maugham's mannerly disesteem for the human race is perhaps best illustrated in the story called "Three Fat Women of Antibes." With unrelenting scorn it exposes the degraded vulgarity of aging women who live for nothing very much besides bridge. The sight of a woman who can eat or drink anything without penalty in the way of added flesh throws this trio into a frenzy of jealousy. They become snarling animals, utterly abandoned to an appalling lust for food. It is good clean fun of the kind that makes one shudder for the human race. . . .

Mr. Maugham is entertaining. But one must be a little like the people who watch the girl dive into the pool to find his

work attractive. For he shows us humanity stripped of the re-
deeming virtues that sentimentalists have attributed to our
kind. He shows us all plunging to our death. ஆ

Mr. Maugham has kept protesting that a writer's chief duty
is to entertain. Since he has a large following and gratifying
sales, he must be fulfilling his obligation. Once more we have
the philosophy that the profits are not without honor. But
it is legitimate to point out to Mr. Maugham that writing is
also communication. For a long time communication with
him has been scattered, incomplete, unsatisfactory. It is as
though the messages he sends us are all interrupted by the
static of the chilly mental atmosphere in which he lives.

When Maugham took up the war theme, in *The Hour
Before the Dawn*, it seemed to me that he was poaching on
ground where a mere entertainer had no right to be. His novel
was a cool, compelling, competently executed melodrama of
English people living under the ominous threat of extinction
in the recent war. But it was rather a large dose of disaster to
take from a man who seems merely to be exploiting the conditions of the moment in pursuit of his self-imposed duty as
entertainer. Because Maugham was too detached and impersonal in his comment on the human plight, *The Hour Before
the Dawn* became merely a vulgar commercialization of the
dramatic shock of war.

With the same cool detachment Maugham skillfully con-
cocted *The Razor's Edge* out of three or four gross, garish
stories loosely fitted into a narrative pattern. He helped himself first to all the shocks and thrills of the great fashionable
world of yesterday stretching from the Riviera to Chicago.
Second, he helped himself to the quiet but intense excitement
of following a mystic through the secret processes of finding
a soul. The result was a superficial and trivial study in counterpoint, setting the melodies of worldliness and other-worldliness
against each other. It was another of the steps which Somerset

Maugham has been taking one after another down into oblivion.

I round out these comments with an article which was not a review of a book of Maugham's, but an effort to imitate his own gift for "summing up."

◄§ The *New Yorker* has published in two installments a "profile" by Hamilton Basso of that most noticeable of writers before the English reading public today, Somerset Maugham.

The individuality that emerges from it is a curiously attractive one. Maugham is reserved and reticent to the point of being inscrutable. John Colton, who discovered the play *Rain* in Maugham's short story "Miss Thompson," has said that in all the years of their association he has never known the mask of aloof urbanity even to slip from its resolutely fixed place. Maugham's own daughter has summed up a fascinating unwritten story of parenthood by saying with a kind of genial resignation, "I really don't know him at all."

Yet Maugham is always courteous, generous, and, within the limits that he sets up, unobtrusively companionable. Many people have taken the greatest pleasure in his hospitality, and he has made surprising gestures of helpfulness toward bustling young writers who have no possible claim upon him.

It adds greatly to his attractiveness as a person of breeding that he has picked up both fortune and fame without being driven into a cataleptic fit of determination to retain permanent possession of either. He has left sizable investments in England and France without any vulgar grieving over their sequestration. What is even more remarkable in one who has had so much success, he contemplates with bland indifference the probability that all his works will be forgotten soon after he is dead. Few men of great prominence have seemed to be so little corrupted in either manners or judgment by a greed for immortality.

There would seem to be little point in nagging such a man

about his place in the contemporary history of English letters. I should not be tempted to do so were it not for the fact that two of his champions, as quoted in the first installment of Mr. Basso's sketch, have accused Maugham's adverse critics of the most trivial malignity in offering their judgment against him.

Jerome Weidman has said that many writers have made wild dashes far beyond the confines of literary criticism in search of abuse to heap upon him. Richard Aldington has complained that, in fits of unacknowledged jealousy, critics have charged that his work is obviously bad simply because it is popular.

I do not know to what writers Mr. Weidman refers, for I have seen in print no irresponsible statement about Maugham that could be called scandal-mongering. Mr. Aldington's assumption seems to me simply silly. It sounds as though it sprang from some martyr fixation of the kind that Maugham himself has so sensibly refused to entertain. . . .

There is just one reason why people who attempt to apply to fiction absolute standards of excellence tend to belittle Maugham: They consider that he has degraded his gifts by making them serve the purposes of pretense, sensationalism, and trashiness.

The pretense that I object to in Maugham is that of having attained a nirvana of intellectual subtlety from which he cannot be tempted to descend. The unfastidious intimacy of identifying himself with the people whose tragic stories he tells appeals to him not at all. He is the all but disembodied observer, to whom the grossness of human life is a depressing spectacle, yet one not devoid of interest.

The sensationalism I dislike in him is evidenced by his willingness to exploit a people's misery in a contrived and obvious melodrama like *The Hour Before the Dawn*. That is quite different from the impulse that overtook Maugham when his own experiences in escaping from France shocked him into the spontaneous warmth of the record that he called *Strictly Personal*.

The trashiness that I dislike in him is revealed in every aspect of *The Razor's Edge*, but particularly in the phase that has to do with the making of a saint. The tremendous theme of the search for spiritual fulfillment is reduced to a handful of episodes each as tawdry as it is incredible.

In his recent books Maugham has created no memorable characters, dramatized no significant crisis satisfactorily. Beginning as a writer of the second order of excellence, he has allowed his facility to degrade him, a little at a time, into a writer of the third or fourth order. The judgment against him has, in my mind, nothing to do with his success. He could be the most genteel victim of the penury which is supposed to be the wages of the pen and I should still believe that his work is meretricious and shabby. ৵

Dream of Unfair Women

ONE of the favorite themes of fiction always has been the battle of the sexes. At least from the time of Aristophanes and his *Lysistrata*, there has been a useful, if neither edifying nor illuminating, formula for the comic presentation of the idea that men and women must forever strive each to defeat both the lower cravings and the higher yearnings of the other. In our own time James Thurber has used the pages of the *New Yorker* in an effort to reduce this hackneyed notion to so ragged and threadbare an absurdity that no one can ever entertain it again with ponderous or pontifical earnestness. His series of cartoons, "The Battle of Men and Women," has shown types that blend the dismaying aspect of the Cro-Magnon specimen of humanity with those of the familiar suburbanite, waging a sluggish and dispirited caricature of the enduring struggle. This satiric *coup de grâce* would have killed the theme if anything could. But it still thrives as stubbornly as a field of quack grass.

In America it is the woman novelist who has kept it alive. To be sure, a writer like Sinclair Lewis occasionally gives it an injection of wit to keep it going. In *Cass Timberlane* he observes that the average American husband "mistakes his wife for the policeman on the beat." It is perhaps unfair to isolate that single line, which reduces to the gross naiveté of radio comedy a point of view that otherwhere in the book has genuinely bright and audacious expression. Yet it does sum up the warning that Sinclair Lewis seems determined to offer to the timorous fraternity of husbands.

It has often seemed difficult for the uncritical resident of suburbia to recognize that he has given his birthright into the keeping of so sly and conniving a monster of neurotic intrigue.

In the years before the Second World War, when each visit of the *Ile de France* or the *Queen Mary* brought us a fresh-eyed European to report that all American women must be regarded as idle, egocentric brats, there was some little reason for the resentment of men against their wives. Women could then be accused, with a degree of justice, of showing a cunning readiness to share their husbands' incomes while they kept their own to themselves. It was sometimes true that they exploited a peculiar form of gallantry which prompted men to display a frenzied, masochistic passion in writing divorce laws that destroyed their own rights. And some ungrateful brides patronized, as culturally inferior beings, the men to whom they allowed no time or surplus energy for the development of cultural interests.

Yet, even at her worst, the American wife seemed to the myopic creature who married her to be preferable, as a comrade, to any sample of femininity he encountered elsewhere in the world. The American husband thought his American wife (or succession of wives) brighter, better dressed, and generally more beneficent in her influence upon his private life than any candidate for sentimental attention he could imagine.

Then, during the Second World War, the American wife seemed to blossom with unsuspected virtues. In quick succession, after Pearl Harbor, she lost her upstairs maid, her cook, and her laundress, without losing her own poise. As these stalwart divinities of the domestic scene disappeared into the defense plants, the American housewife multiplied her physical efforts, while her complaints ironically diminished. Sometimes she even followed the cook into the defense plant, or she put on the uniform of the Nurse's Aide or the Gray Lady and rushed out to feed other people's babies with a zeal and a patience which she had, perhaps, never found time to display in feeding her own. The American wife became such a zealous combination of chauffeur, gardener, airplane-spotter, clerk, and menial servant that such of her adverse critics as the late Margot, Countess of Oxford and Asquith, would have been quite incredulous about her mercurial transformation. Yet it is pleasant to reflect that in the midst of all this activity she neglected neither her permanent wave nor her bridge game. Not the least impressive of the war's victories was that won by suburbia over its reputation for sluggishness.

But this story has yet to be told, except in the baldly sentimental terms of Hollywood or in the pages of magazine fiction. The record left by the lady novelists of the past two decades is still a wild, neurotic dream of unfair women.

The battle of men and women has been fought by such shrewd, not to say shrewish, girls as Nancy Hale, Clare Boothe Luce, and Dorothy Parker according to rules of their own devising. It is no simple, ideological affair of blaming one sex for the discomforts or the sense of insecurity suffered by the other. All these women see the two sexes engaged "in dubious battle," with blame for treason and betrayal to be issued in equal amounts to both men and women.

Nancy Hale

NANCY HALE comes of a distinguished family of artists. Her grandfather was Edward Everett Hale, whose name will never be forgotten as long as mildly skeptical, mildly fascinated seventh-grade students are required to read his story, The Man Without a Country. Her great-aunt was Lucretia Hale, whose Peterkin Papers remains an endearing masterpiece of American comedy. Her father was Philip Hale the painter. She herself has been editor, reporter, short-story writer, and novelist—a serious and copiously productive woman of letters during the years of her youth while she has had also a strenuous and absorbing private life.

After an early appearance with a pretentious and irritating sub-deb first novel (its body was anemic and its narrative dress as flimsily unprotective as crepe de chine), Nancy Hale matured into an intensely sober observer of American society. In her bulky novel *The Prodigal Women* she presented her strangely distorted, but far from trivial, view of American society.

◄§ Nancy Hale has written a long, long novel about women: how they torment one another, steal each other's lovers, exploit men, are exploited by men, and act at all times under the dictates of a thoroughly depressing negativism. It's the sort of book that makes a man wish he were somewhere else, as though he had been caught inadvertently in the powder room. It makes him also feel inclined to mutter under his breath, "Miss Hale is just prejudiced. Women aren't as bad as that. After all, some of my best friends are women."

I suspect that Miss Hale felt she was being sternly just about something. Her title and a note on the jacket suggest that she is thinking of the feverish wastefulness of our American life in a period that was somehow doomed and damned. But that doesn't make matters much clearer, especially when she undertakes to prove her point by a minute examination of lives that seem corrupted not so much by any disease of the era as by their own triviality.

Leda March, one of the central characters of *The Prodigal Women*, begins by being an unhappy little prig and ends by being an unhappy little prig, and all that has happened to her in between has merely confirmed her in a sense of specialness to which she must cling in order to know beauty and virtue. Susan Glaspell once had one of her characters in a play call this formidable psychological state "my by-myself-ness." It is pretty unattractive viewed from without, no matter how serene and inviolable it may seem from within.

Another of Miss Hale's characters, Betsy Jekyll, is presented as an outgiving little thing, a touch on the vulgar side, but copious in affection. All this gets her is a succession of drunken amours, some inside and some outside marriage. Her uncritical togetherness, to invent another unpleasant word to match Miss Glaspell's, lacks continuity, lacks dignity, lacks point, and must therefore be set down as merely another kind of alienating negativism.

The third figure on whom attention is centered, Maizie Jekyll, is the most negative of all. Her weak, concessive femininity forces her to become the emotional slave of a glittering male who jauntily robs her of self-esteem, health, and finally sanity.

To present these women as typical of the weakness of the times is equivalent to saying that the entire female population ought to be hurried as quickly as possible into the psychopathic wards of the nearest clinics.

Fiction at its most moving, most memorable, most true, always reminds us of the core of simple humanity that lies at the center of even the most complex character. In reading Tolstoy, for example, it is the pleasure of recognition that illuminates every comment on human psychology, whether the figure be as complex as Napoleon or as simple as a soldier on the field. It is the mark of a lesser novelist to love obscurity and bewilderment.

Miss Hale loves the dark and inexplicable so well that she does not bother to cover her transitions in the way a less intensely subjective writer would feel obliged to do. Leda is a social failure; presently Leda is a great social success. Leda is unattractive; Leda is dazzlingly beautiful. Miss Hale seems to feel that a desire to have these changes accounted for is mere literal-mindedness.

Her blithe irresponsibility in this particular touches even upon the sacred snobbery of Boston. The Jekyll family, interlopers from the South, are unwelcome within the gates, and then suddenly they are inside the gates without any explanation of the miracle. This constantly mars any effect of social satire at which Miss Hale may be aiming. None of the backgrounds of the novel—not Boston, New York, or rural Virginia—seems really to belong to terra cognita. They all merge into that large, vague, subjective world in which foolish people are tormented by cold or violent people in ways that enable Miss Hale to record some startling scenes.

Oddly, Miss Hale is a sensation seeker. In a style that seems cold and ruthless she intently explores those aspects of the relations of men and women that produce the greatest amount of discomfort for everyone concerned. Typical of her method is a scene toward the close of the book in which a psychoanalyst, in the presence of his patient, questions her unfaithful husband and his mistress about their past misbehavior and future intentions. The mistress (it is the superb Leda, of course) is cruelly articulate and candid. But it remains for the husband to twist the scene into its most striking moment of incredible misery and meanness. He has been represented throughout the book as a cozy combination of sadist, satyr, and sentimentalist, and now, to top off his impudence, he shows in a fluent outburst that he is the one who has been wronged, all the time, by both women.

These dizzy reaches of the higher madness are just a little too much for the reader who does not know his way about in the psychopathic ward.

The Prodigal Women is 704 pages long. It will be read by others (even as it has been read by me) with the worried feeling that anything so long, so earnest, and, of course, so skillfully written must have a legitimate point. But I still don't know what that point is, and I suspect that the prodigality is not so much Leda's or Betsy's as Nancy Hale's own. She has squandered on an exhaustive and exhausting study of maladjustment in trivial people the gifts she should have saved for the short stories with which she is so much more successful. ह᠍

The Prodigal Women might be described as a sort of monumental portrait of Columbia as a nervous wreck. The difficulty with it was that its ambitious, but vague, design gave the author herself the uncomfortable feeling that she must be, in all its many pages, portentous and full of a mighty rage. To adapt one of her own delightful phrases, her approach to her story seemed to be "sad and disapproving and somehow ominous." Then within a few months Miss Hale reappeared before the reading public with a less pretentious but far more important book. The short stories brought together in *Between the Dark and the Daylight* revealed her talent at its best.

ᚣ§ The Nancy Hale who wrote the stories in *Between the Dark and the Daylight* is essentially the same Nancy Hale who wrote *The Prodigal Women*. The themes are the same: mental suffering, nostalgia for childhood, distaste for men who at thirty-odd manage to be spoiled brats, pained and angry protest against prejudice. But in the stories Miss Hale feels no obligation to be a great big girl with a beacon in her hand, lighting the way for the sisterhood of women. She is content with a more casual and a more plausible role, that of a shrewd woman lighting a candle in a naughty world. Sometimes her candle is intuition; sometimes it is impish humor; sometimes it is even tenderness. But always the ground illuminated seems to be surely and unchallengeably Miss Hale's own.

And so one feels no resistance to the points she wishes to make, despite the fact that these are often bitter in essence. In "The Six-Fifteen" a child's innocent passion for her father is shadowed by the meager, fear-ridden imagination of a grandmother. In "Sunday—1913" a lonely, frightened girl feels her spirit being crushed beneath the weight of a husband's gross selfishness without herself perceiving clearly that behind the mask of playfulness and piety he is a ruthless tyrant. In "Book Review" a young woman of spirit stands alone against the cold, contemptuous force of American Fascism and in the night of panic that follows lies sleepless with the thought that she knows too little to combat its shameless confidence. In

"Who Lived and Died Believing" a woman whose mind has crumpled under the destructive impact of love comes slowly out of her insanity to find that the calm young nurse who helped her through has gone down before the same destructive onslaught. In "That Woman" the whole social system of the South, which, in Miss Hale's opinion, makes self-indulgent, insensitive boors of many men, is neatly and completely demolished. In "Georgetown Nights" a nice, outgiving girl is subtly corrupted by the spirit of prejudice against the Negro.

These, obviously, are serious stories. Though Miss Hale has written successfully for the popular magazines, she has never surrendered her talent to the demands of editors with pet formulas. She writes her own stuff and she writes it exceedingly well. It is hard to see how her work could be improved upon from a technical standpoint. Her use of the symbol (like that of the highboy in "Sunday—1913") fulfills expertly all the demands of the fiction writer's husbandry. In "Who Lived and Died Believing" she offers a fine example of how two narrative themes may be drawn together without any evidence of strain upon the artist's resources. But it is her ability to sustain a particular mood—of intense, simple passion, of complicated mental torment, of glittering social irony—that makes Nancy Hale seem to be so far ahead of most of her fellow practitioners in the short-story field. ⧽

Clare Boothe Luce

CLARE BOOTHE LUCE is one of the most noticeable women before the American public today, first because she is a beautiful woman, and second because she is a woman of restless and demanding ambition. Into what is clearly only the beginning of an important career, she has crowded the choicer excitements incident to the life of actress, editor, playwright, war correspondent, and member of Congress. Like Nancy Hale she has had a private life which has been similarly packed with excitement, sudden transformations of outlook, tragedy, and triumph. Some hints about the shocks of her personal experience she has confided in her plays, particularly in the only one among them that enjoyed no particular success, *Abide with Me.*

The representative examples of Clare Boothe Luce's work deal with the struggle between men and women. Her play called *The Women* describes the battle, so to say, from the vantage point of the powder room. No men penetrate into it, though the shadow of many falls over the figures at the bridge table and in the beauty parlor. The comedy shows women living in a vacuum of ideas or of values, tormenting one another in much the same ways that Nancy Hale's prodigal women torment each other.

In *Kiss the Boys Goodbye* Mrs. Luce allowed men to come upon the scene, but only to complete their own ruin by exposing themselves as squalid and conniving amorists, as petty persecutors of anything resembling a principle, and as sluggish, niggardly partners in any human enterprise. The men of *Kiss the Boys Goodbye* are a depressing lot, but again, their wives are rather worse. Clare Boothe Luce seems to have had no point to make other than that once more the battle of the sexes has ended in a draw.

Both *The Women* and *Kiss the Boys Goodbye* are littered with clever bits of theatrical improvisation and with machine-made epigrams. But from the evidence that Mrs. Luce offers of the weak, neurotic character of one kind of American life, only a reckless analyst would attempt to draw any sort of general comment.

My conviction that Mrs. Luce has never learned what to do with her glittering talent was summed up in an article written when she presented herself in a new theatrical role, as rouser of a political convention at Chicago in the summer of 1944.

When Clare Boothe Luce came trailing clouds of glamour into the political arena in Chicago, she made an unquestionable contribution to the showmanship of the old and usually somewhat untidy institution of the convention. She must have looked handsome and chic as she stood up before the delegates, because she never looks any other way than handsome and chic. But even to one who merely heard her speak over the air, the occasion of her debut as a power within the inner circle of the Republican party had many of the beguiling features of an encounter with an extraordinarily attractive woman.

Possibly no one in our public life uses the assets of the human voice more artfully. Mrs. Luce's diction is perfect. Every syllable she speaks has a ringing clarity that is delightful to hear. Yet there are absolutely no eccentricities or artificialities to her speech. All the devices of timing and of emphasis are at her command. As a child she had some training for the professional stage, and either she remembers her instruction well or an instinctual aptitude for the platform has made her an accomplished actress even without benefit of the ordinary discipline.

Further, Mrs. Luce's experience as a playwright, with many solid successes on her list, has given her a sense of form that must be the despair of older statesmen. The architecture of her speech before the Republican convention was as skillfully designed as was her cleverly constructed play, *The Women*. Like the accomplished artisan of the theater she is, Mrs. Luce showed that she knew how to deal with the problems of exposition and how to present her material in a succession of dramatic scenes, with appropriate climaxes to match. It would not be in the least surprising to learn that Hollywood is bargaining spiritedly for the dramatic rights to Mrs. Luce's speech.

But with these acknowledgments admiration of her performance as a work of art must abruptly collapse. Mrs. Luce is still having trouble with the three deficiencies that have made her work in the theater seem less than distinguished: a lack of taste, a lack of sincere sentiment, and a lack of ideas.

Surely it revealed a lack of taste to attempt to play upon the tragedy the war has brought to so many American homes by suggesting that all the dead soldiers of the Pacific and European battlefronts had made her their mouthpiece, to speak, in astonishing unanimity of feeling, their most sober sentiments. For one woman to stand up before a serious gathering and pretend that she spoke for all the war dead was a startling impertinence.

Only the kind of harsh, brittle, and frivolous cerebration which has always been Mrs. Luce's literary stock in trade could have inspired such a vulgar assault on the privacy of grief. The impulse to make slangy epigrams out of the tragic sacrifices of this hour reveals the same insensitivity to the pulse of human emotion that has made Mrs. Luce's plays seem so hard and shallow.

Throughout its whole neat stretch the speech showed the same negative approach to anything resembling an idea that made The Women a second-rate piece of satire. Ingeniously put together as it was, that play had no real originality. If you try to find a theme in it, you must settle for the statement that idleness sometimes makes women behave like malign and predatory brats. That might have strength enough to carry the weight of a door-slamming farce. But The Women set up to be something much more, an intellectual satire worthy of attention for its wit. Because her wit was more seeming than real, because she let it glitter to no point, Mrs. Luce sacrificed first one's sympathy, then one's patience, and finally one's interest.

For many who heard it her speech must have passed through the same routine. The idea of the dead soldier's coming arm-in-arm with the shade of George Washington to attend a political rally is so banal and stereotyped that even Hollywood would have it "treated" with some show of originality before it could be accepted at a story conference. The theme of reproach for political ineptitude, which Mrs. Luce tried to weave into her conceit, was repeated over and over again in completely negative terms. Her old problem of paucity of everything but spite seems to be no nearer a satisfactory solution.

On the basis of her convention speech the judgment must still stand that Mrs. Luce is a second-rate dramatist. ࢡ

Her recent retirement from the political scene, after being accepted into the Catholic church, was in itself an extremely dramatic climax which leaves one puzzled, curious, and, inevitably, not a little impressed with what appears to be a new seriousness. If fate and faith have collaborated on the final, public scene of Mrs. Luce's "strange, eventful history," then perhaps we shall have to regard her plays as the early indiscretions of one who reached spiritual fulfillment by the same devious path as that followed by Saint Francis of Assisi.

Dorothy Parker

LIKE the others in this group of women writers, Dorothy Parker is the product of a privileged world. She did not force her way toward a conspicuous place in the literary scene with the avidity of one who seeks escape from a hated or squalid obscurity. Her early education, if it did not offer a particularly rewarding intellectual experience, at least gave her a time of security in which to rally her own intellectual forces.

In her mature years she has been editor (by an odd, and perhaps significant, coincidence, she was once employed by the same smart monthly magazine which Nancy Hale and Clare Boothe Luce also helped to produce), versifier, short-story writer, scenario writer. She has had successes of many kinds, some of which have seemed to her exacting and fastidious intelligence grotesquely unworthy of enjoyment, and others of which must greatly have eased the burden of living.

Like Clare Boothe Luce, Dorothy Parker is a wit; like Nancy

Hale, she has always been preoccupied with the theme of the demoralizing, even degrading, pettiness of the life of women.

Yet there is this very sharp difference between Clare Luce and Dorothy Parker: The satires of the former always seem shallow, empty of emotion, devoid of values; those of the latter, though they may be quite as devastating in their treatment of an individual figure, always carry the implication that some positive good, inherent in human nature, has here been trod upon ruthlessly by an insensitive savage.

Excursions into the field of biography would show that Clare Luce believes herself to be in possession of positive values quite as much as does Dorothy Parker. To choose at random among the efforts of each to champion causes, it would be fair to mention that Clare Luce is deeply concerned with the place of America as an air power in the world of tomorrow and that Dorothy Parker was an active supporter of the republican government of Spain at the time of the revolt of Franco. But the literary analyst has no right to allow his glance to wander from an artist's actual product or to attempt to reappraise its worth in terms of unrealized intentions. Mrs. Luce said in the preface to *Kiss the Boys Goodbye* that the play was intended to warn America of the development of a native form of fascism. But on the basis of her characters' performance within the three walls of the stage, she might as well have said that it was designed to dramatize Einstein's theory of relativity. What one sees on the printed page or hears in the theater is simply "a tale of bawdry," reported in her best drawing-room manner by a shrewd and completely compassionless woman. Dorothy Parker has frequented some of the same drawing rooms and come away with equally unfavorable impressions of the people she encountered there. But her fundamental purpose in devoting her time and talents to this Park Avenue slumming is very different.

⋐§ It is a little startling to realize that Dorothy Parker, even while she lives and continues to write (now and then), has achieved the kind of celebrity that belongs only to a few very great writers, like the contributors to the Bible, Shakespeare, and Alexander Pope. That is to say, Mrs. Parker is the sort of person who is always suspected of being the author of a famous, but elusive, quotation.

Whenever one is asked to identify a ringing line notable for its frightening sagacity, one automatically risks the guess that it must be from the Bible. When such a quotation bowls along competently in iambic pentameter, the ear whispers to the mind that surely this must be Shakespeare. If the point of a saying tinkles out its passage in a rhyming couplet, one draws a deep breath of relief and says, Alexander Pope. But if wisdom puts on a wry-lipped smile and expresses itself with a startling aptitude that rocks the mind momentarily out of its usual mood of somnolent acceptance, one blinks and says, Dorothy Parker.

There cannot be much doubt about it now. Dorothy Parker is one of the few writers of our time who is destined for immortality. It is nice for us who have always cherished her gift to know that in centuries to come she will represent the sad, cocky, impudent mood of our tragic era. Waking from our graves five hundred years from now, we shall be pleased to see Dorothy Parker strolling Olympus, perhaps in the company of Marguerite of Navarre and Madame de Sévigné. Proudly we shall say, "We knew her when she was just a quick-witted girl who kidded around with Robert Benchley and wrote pieces for the *New Yorker*."

This slightly oracular prediction is suggested by the fact that a neat new portmanteau volume is crowded with most of Dorothy Parker's best stories and verses. A handful of them are brand new, though no point need be made of that. There is novelty enough in the oldest and most frequently reprinted of them, like "You Were Perfectly Fine" and the verse about how women and elephants never forget.

Dorothy Parker has a kind of admirer whose praise must

make as shrewd and fastidious a person as her work shows her to be wish actively that she had never been born. This misguided enthusiast assumes that Mrs. Parker feels a devastating contempt for the human race, and that her scorn is directed in particular toward the half of the race that belongs to her own sex.

It must often depress the author of these deft sketches and poems to realize how superficially her irony has been read. Mrs. Parker does not belong among the haters. Only inferior talents can be prostituted, year after year, to the expression of merely negative feeling. The responsible satirist never uses his weapon to demonstrate his own skill at inflicting pain, but rather to punish a pretension that has too long masqueraded as innocent and winsome grace.

Dorothy Parker's sketch called "Arrangement in Black and White" is typical of her method. It introduces a fatuous woman who pretends to be ever so magnificently unprejudiced when she consents to meet a fine Negro artist at a social occasion. But her babble, as she praises her own superior sensibility, exposes a mind that is callow and callous, inept and vicious. With a deft and unobtrusive hand Dorothy Parker lifts the disguise to expose the Nazi mentality. If this character could become independently sentient and aware of her creator, she wouldn't know that she had been hurt by these attentions. Yet a reader cannot fail to perceive the point. That is art.

But even when she is operating on folly with her most uncompromising surgical completeness, Mrs. Parker seldom seems vindictive toward her subject. The sketch called "From the Diary of a New York Lady" exposes the tawdry private emotions of a complete parasite. Nothing concerns the diarist except her program of pleasures and the tragedy of what an inept manicurist has done to her nails. But she does not exist, like the vicious women of Clare Boothe's plays, in a moral vacuum. Subtly, Mrs. Parker is able to show that already the shrill, insensitive temperament of this creature has alienated all normal people, that she is alone, and that her destiny is a bleak one. It is this respect for poetic justice and this acknowledgment of a set of positive values which are being violated, that give Mrs. Parker's satire its point.

Her gifts include, beside the satirist's insight, the poet's imagination and the high-spirited person's love of improvisation. She says of a chic and lovely woman, "her body streamed like a sonnet." Into the mind of a girl whose dancing partner is apelike and insistent and whose name she doesn't even know, she puts the thought, "Jukes would be my guess from the look in his eyes. How do you do, Mr. Jukes? And how is that dear little brother of yours, with the two heads?"

But it is not this glittering gift that makes her work worth reading and re-reading. Rather it is the fact that Dorothy Parker has a mature mind and a will to protect the dignity of man from the assaults of the insensitive. ॐ

If one were to judge American life as it has been lived through the past two decades solely on the basis of the observations offered by Nancy Hale, Clare Booth Luce, and Dorothy Parker, one would be forced to agree with such critics as Count Keyserling that many of our wealthy folk have too little responsibility for their own good. It might even be necessary to concede that Heinrich Hauser was right when in his fatuous and impudent book, *The German Talks Back*, he declared with a snarl of satisfaction that Americans are a profoundly unhappy people whose restlessness indicates their dissatisfaction with their own values.

It is difficult to discount the evidence offered by these three shrewd women. Though their methods of analysis are different, they reach approximately the same conclusion. Nancy Hale's approach is clinical, Clare Boothe's merely cynical, while Dorothy Parker's is that of a critic who champions positive values by the indirect method of holding negative ones up to ridicule. Yet they agree that negative values exercise a corrupting influence in the lives of people who should be our most healthy, because they have been our most carefully nurtured, citizens.

I take it to be merely a symptom of a certain immaturity in our culture that these women have concerned themselves with a tiny fragment of society and with negative themes. While they have attempted to create literature in terms of the gossip of the cocktail hour, their English contemporaries have been energetically turning over whole cultures to find their material. Simply as artists, two of these American women novelists are more adept than three of their English sisters. Dorothy Parker writes far better than Vera Brittain, and Nancy Hale is a closer analyst, at her best, than was Winifred Holtby. Yet they have held off from the bold attempt simply out of self-consciousness. They show the nervous apprehension of the very young, lest they be suspected of indulging in swank. One can almost hear Dorothy Parker murmuring,

> I will not be a *femme savante*
> But leave that to my maiden aunt.

At the moment one can only regret that nothing in our tradition has compelled Dorothy Parker to write a novel about an American's attitude toward revolution in contemporary Spain, and that Clare Boothe Luce has not devoted a little of her time to a serious study, however ribald she might wish to make it, of the adventure of a woman in Congress.

Our shrewd girls seem still to need time in which to grow up to their talents.

Hypatia at the Helm

Nothing, with the possible exception of headgear for women, goes so completely out of date as satire. Loyal Savoyards still like to remind themselves of the verbal ingenuity of W. S. Gilbert's song in *The Mikado* about the "little list" of folk who "never would be missed." Among them he mentioned prominently "the lady novelist." Today we cannot dismiss her so lightly. Indeed, in England the chances now seem to be far greater that the gentleman novelist will offer something vague, innocuous, and, in any exacting sense, meaningless than that the lady novelist will turn up with such a book.

One of the most striking phenomena of the literary life of England since the First World War is the fact that the novels of breadth, scope, and earnestness in the examination of the social scene have been the work of women. There have been brilliant men in England, but they have devoted their talents to the philosophical novel or the novel that specializes in the interpretation of a set of personal values. When one takes down from the library shelf an armful of contemporary English novels which clearly intend to deal with the human comedy in its basic aspects, which dramatize essential conflicts and significant political crises, one finds that one has, all unwittingly, invaded a salon of *femmes savantes*. The lady novelists of England seem to have exclusive possession of a sense of social responsibility.

The explanation of this inequality of intellectual fortitude on a basis of sex is probably twofold. There is one reason why the minds of English men have gone slack and flaccid and another why those of English women have acquired new vigor and adventurousness. Of the first aspect of the problem a sentimentalist would certainly say that the flower of English manhood was killed in the First World War. It seems not unlikely that a psychologist would support this general view by saying that the male population between wars suffered from fatigue and disillusionment.

The truth about English women may very well be that they are enjoying their own private Elizabethan age. For them the period since the beginning of the First World War has been one of emancipation, of greatly broadened outlook and enlarged opportunity. To be sure, only a small proportion of them availed themselves of the new freedom in the years between wars; the rest continued dutifully to trail their husbands along the path of ideas, as they remained content to trail them into restaurants and theaters. No doubt the crisis of the Second World War has enrolled many more young women in the company of potential leaders.

But for the woman of genuine intellectual capacity the decades of the 20's and 30's were a time of excited exploration and discovery. There were no seas to conquer such as their Elizabethan forebears had had in another day of great restlessness and inquiry. The belated Elizabethans among English women accordingly set out to explore the unknown countries of the mind. Because this was a new exploit to them, they brought to it all the eagerness and energy that human beings have ever displayed in the quest of understanding. I do not mean to exaggerate the importance of their contribution. There has been more earnestness than originality in their work, more of analytical fervor than of creative brilliance. But women like Winifred Holtby, Vera Brittain, Phyllis Bentley, and Storm Jameson stand with dignity and resolution for the best that has been accomplished by the English novelists of our time.

Winifred Holtby

THE first two members of this group happen to have been closely associated and both have set down personal records of the most revealing kind. Vera Brittain, after the death of her friend Winifred Holtby, edited a volume of the latter's letters, a series which reveals with exuberant and touching spontaneity exactly what were the absorbing interests, political convictions, and emotional values of these earnest women of the 20's.

◄§ With just a little more slyness in the editing, *Letters to a Friend* might have been given the pattern of a novel, with all the proper climaxes in their inevitable places. It would then turn out to be the story of three young lady musketeers who in the years just after the war undertook to storm artistic London and had a gratifying success.

The story concerns Winifred, Vera, and Clare. The first two had served in the war, returned to college afterward, and then settled down to enjoy the intellectual life in a modest flat. Clare was younger, the carefully nurtured sister of Vera's fiancé, who had been killed in the war. They were all very independent young women who believed intensely in social reform and the League of Nations and the importance of literature. They talked about all these interests endlessly in public and private, took a hand in politics, wrote feverishly at their novels and their stories and their articles, believed ardently in the duty to reclaim society from disaster.

It looked for a time as though they might all live out their lives in sober, intellectual spinsterhood. Then suddenly a new lover appeared for Vera. He had liked her books, and wooed her first by letter and then in his own quiet person. Winifred was the ideal chaperon, sympathetic and fond, romanticizing the lovers as much as they romanticized each other. She bought a dress for the wedding and was wistfully humorous about her own lack of physical attractiveness.

Clare got on too, establishing herself as an artist whose work was in much demand. Winifred's novels received mixed notices and earned almost nothing at first. But when the volume ends, she is setting out to visit Africa, where she will write the best selling novel of her career. Life has given her its compensations too. She is a professional aunt to the children of her friends; she is seriously regarded in the writing world; she is a firm-minded intellectual who has served faithfully and well the ideals she espoused.

This, I think, would have been an interesting and significant story even if it did not have the added attraction of being a true one. The three young lady musketeers were Winifred Holtby, whose *Mandoa, Mandoa!* and *South Riding* are likely to endure past our own time; Vera Brittain, author of that extraordinary statement made for the war generation, *Testament of Youth*; and Clare Leighton, whose book *Country Matters*, for which she did both text and illustrations, is a genuine delight.

Winifred Holtby told of the excitements and intellectual passions of their joint lives in a series of exuberant letters written to an old war associate turned schoolmistress in Africa. Because her friend was out of the country, there was sufficient reason for discussing every aspect of the life of London—its political crises, its literary sensations, its theater, its personalities, its movements, moods, perplexities. Without an undue amount of self-consciousness, Winifred Holtby sent off to Africa a series of intimate snapshots of postwar society in intellectual London.

She gives also a vivid portrait of herself, and a most attractive person she proves to have been. What one likes is her ardor. Winifred Holtby wanted the world to be better and she went racing from meeting to meeting determined to make it so. She loved literature and read everything she could lay her hands on. She was devoted to her friends and did them innumerable services, small and large, to make their lives more comfortable.

The letters are far from being brilliant. They are as sententious as the letters of a young and very bookish lady, written to a schoolmistress, would inevitably be. They do not reveal extraordinary critical insight. Winifred Holtby liked most of the things she read. To the realism of Arnold Bennett she indiscreetly applied the adjective "exquisite." The style of Cabell in *Jurgen* "went to her head." But it is her vitality and generosity that one finds quite irresistible in these letters.

This youthful portrait of Winifred Holtby remains something to be treasured. Despite the gushing youthfulness of the letters, one catches a glimpse of just the sort of resolution and idealism that is still the hope of the harassed, stubborn, and not overbright world. ₰

It was in *South Riding* that Winifred Holtby showed herself to be in full command of the tactics of the interpretive novel.

₰ Shortly after she had completed this magnificent book, Winifred Holtby died. Her death was a shocking betrayal of what, in our more mystic moments, we like to consider the purposes of human life.

Her last book was her finest. It would inevitably be so, because Winifred Holtby was an artist whose imagination sent roots deep into the soil of human life. Her work became riper and more flavorsome in each phase of her development. *South Riding* is an impressive social document, as copious in detail, as varied in interest, as is her *Mandoa, Mandoa!* but more significant because less fanciful. The vein of satiric extravagance which ran through her earlier books apparently exhausted itself in *The Astonishing Island*, making Miss Holtby ready to deal with an ambitious social theme in a realistic and compassionate style.

It is the likeness of a whole community that Miss Holtby has painted on her huge canvas. Wishing to give a complete view of a typical English way of life, she has taken the commanding view of South Riding's activities and problems that is open to members of a county council. As the functions of government proceed in their usual intermittent and wavering way, they sometimes run parallel to, sometimes collide with, the interests of private individuals. Very artfully and dramatically, Miss Holtby seizes the opportunity she has made for herself to tell the stories of those individuals. Though each is a fairly typical product of modern society, each is depicted in sufficient detail to give him his own identity.

The problem which the council faces in its deliberations on educational matters is dramatized in the appointment of Sarah Burton as headmistress of the Kiplington girls' high school. She is a highly competent spinster who has poured into her zeal for improving methods of instruction all the vitality which has been denied any other outlet. This portrait is Miss Holtby's tribute to the modern woman of sensitive social feeling. It would be hard to imagine a better picture of intellectual hardihood, divorced from sentimentality.

There is perhaps a trace of biography in the study of Mrs. Beddows, a woman of seventy who continues valiantly to serve her community as alderman, generously and intelligently concerned with the complicated problem of making human life livable. South Riding is dedicated to Alderman Mrs. Holtby, the author's mother.

Never very far from the center of the scene is Robert Carne, gentleman farmer and conscientious reactionary. He suffers the fate of all well-meaning men who are out of sympathy with the spirit of the time. Complicating his existence all but unbearably are the financial and emotional problems of his private life. Carne is far too scrupulous to profit by his official position in the community and must stand by, helpless, while men on the make work cheerfully for his ruin. His difficulties culminate in a great orgy of disaster when he loses his home, fails to be re-elected to the council, and sees his neurotic wife collapse into insanity. Miss Holtby did not, however, set on her hero with the sadistic violence of a writer determined to fake a tragedy. Carne's misfortunes and those of his wife spring inevitably out of the very nature of their maladjustment to the world in which they live.

There is no aspect or problem of community life which Miss Holtby does not investigate with the shrewd intuition of one who has devoted a great deal of her life to the study of social conditions. Poverty, insanity, incompetence, disease— all the ills which conscientious men and women have tried so hard in our time to cure or alleviate are examined once more in their significant and universal aspects. *South Riding* is a great comprehensive social survey in novel form. Though it describes conditions in an English town, there is nothing in the implied generalization of the report that does not apply equally well to the conditions of an American community. Readers in this country will find it no less engrossing, and no less disturbing, than the author's fellow countrymen.

If there is a formidable and forbidding sound to the description of the book as a comprehensive social survey, ignore it. The individual histories have been developed with such compassionate understanding and with so much feeling for drama that their interest, simply as human documents, is powerful and compelling. No English writer of our time has developed the social theme in the novel with so much art and so much warmth. ❧

Vera Brittain

VERA BRITTAIN is the most earnest and the least humorous of this group of women writers. Her deficiency of grace in small matters of sympathy and understanding is the defect of her fine quality: an all-encompassing desire to serve.

Both the earnestness and the humorlessness have stood in the way of her personal ambition, which has been to become an accomplished artist of the novel. Miss Brittain has a way of going about with a soap-box strapped to her back. She can slip out of it and she can mount it, all at a moment's notice. Her ideas are interesting, challenging, unconcessive, but they elude translation into fiction form.

She was certainly at her best in the book with which she first claimed wide attention. *Testament of Youth* described how a young woman came through the ordeal of the First World War, having suffered much more than an average share of shocks and bereavements, to become a champion on the platform of the ideals of internationalism.

⁓§ Vera Brittain is a novelist and when the idea of telling her own story first suggested itself to her, she thought of casting it in fiction form. But after several attempts that proved the folly of trying reticently to hang veils over the reality she had lived, Miss Brittain abandoned all subterfuge. Here is her autobiography, and it is the sort of book each of us would like to have written about his experience: a complete evocation of an intimately known way of life.

Miss Brittain came of a stodgily respectable upper middle-class family from the vicinity of the Five Towns. The Brittains knew and thought "quite ordinary" the family that produced one Enoch Arnold Bennett, who did rather well later when he went up to London. The Brittains, however, continued to have their own opinion. This proves as well as anything could how perfectly they lived up to the backbone-of-the-nation tradition.

But into Vera Brittain had mysteriously been born the new-woman impulse. She left the bridge table for higher education, got on well with the intellectual friends of her brothers, became engaged to one of these, and found herself facing the future in 1914 with as much anticipation as a self-conscious, introspective child of the times could permit herself.

The increasing fury of the tragedy that rode down and trampled on all these pleasant, harmless hopes is entirely familiar. In its essentials, this story has been told many times before. But its pathos does not grow less. Something about the intimacy of this quiet confession makes it genuinely and deeply moving.

First the fiancé, then the brothers, then two intimate friends were killed in action. Vera, who had given up studying temporarily, was nursing in various places—in London, in Malta, in France. As these brutal finalities snuffed out one significant relationship after another, she had to live on alone in an atmosphere of tense suspension of hope.

There are many dramatic incidents. On Christmas she sat half the night waiting for a telephone call from her fiancé, who was expected to arrive at any moment on leave. In the morning a telephone call came at last, but it was from her fiancé's sister to announce his death in action two days before. . . .

At first the peace was rather worse than the war had been, partly because it was a "thoroughly nasty peace," but partly too because the weight of tragedy had depressed Vera Brittain to a level of sluggishness on which all experience was irritating. Still, there was Oxford to go back to, a little resentfully because the war seemed to have made so little difference there, then teaching and lecturing for the League of Nations, and finally a passion for a literary career.

The perfect pattern for fiction is here, even the happy ending. For at the close of the book, Vera Brittain is well established in a writing career and she is about to marry appropriately.

It is a strange odyssey and a genuinely affecting one. It will be said many times that this is a significant book because it traces the changes that have taken place in society, in its thought, its manners, and its morals, as a result of the war. But it is a significant book also because it speaks so directly, so passionately, so honestly, of the emotions and the needs that dominate all human lives. The background happens to be of special interest. But any life story told as simply, objectively, and unpretentiously would be equally interesting. Miss Brittain has succeeded admirably because, having decided to tell this story, she tells it without reserve, lets us see her in her moments of frustration and pettiness as well as in her moments of dedication and gallantry.

And the end of this remarkable exercise in truth-telling is that one admires human nature the more because it can endure so many assaults on its faith, on its dignity, on its vitality and yet find life livable. ße

To the all but unendurable crises of the First World War, which Vera Brittain survived with dignity, there were presently added, as for everyone else in the civilized world, the excruciatingly painful anxieties of the second global conflict. These included separation from her children, evacuation from her home in London after the surrounding area had been bombed, and the distrust of her own government when she expressed unpopular views.

Repeated onslaughts upon her passionately held faiths resulted in the final collapse of the artist and the emergence from the novelist's ashes of the unapologetic propagandist. In *Account Rendered* every incident of the story was intended to demonstrate a theoretical point.

ße The last time Vera Brittain was in the news she appeared as one of the pacifists of England protesting eloquently against the obliteration bombings of the German cities.

She is still in that somewhat curious state of mind. Her new novel, put together not so much to tell a story as to communicate her ideas on the psychopathology of war, reiterates that protest and goes on to express the view that civilization itself is the real war criminal. Leaders in every country have blundered so badly that a totally unnecessary war is the result. Those who failed to correct the political evils in their own countries must share the blame for the war with the Nazis.

It is brave of Miss Brittain to stand so stanchly by her fundamental principles even while the prosecution of the war continues. But the program of the pacifists still seems maddeningly unrealistic. To talk hysterically about putting civilization on trial for war guilt is absurd. The pacifists, who would prolong the war by denying us the use of the weapons that alone can bring it to a close, seem to be determined to scurry brightly off into the millennium, taking along our hopes of a peace whereby we can live in this century. For if they brand as criminal the only civilization we know, people with modest and reasonable expectations of reform are likely to become disheartened and drop any effort at progress.

Sometimes idealists seem to be just a little too garrulous. . . .

Miss Brittain has been so determined to set forth her theories and to lash the reader about the head and shoulders with her moral precepts that she has quite forgotten how to behave like a creative artist. Her characters never come alive. There is even something alienating about the chilly and devitalized correctness of the two principals among them. Miss Brittain is never able to make their plight seem pitiful, partly because she herself is ever present, pointing out through one mouthpiece or another how pitiable it is. . . .

One of the characters in *Account Rendered* remarks on the absurdity of the situation which prompts a great country in the midst of the threat of extinction to spend several days and many people's time exploring the state of mind of a mentally disordered individual suspected of murder. Similarly there seems to me something a little disproportionate about Miss Brittain's taking a year and a half out of her life in the midst of the same crisis to draw up an indictment of society on the basis of the suffering it has caused one neurotic. ❧

Phyllis Bentley

PHYLLIS BENTLEY is the least personal, the most academic, the most learned of all these strong-minded English women. Her voice has the steady, practiced intonation of the professional teacher of history, the disciplined lecturer on public affairs.

This cool air of knowledgeability and thoroughness is quite

different from the manner of the others in this seminar. Winifred Holtby's utterance had always an overtone of personal amusement. She had begun as a writer of fantasy and even her most realistic studies of English society retained something of the flavor of an indulgent love of the absurd. If it did not sound patronizing, one might almost say that there was a faint, beguiling echo of girlish laughter in all her expression.

Vera Brittain has never been able to escape from a personal quality in writing that edges toward hysteria. One feels that she would rather like to be a martyr to something; that her nostrils widen, scenting the not altogether unwelcome hint of the sacrificial flames.

Miss Bentley has put resolutely away any temptation to exploit her own individuality. She is a creative artist, and her best books are crowded with genuinely vital creatures of her imagination. But they are built up not so much out of the writer's intuitive apperceptions of the intimacies of human psychology as out of her orderly awareness of man's relationship to the social world of which he is a part.

The themes of Miss Bentley's novels have been drawn from various sources. The historian in her has prompted her to point out parallels between the crises of our time and those of the days of Caesar and of Cromwell. But in her most characteristic books she is concerned with England, with an account of how the world she knows emerged out of the industrial revolution.

Unlike Gilbert's lady novelist, who, as he might have said, was more concerned with tea and crumpets than with bugles and trumpets, Miss Bentley has taken up her post in the very center of the economic struggle. Her people have never been the magazine writer's brittle neurotics living in a world that floats somewhere out of reach of all such gross crises as business failures, bank collapses, and economic depressions. Her men and women are credible representatives of the class of people in English society who make goods, undertake to sell them, husband their profits, hedge round their security, and very often cut their neighbors' throats in the process.

Phyllis Bentley was introduced to American readers as the author of the novel *Inheritance*, a long, thorough, and persuasive account of England weathering a great economic storm. It was an acute and subtle analysis of the twofold fight between man and the machine and between man and money. Yet through the whole troubled course of the richly detailed novel the human element dominated, making each character believable and each in his way appealing.

But a greater social storm was in the making, and two years later Miss Bentley, with the conscientiousness of an artist who was also part historian and part economic interpreter, undertook to dramatize in *A Modern Tragedy* the story of how the depression affected the manufacturing world of England.

◄§ If novelists were like wine merchants they might, I think, very easily name the "good years" of the twentieth century. The good years for a writer are almost necessarily the bad years for everyone else, because what the creative artist wants is the spectacular event, the dramatic interruption to the monotonous routine of living. The years 1914 to 1918 were good years because they distilled excitement. Scarcely less stimulating have been the years 1929, 1930, 1931. For, like the war, the depression has reversed many values in the life of the modern world and set society the task of re-creating itself in new terms.

Inheritance, Miss Bentley's most important previous novel, was an ambitious chronicle describing the growth of a great textile manufacturing business through several generations in the lives of its owners. She brought that story down to our own times, but the chapters dealing with the present were sketchily written as compared with the richness of design in the earlier part. Now she makes good that defect, for *A Modern Tragedy* is really an extension of the same material. Though she calls her characters by different names and moves them to a new town, both the people and the background are so closely related to those of *Inheritance* that there seems to be almost no interruption to the continuity of the discussion.

The men are the important figures. Each of them represents a special group within the industrial struggle. Henry Crosland is the hereditary aristocrat of business, an honest manufacturer who conducts his affairs according to the rules that have made his predecessors powerful and respected. His rival in business, but an ally in matters of ethics, is Arnold Lumb, a rugged, conscientious, middle-class manufacturer.

These representatives of the substantial manufacturing class, which understood its responsibilities as well as its opportunities, are pitted against Leonard Tasker, the ruthless, conniving man of affairs whose philosophy is that of bleeding society for what he can get, taking no thought for the final effect upon its health. It is he who carries the whole group down to complete disaster by his unscrupulous methods of exploitation.

An ambitious young man becomes his tool. Trained in the Lumb employ for honest service, Walter Haigh is dazzled by the opportunity Tasker offers him to rise quickly in his world. He becomes the manager of Tasker's mill, through which the employer hopes to drive Lumb out of business. The drama of ruthless competition begins. Wages are cut and the community suffers. Led by an eloquent radical, Milner Schofield, the workers rise in protest. The society which had functioned smoothly, providing comfort and contentment for everyone, is suddenly a chaos.

But the depression is operating constantly against Tasker. The upturn he has counted on to rescue him does not come. Misrepresenting his assets, he floats a stock issue. Walter Haigh, deeply involved with his employer now, does not protest and even the honorable Crosland becomes innocently involved. The crash overtakes Tasker in the midst of his machinations. Everyone is ruined. Crosland commits suicide. Tasker and Haigh are sent to jail.

The impressive thing about Miss Bentley's book is her ability to make the details of business constantly interesting, humanly dramatic, and socially significant. She has conceived her tragedy on the grand scale. It is the tragedy of the community rather than of the individuals. Her picture of the industrial town, utterly demoralized by the ruthless ambition that has betrayed its interests, is detailed and pitiful. Spiritual depression follows the economic depression. The workers, unused to idleness, become dispirited; the line at the employment exchange grows longer and longer. The face of the community becomes weary, anxious, looking for hope from it knows not what source.

Neither does Miss Bentley know. For in the epilogue to her drama she makes one of her women characters offer this pale consolation: "And I can see that not till men have learned the mutual love which casts out fear can the economic problem be solved, and as long as it remains unsolved, fears will multiply. Let no one seek his own, but every man another's, wealth."

Though it is not quite what she says, Miss Bentley means that we must create a world in which the common good will be the objective of everyone. It was the will to seek and grab another's wealth that ruined the pre-depression world. ஐ

Storm Jameson

MARGARET STORM JAMESON sums up in her luminous intelligence the excellences of all her confreres—or, if the Academy will permit me to enrich the French language in the interest of women's rights, her *consoeurs*. She has the humorous intuition of Winifred Holtby, the earnestness of Vera Brittain, and the solid knowledgeability of Phyllis Bentley. To these she adds a quality of her own which one must be reckless enough to call richness of spirit.

It is this breadth of view that makes it possible for her to achieve complete spontaneous identification with every aspect of the human plight, down to the meanest and the most distressing. She is precise and exacting in the standards to which she wishes to hold the behavior of the race, yet generous in the allowance she makes for its failures. Indeed, she is the true Hypatia, a woman of genuinely philosophic mind, illuminated by the poetry of intuition.

She is the most feminine of all the creative artists in this group, enclosing all human effort in a sober, contemplative absorption that is distinctly maternal.

Man, the fighter, the destroyer, the creature of restless and uncritical rapacity, has always felt an impulse to represent his aspirations toward justice and peace as having the forms of women. The symbolism of this is complex. Among its implications are that certain values are passive as women are passive, and that man must ever woo them with the same intermittent passion with which he woos women.

A writer like Storm Jameson does credit to the tradition of woman as the conservator of ideals, for she is concerned with the welfare of the whole human family and is stubbornly, valiantly hopeful of its ultimate success. She seems in her writing as shrewd, as discerning, as impartial, as we would ask abstract justice to be. But what is better, she gives one the impression of feeling that the race is her child, and in the warmth of her consideration of its perplexities the aloof virtues come attractively to life.

Her themes have been many and her scenes far flung. But the European mind has been the absorbing interest of her life. In *Then We Shall Hear Singing* she wrote a fable addressed to conquerors and intended as a warning that mind is indestructible and will always be an implacable counterthreat to tyranny.

~§ Storm Jameson has long been preoccupied with the confusions, antagonisms, betrayals, and violences of European politics. But she does not turn this interest into fiction of the ordinary types, either the kind that develops into an elaborate game of ratiocination or the kind that degenerates into a game of spying and escape. What she is after is a dramatic interpretation of the complex psychological state of mind out of which these outrages spring.

Her new book is the most ingenious she has yet produced, a tragic and poetic study of a conquered country struggling to be reborn. The book is many things in one, a fantasy, a parable, and a prophecy. But I like it best of all, I think, for its sensitive study of the function of memory and of how it nourishes the mind and sustains the heart so that there can be no such thing as defeat for those who will only remember.

With that audacious resolution which has always characterized her imaginative processes, Storm Jameson begins her story with the assumption that the democratic countries have given up the struggle in Europe and that the war is over. (She never names her conquered country and she does not specify that Germany is the invader, but this is simply to keep the theme on the abstract level and not allow it to get involved in all kinds of cluttering, realistic concerns.)

The "Protectorate," which, like Czechoslovakia, was never permitted to defend itself, has accepted the gross, obvious terms of defeat, maintaining its integrity only in its inner mind. In secret the people preserve their language, their songs, and the memory of their brief, glorious moment of freedom.

But a scientist of the conquering people discovers a method by which he can hasten and, he thinks, ensure the enslavement of this people so that it will no longer be necessary to maintain an army to keep them in subjection. He treats them in his laboratory in such a way that the higher functions of the brain are destroyed without affecting the body. Thus they become like vigorous children, able to work well for their masters, but uncritical with regard to their own social welfare or destiny.

First a few carefully chosen specimens are thus divested of the more inconvenient aspects of mentality. When they have been turned successfully into slightly boisterous but docile children, the rest of the community are similarly treated. Only a few escape, an old woman who is not thought worth the effort and a few young women who take their children and flee. In them memory is preserved. Especially the old woman, Anna, becomes a kind of living repository of her country's history.

But Storm Jameson's point is a subtler and better one than that memory can be preserved in a single loyal mind. She wishes to suggest in a vivid and poetic way that the higher functions of the brain cannot be destroyed as long as people live together in any kind of sharing. Spirit touches spirit into life; the evolutionary process of reaching adulthood of mind begins all over again; and presently the dull and docile child will be restored to manhood, demanding decency and freedom and something of grace in his way of life.

There are many fine passages in Storm Jameson's novel. The moments of domestic drama at the start, which show a conquered people trying to piece together a life of emotional fastidiousness out of the ruins of their loves and their loyalties, have a lightness of touch that belongs to the finest tradition of the literature of sentiment. The psychological analyses of the old, exhausted warriors of the conquering nation, who actually apologize for their cruelties while they seem to justify them, are full of insight and wisdom. The portrait of the doctor, who feels an intoxicating sense of power in degrading his fellow men, brings out all the grossness of the inferiority complex. The doctor's eloquent defense of the rights of the master race is cleverly designed to make all the routine Nazi propaganda utterly fatuous and ridiculous. . . .

This is a fine-spirited book with no falseness of sentiment

in it. *Then We Shall Hear Singing* reminds us merely of our right to believe that no matter how grossly it may sometimes be corrupted, the wisdom of the race endures indestructibly. ৪ই

Even more characteristic of Mrs. Jameson's generosity in viewing the failures of the European intelligence and her belief in its ability to be reborn after each death, is the novel *Cloudless May*.

ই Once more Storm Jameson has demonstrated that she is by far the most intellectual of the novelists now serving the British tradition. Her latest work is a rich and detailed study of the moral climate of France during the deceptively perfect serenity of that "cloudless May" just before the debacle. . . .

Because it deals with a defeat which was moral as well as physical, *Cloudless May* will make grievous reading for Frenchmen or for devoted lovers of France. It shows a small, typical (though imaginary) community of the Loire Valley clinging stubbornly to the normality of its ways, bargaining, plotting, dining, deeply engrossed in affairs of finance and of the heart. No effort is being made to prepare for the approaching test of strength because no one believes in his physical strength and almost no one has a philosophy from which to derive any sort of moral resolution.

Storm Jameson has built up original characters, full of individual quirks, oddity, and interest, which have as their foundations those weaknesses and perversities of which Pétain and Laval are the embodiments. She is, I think, completely fair, for she has also created characters that are counterparts for the brave and unyielding young men who have escaped from France to fight again from England or in Africa. . . .

It is no mere parable of defeatism that Storm Jameson has written, but a full-bodied social novel. The people of the town of Seuilly have not been created merely to conduct a sort of town meeting discussion of abstract issues. Their personal histories have been fully imagined and their personal passions are fully explored. They act and react upon each other before one's very eyes. The fact that their lives are enclosed within a pattern of crisis about which we know the beginning and the middle, if not the end, does not make them seem to behave automatically or to be jerked on puppet strings.

Storm Jameson has managed to look at recent events in France as though she were far enough removed to judge them both judicially and sympathetically. At the same time she looks at her material as though she were close enough to know its every detail. The war that has put an end to the limitations of space, so that we are all occupants of one little world, has also rubbed out time. The novel of contemporary society is nowadays a historical novel too. 8~

Stanch defenders of the faith in art exclusively for art's sake tend to look with sniffish distrust upon the novel of social significance. They think it a machine-made affair that moves with a noisy and insistent grinding of gears. For them it lacks the placid attraction of the work of art which, as Oscar Wilde declared with his own special kind of snobbery, has absolutely no importance.

Such observers might be distressed if they realized that in our boisterous and ungracious day even women have been seduced away from the universal themes of the day of small things. Jane Austen, they point out, achieved literary master-pieces without once referring to the vulgar and distressing crises of social significance stirred up by Napoleon's mischievous hand.

But perhaps if the news of the war had been brought to Jane Austen through sixteen hours out of every twenty-four, in the tense yet manly and refined accents of a radio analyst; perhaps if it had been deposited on her doorstep in the form of a delayed-action bomb, she too might have felt obliged to emerge out of her village security. It is even possible that she would have exchanged her persistent interest in the difficulty of getting married for concern over the problem of keeping the race from committing suicide.

Alert human beings must always live the life of their time. Our time has been one in which people of sober and responsible mentality have become aware of the obligation to forgo some of the values of our several national loyalties in favor of those of an international society. In England no one has seen this truth more clearly or steadily than this group of women. They have been as useful as any of the intellectuals their country has produced in our strenuous day.

We Walk in Anguish

THERE is a cycle to the development of a society as there is to the development of an individual. A young culture, like a young man, is eager, curious, vigorous, and naive. A middle-aged culture is meditative, and, whether the balance of its philosophic attitudes inclines toward the skeptical view of life or the sanguine, its attention is fixed upon intellectual values. A senile culture is devitalized and, in a half-bored, half-fearful restlessness, is chiefly concerned, often on a low level of superstition, with other-worldly matters. When the cycle has been completed, if the culture itself does not disappear completely, it begins all over again.

In our crowded and tumultuous century we have seen the progress of the cycle dramatically speeded up in at least one instance. The old Russian culture, having reached a maturity to which Dostoevski, Tolstoy, and Chekhov gave expression, moved on into its senility, to which Tolstoy also gave a maundering tongue. Then, after the Revolution, its society began a new cycle, the spirit of which is represented by the young writers of the USSR, who are for the most part explorative, hopeful, and full of projects which leave them very little time to devote to abstract ideas.

American culture may be said to have passed out of its youth and to be on the threshold of maturity. The writers who express our ideas for us are through with the myth of limitless and universal prosperity. They are at the moment engrossed in the task of gathering up and arranging for closer study all the souvenirs of our progress from our beginnings on this soil up to the present time. Our period of richest and most sober interpretive writing is ready to begin. Having lately come of age, our culture is soon to start the task of codifying its beliefs.

The mind of Europe is still the best philosophic mind our world community has produced. In its apprehensions and hopes we may discern the pattern that our own philosophic development is likely to assume.

In the critical years between 1914 and the present, Europe has undergone a series of special convulsions so violent that it is difficult to see how anything of its culture has been able to survive. Those who take a masochistic satisfaction in repeating the incantations of death, saying "All is over," go on the assumption that nothing of significance has survived. Germany, such observers say, has at last fulfilled its long-cherished impulse to commit suicide. Italy, having played the role of subnormal confederate to gangsters and gone along on a larcenous adventure "just to drive the car," is fit only for reform school. Spain is in the midst of a tense and demoralizing family feud. France, in a mood of decadent sluggishness, allowed her convictions to be discarded and her integrity to be destroyed. The ruins of Europe's cities are merely the "outward and visible sign" of an inward and spiritual disgrace.

But neither the shape of a society nor the power of its mind appears to be as feeble and as fragile as such woebegone analysts imagine. Despite the threat of starvation, despite every other acute discomfort to its body, Europe is making as good an intellectual recovery from the war as is the rest of the world. And as far as things of the mind are concerned, even the worst offenders among the misguided nations can rejoice in the character of the exiles into whose keeping the best of its intellectual capacities have been given. From Italy have come such preservers of the conscience and intellect of humankind as Sforza, Salvemini, and Father Luigi de Sturzo. The shores of our continent have received from Spain such uncorrupted spirits as Isabel de Palencia. Against the decadence of France, Saint Exupéry set the example of his physical, as well as his intellectual, resistance. And from Germany itself there came such representatives of the tradition of free inquiry and judgment as Einstein and Thomas Mann.

No matter what may be said in legitimate protest about Europe's failure to protect the liberal spirit against betrayal from within, the distinction of the exiles testifies to the fact that the European mind is still a source of strength from which our generation will continue to draw nourishment through the rest of its own time on earth.

Thomas Mann

THE history of Thomas Mann is, I think, the history in essence of the intellectual living through the exacting crises of a revolutionary period. His distinguished qualities as observer and chronicler of the human experience declared themselves when, as a very young man, he wrote the brilliant family history called *Buddenbrooks*. The command of the tactics of the novel which he demonstrated in his first book was matched by his command of the emotional resources of storytelling when in later studies like *Death in Venice* he wrote of the subtle enemies that attack the integrity of the human spirit.

These achievements would, in any orderly world, have given their author a secure position from which to direct other campaigns intended to conquer wide fields of human understanding. But the consistent development of Thomas Mann's artistic career was interrupted by the First World War, during which he conceived it his duty to remain a loyal German. By the narrow margin of emotional commitment, he missed the opportunity which his brother, Heinrich Mann, seized, that of speaking out for abstract values even in defiance of the sentimental attachments of heritage.

In the period between wars Thomas Mann gained a higher place than ever in the estimate of the world community of letters by writing a peculiarly fascinating book which still offers a model for anyone who undertakes to explore the possibilities of the philosophic novel. *The Magic Mountain* is a unique achievement in the literary history of our time.

Then, when the hostilities that resulted in the Second World War began to gather their poison, Thomas Mann was ready to play the role of the leader of thought who stands above the battle of immediate loyalties and lends his strength to the support of abstract principles. He became a voluntary exile from Germany and as such a chief example of the incorruptible keeper of the conscience of humanity.

As a comment upon his intellectual significance, I offer these lines written when he visited the University of Minnesota to speak before its community of students and alumni.

◄§ To those who have regarded the author of *The Magic Mountain* and the Joseph novels as the titan of our time in the field of literature, the visit of Thomas Mann to the University of Minnesota could seem like nothing less than a major event of their lives.

He stood among us for an evening, an authentically great man, one whose abstract convictions have been supported by acts of almost unexampled courage and beauty. And when he spoke to us, it was to justify all the depth of our respect for his mind and his spirit. From first to last he was earnest, tender, and wise. The opportunity which the platform offers to the man of reputation has been so often betrayed by the shallow exhibitionist that simply to hear Dr. Mann speak, almost as though he were hypnotized by reverence for the greatness of his theme, was in itself a moving experience.

He enclosed his thought in a radiance of phrase that made even his most difficult speculations luminously clear. Yet there seemed to be no mere technical expertness involved in his enormous effectiveness. As he spoke, quite without heat or nervous emphasis, on "The Problem of Freedom," his voice seemed to assume the authority belonging to the prophet.

The point which is fundamental to Dr. Mann's philosophy is the belief that democracy can and will reconcile within its program the needs of the individual and the needs of society, the ideal of freedom and the ideal of equality. It is not, he was scrupulous to observe, a task which can be accomplished by anything less than the heroic exercise of man's best powers.

There are, Dr. Mann pointed out, two attitudes which the thinking man may take toward human life. Both are tinged with pessimism, yet there is the greatest difference between them. One looks with reverent compassion upon "man's dark lot" and says, "It will never be better." The other, unmoved by what it sees as a grim plight, says, "Life shall never be better."

It is the first of these attitudes that Dr. Mann takes as his own, coupling it with the determination to struggle for the amelioration of the human plight, which he views as tragic. It is the second of these attitudes that he discerns in the minds of the leaders of Germany, most particularly in "that fatal man" against whose strange teachings Dr. Mann was protesting even before he left his native country. . . .

As with any very significant utterance, there were points upon which equally earnest philosophers might not wholly agree. The passage in which Dr. Mann spoke of the limitations that must be put upon tolerance must have created a momentary division in the mind of his audience, delighting many of his hearers and giving others perhaps a twinge of doubt. But as to the general pattern of his thought, there could surely be no other opinion than that it was earnest, moving, hopeful, and noble. ⧉

Antoine de Saint Exupéry

ANTOINE DE SAINT EXUPERY was perhaps the most consistent and most vigorous of all the poet-philosophers who undertook to be the preservers of the European conscience. Not only did he write uninterruptedly in defense of the ideals of brotherhood, but he sacrificed his life as a pilot fighting to reclaim the freedom and the integrity of his native France. *Flight to Arras* was his last and his most characteristic book.

᭰§ With three books, *Night Flight, Wind, Sand and Stars,* and *Flight to Arras,* Antoine de Saint Exupéry established himself as a sort of metaphysician of the adventure of flight. Each of his books had the same basic structure. All of them described journeys which, though they were brief in time, were crowded with a sense of spiritual crisis and before the end with a sense of revelation.

The first two seemed momentous when they were produced, but neither of them can have been for the author an experience as strongly accented with emotions as the third. In *Night Flight* and *Wind, Sand and Stars* Saint Exupéry found himself trying to arrive at a conclusion about the value of human life, prompted by the possibility of its being sacrificed in the midst of a physical adventure over mountains or over a desert. But as he took off for Arras he was struggling with a more desperate speculation: whether or not human life had any value at all. He had faced death before; this time he faced the corrupting and demoralizing defeat of all his faith.

The time was May 1940. The occasion was a sortie ordered by the staff of the already defeated French army. No one, least of all the major who had to order his pilot, observer, and gunners into the air, believed there was any point in the mission. A report about the position of the German forces could not be news for more than a flurried moment or two because the position became more furiously menacing every hour. With the passivity of men who had ceased to believe in the meaning of anything, they took off.

So the flight, like those of the other books, became a kind of parable of faith lost and won again. During the time that Saint Exupéry and his men were in the air they had several adventures of a physical sort. The controls of the machine were frozen; the struggle to release them nearly cost the pilot his life, because it is not possible to make great straining efforts at such an altitude. Again, the plane barely eluded a force of German fliers. Still again, it was subjected to the tragic irony of being shot at by Frenchmen, who assumed, reasonably enough, that since France had so few planes any that was seen in the air must be German. These incidents lent dramatic tension to the narrative. But their purpose to the book, as Saint Exupéry conceived it, was merely to keep attention fixed on the figure of a lonely, desperate man struggling to regain something by which he could live if he should return to earth from this flight with despair.

He did find it. Although Saint Exupéry felt a terrible and crushing guilt in the defeat of France, he reached out to accept that guilt and to learn to understand "the profound meaning of the humility exacted from the individual."

"Each is responsible for all," he wrote. "Each is by himself responsible. Each by himself is responsible for all. I understand now for the first time the mystery of the religion whence was born the civilization I claim as my own: 'To bear the sins of man.' Each man bears the sins of all men." ع

André Malraux

ANDRE MALRAUX is another young writer of distinguished gift who has given not merely of his intellectual capacity but of his physical strength also, to support his belief in the best the European mind has been able to devise as a pattern for human society. He fought in the underground movement as a Maquisard and, fortunately for his country and for the struggle to keep intellectual values alive, he has survived that superb recklessness. Days of Wrath is the book in which he expresses most effectively the philosophy of the man of conscience faced by the obligation to defend the positive value of man's fellowship against the negative threat of man's cruelty.

André Malraux's book is touchingly dedicated: "To the German comrades who were anxious for me to make known what they had suffered and what they had upheld."

In this short but intensely emotional novel the author of *Man's Fate* takes up another tragic story. In a manner that is all but unbearably poignant, he describes the suffering and the despair of one who earns the ill-favor of Nazi officialdom and is flung into a concentration camp.

Malraux has chosen as his central figure a significant person. Many of the actual accounts of torture in the Nazi prisons have been written by men who were either victims of the prejudice against their race or victims of the idlest kind of malice. Kassner does not belong to that group. He is an active worker against the Nazi party and therefore its enemy.

The act for which he is thrown into prison is simply that of entering the headquarters of his fellow workers and destroying a list of names which would have incriminated other men. There follow the perfunctory examination, imprisonment, beating—all in the routine that is distressingly familiar.

After nine days in which Kassner fights a desperate battle to retain his sanity, he is released through the sacrifice of a fellow worker who gives himself up pretending to be Kassner. The organizer makes his escape out of Germany. But it is only for a moment's respite. He sees his wife and child once more and then prepares to return to the struggle.

The book is very short and Malraux has deliberately transferred the emphasis from the physical plane to the spiritual. He does not wish to make one's blood chill, all over again, with extended descriptions of Nazi boots kicking at human flesh and ribs. Each incident is given a sort of symbolical treatment so that its meaning as a part of the human struggle for preservation of its finest ideal of brotherhood may become apparent. Kassner in the concentration camp is not a mass of bruised, tortured flesh. He is a spirit, released by suffering and so more conscious than ever of his duty to the mass of men.

229

There are many moments of tragic intensity in the book. The moment when Kassner in his cell thinks that he must take his own life by sharpening his nails on stone and slashing his wrists is intensely dramatic. Very vivid is the description of the airplane's desperate flight through a storm that, from moment to moment, threatens pilot and passenger.

Tremendously effective in a different way is the meeting between Kassner and his wife. They are two people who are intensely aware of each other. Yet each of them is aware of something infinitely greater: his responsibility to the fellowship of man which is their common faith. Supported by that belief, Anna is able to see Kassner go back to dangers like those from which he has just escaped.

In each of the other episodes one feels the same desire on the part of the author to make it a symbol of the spiritual struggle through which man is passing.

Kassner thinks, as he looks on at a meeting of people come together to try to free political prisoners:

"These people had chosen to come here, and not to seek pleasure or sleep, because they wanted to give courage to those entombed in the prisons of Germany; they had come because of what they knew and did not know, and in their unbreakable determination . . . could be found their reply to the challenge of that body beaten to death against the wall of the cell and to the unceasing voice of man's suffering that rose up out of the earth. . . . No human speech went so deep as cruelty. But man's fellowship could cope with it, could go into the very blood-stream, to the forbidden places of the heart where torture and death are lurking."

This is the faith that Malraux has written this novel to express. ৪৯

Jules Romains

THE most thorough and consistent effort to interpret the positive and the negative values of contemporary European society in terms of fiction has been made by the philosopher-novelist Jules Romains. The threads which Romains has been slowly weaving in his long series of novels are now drawing into a tight pattern. The question, still unanswered, is this: Does a man deceive himself when he attempts to work "in terms of the eternal," or can "the rational will of mankind" influence its destiny and affect its history?

For nearly fifteen years Jules Romains has been engaged, in a leisurely yet thorough fashion, upon a monumental project, a history of contemporary France in fiction form. The first novel of the series to which the all-embracing title, *Men of Good Will*, has been given dealt with events of the year 1908. Now in the twelfth volume, *The Wind is Rising*, Romains has penetrated into the days of unrest, two decades later, when Europe was beginning with perverse zeal to prepare the background for the tragedy of the Second World War.

In the years 1928 and 1929 the dissatisfactions of several different groups of people produced in France what Romains calls "the gathering of the gangs." The Communists were attempting to spread their faith among the workers; men of the right were worriedly watching this drama of unrest; and between these extremes were the improvisers who were later to play so important a role in the betrayal of France from within. Among them were many leftists, men of theatrical temperament and overweening personal ambition who, finding that they were more likely to be used by the Communist movement than to be able to use it themselves, turned back toward the right with their wits sharpened and their principles blunted.

It was out of such connivings and confusions that the chaos of the days just before the fall of France was created. Jules Romains has transported his readers backward in time to that period of jaunty irresponsibility.

A less skillful artist, knowing the end of the story, would

have been unable to restrain an air of special knowingness, seeming to say by implication all through the book, "See, this is how it came about that Laval was able to insinuate himself into a position of such power," or "Now you understand Pétain." The subtlety of Jules Romains's philosophic mind has made it possible for him to resist such oracular implications. The years 1939 and 1940 will in time take their place in his series. At the moment he is content to do no more than re-create the special atmosphere of 1928 and 1929.

His improvisers, like the maladjusted young man of fashion, Nodiard, and the ex-Communist, Douvrin, seem to think of themselves as living in a hermetically sealed world outside which the effect of their actions cannot be felt. Cynicism and decadence are their glittering playthings. Both in public and in private life they invent reckless games, the ultimate effect of which is to destroy values.

They are the most vivid figures of this book because such action as it contains springs out of their plots. Touching them not at all closely but observing them with distress from a distance are men of mature intellect, brought in from Romains's other books: Jallez, the journalist, and Jerphanion, who has served his government from time to time in ministerial posts. Touching them also are the men of affairs, like Haverkamp, owner of a health spa and war profiteer. He is ready to use the unrest of the times in any way that is likely to serve his interests.

It would be a mistake, I think, to try to identify these figures too closely with those of actual life whom they obviously resemble. As an artist Romains is interested in imaginative figures whose mental life he is at liberty to create completely; as a philosopher he is interested in creating men who embody the spirit of the time.

The value of the book as interpretation would be blurred if one were to insist stubbornly on regarding it simply as an exercise in the upper reaches of gossip peddling.

This is truly a philosophic novel in the sense that all its interests are translated into terms of ideas. The bulk of the book is given over to the discussion of values. The middle-aged or elderly men of intellect consider the threatened breakdown of French institutions and what may be done to combat it. The young improvisers, who have neither plan nor principle, debate at length about the techniques of seizing power; as potential fascists they are fascinated by the mental tricks of their trade. Even the young girls of the book involve themselves in explorations of the changing status of women and the relations between the sexes. Yet none of this is pompous, pretentious, or ponderous. Jules Romains has the gift of translating ideas into the language of spirited, idiomatic, and pointed talk.

When he turned from the teaching of philosophy to the writing of fiction as a life work, Romains became the sponsor of a literary principle to which he gave the name "unanimism," designed to show that as far as literature is concerned the interests that have animated humankind can be dramatized in the life of a group better than in the lives of individuals.

The mood of our times has served his idea well, for fascist movements have been group movements, and it is as a world community that fascism has had to be fought. The group, then, is the protagonist of his book. But that does not mean that Romains has failed to individualize his figures. Though they do not have faces the oddities of which one remembers, they have mental lives the details of which one cannot forget.

Several men in our time have attempted to write series of novels which dramatize the great movements and impulses of whole societies. The Forsyte novels of Galsworthy and the Lanny Budd books by Upton Sinclair were inspired by the same brave concern with the fate of society. Neither of these other writers, however, had either the mentality or the vitality to carry the project through to genuine success. Galsworthy's books dwindled off into trifling drawing-room drama and Sinclair's into bustling, naive melodrama. Only Jules Romains has had the intellectual hardihood to give real dignity and spaciousness to his tremendous project. The *Men of Good Will* series makes up one of the few literary masterpieces of our time. ૩✑

Erich Maria Remarque

NOT all the observers of the threatened total breakdown of the European conscience have discussed the crisis in terms of abstract ideas. In his completely characteristic novels, Erich Maria Remarque has avoided speculation and philosophic comment, to concentrate closely on telling the story of man's inhumanity toward man in terms of simple, objective drama.

Only in his most recently published novel, *Arch of Triumph*, has he departed from this method. The central figure of the book is a German refugee doctor, forced to live in Paris under the most humiliating conditions a man of spirit can face. Secretly wooed by incompetent French surgeons, he must be content to do their work for them while he is publicly classified as an outlaw. Such a mature and sophisticated man inevitably finds much to say about the indignity of the human plight when ruthless and perverse power assumes control. What Remarque's character says is intelligent, thoughtful, and often appealing. Yet the stream-of-consciousness technique seems to be essentially unsympathetic to the author's style. Remarque succumbs to all its dubious attractions, permitting himself to be florid, opulent, and, finally, overblown.

The earlier books were more satisfying because, despite their reticence and objectivity, they dealt movingly with the question of whether or not man can manage to live his life in terms of the eternal.

৯§ With *Flotsam* Erich Maria Remarque re-establishes himself as one of the novelists of our time who has a claim upon one's deepest respect. Again, as in his first book, *All Quiet on the Western Front*, he has examined an unendurable human plight and shown with dignity and even with humor how the world's stoutest-hearted men and women have managed to endure it.

There is a curious resemblance between the two books, one of which examines fortitude under the impact of war and the other, an equally impressive fortitude under the demoralizing influence of race hatred. Each book weaves together the threads of many lives and makes the completed design reveal something touching and hopeful about the basic qualities of human nature.

The figures of *Flotsam* are, of course, the homeless people driven out of Germany, in the years before the war, for no reason other than that they were either Jews or enemies of the Nazi party. Deprived of their wives, their means of making a living, their very nationality, they are pushed across one border after another, finding no country that is willing to run the risk of receiving them as wards. Like criminals they are hounded from one place of hiding to another, forever in fear of the police, dodging an endless succession of traps—a lifetime of restless, exhausting flight their only prospect.

Remarque has managed to concentrate the terrifying incidents of this unending odyssey into the lives of two men and of the women they love. Steiner is a man in his middle years who has lost a solid position and the wife he loves, along with the right to carry a passport. Kern is a boy of twenty-one who has been forced to follow his father into exile, leaving behind a promising career in the comfort of a middle-class home. Their paths cross frequently as they run round and round in a circle that centers about Vienna but which takes them sometimes into Czechoslovakia and Switzerland. When they can escape from detention here and there, they try to help one another, peddling odds and ends, working as fakers in amusement parks, doing any small, inconspicuous job that will not immediately attract the police. Their casual feeling of brotherhood gives a warmth to Remarque's pages which recalls the very best of *All Quiet on the Western Front*.

They suffer many hideous and humiliating ordeals. Kern is robbed in his peddling by people who know that it is safe to exploit his helplessness. Steiner compromises with his integrity to cheat cheaters at cards and runs the risk of being physically beaten for his success. Both men are denounced by the spies in whom they have been forced to trust.

Yet there is a curious camaraderie on this dismal road. Steiner and Kern meet with moments of generosity and gallantry not merely from their fellow sufferers, but also from an occasional man in whom good will and common sense have not been snuffed out by the conditions under which all Europe has had for so long to cower. Kern even manages to fall in love with a fellow wanderer. Through sickness and betrayal, he and his Ruth cling loyally to each other. In the end they owe to Steiner their escape from the hopelessness of the new bondage. All of Remarque's central figures toward the close reach Paris. Steiner has used his remarkable resources to gather together some money. He has a brief reunion with his wife and sees her die in the peaceful thought of his security. But he is actually in custody once more, and this time he prefers to die, leaving his resources to his young friends that they may take their unextinguished hopes to Mexico.

What is remarkable in Remarque's work is not style. His translator, I imagine, correctly renders his intention, which seems quite clearly to be aimed at blunt, unsentimental directness. Nor is his gift that of philosophic intensity of feeling. It is interesting to think what a torrent of rapture about the lostness and brokenness of these people Thomas Wolfe would have poured out. Quite simply, Remarque is a brilliant narrator. . . . With candor, audacity, tenderness, and ruthless honesty, he has written this full, rich statement of what the soul of man may become under the discipline of tyranny. ᘔ᙮

Arthur Koestler

In the work of Arthur Koestler one finds a mixture of Remarque's aptitude for drama with Romains's skill in philosophic interpretation. This young internationalist has crowded into his forty years samples of all the sufferings, excitements, loyalties, faiths, and disillusionments of our time. Born in Budapest and educated in Vienna, he has traveled all through Europe, the Near East, and Central Asia, telling as a journalist the stories of the revolts, the perturbations, the hopes of our century. He has been, by turn, a dedicated Communist and a relentless uncoverer of what he takes to be its weaknesses. His sheer physical vitality will not permit him to succumb to the counsel of despair, and wherever he has found a struggle involving the destiny of mankind, he has been in the midst of it—in Spain, in France, in the Second World War. His own inner life has been a perpetual conflict between skepticism and faith. Yet, though he inclines toward the view that the recurring motif of mankind's experience through the ages is the cynical readiness of the powerful to beat down, exhaust, and finally devour the less powerful, nonetheless his own apparently inexhaustible mental health makes him unwilling to accept this judgment as final. He hopes, in spite of all the doubts his eager, uncompromising intelligence can produce.

In *Arrival and Departure* Koestler quite brilliantly dramatized this struggle between skepticism and faith, allowing faith to win by the narrow margin with which, in the minds of courageous and intelligent men, it must always manage to come through the threat of extinction.

᙮᙮ Ever since the beginning of the Second World War the earnest have been protesting, more in sorrow than in anger, that the greatest conflict in the history of mankind has produced no fiction of major importance.

These grievously afflicted observers of contemporary history may now retire to their studios and reconsider their decision. For in *Arrival and Departure* Arthur Koestler has written one of the most important novels of our time. It is a genuinely thoughtful and moving comment on the crisis which every intelligent young man must face before he surrenders his private will to the service of the race of man.

The story is of a modest hero, Peter Slavek, who has fought the good fight against Nazism from his earliest days as a student and who has suffered the full weight of vengeance from the leaders of the Hitler movement. Slavek has been in the hands of the Gestapo and knows all that these representatives of the philosophy of cruelty have to contribute to the story of human fate. Having escaped from them at last, he reaches "Neutralia" intending to make his way immediately to England, where he will continue to struggle against the Nazi ideology of waging war against idealism in all its forms.

In Neutralia, however, he has a succession of disturbing experiences. England is by no means in a hurry to accept him as a soldier, and he must cool his heels awaiting word that he has been found acceptable in the sight of a curiously cautious democracy. In the meantime he, being young and full of undischarged vitality, has a love affair which proves to be greatly disquieting.

When his young woman suddenly and unexpectedly deserts him, Peter indulges himself in a long overdue nervous collapse. With the aid of a psychoanalyst he explores the unhappy past, the crucial misery of the present, and the prospects for the future in an effort to restore his afflicted mind to normality. He finds that the grim resolution which has helped him to face the Nazis has come as the result of his maladjusted childhood. As a boy he had a sense of intolerable guilt because of the dislike he felt for a younger brother. Having once indulged the juvenile notion that it would be pleasant to have injured this helpless creature and having later inadvertently happened to injure him, he has gone through life trying to make amends for a crime which he considers to be unforgivable. From this sense of guilt all his stalwart idealism has sprung.

This revelation is at once releasing and distressing. If the total of his desire to serve the race amounts to no more than an impulse to appease his own conscience, then Peter considers he is free of any obligation to be a hero. He can forget the fight against Nazism; he can follow the girl he loves in her flight to security in America; he can enjoy himself as he sees fit in a sheltered world. Together, he and his psychoanalyst cure him of the hysteria which has made him seem to be paralyzed by the old wounds of Nazi torture. He will rise from his bed, go to America, and put behind him every souvenir of his old obsession with the fate of man.

But he has no sooner begun to give himself the comfort of this decision than his social conscience reasserts itself. He meets a Nazi theorist who describes the superstate in which a kind of ruthless god of scientific lore rides over all human rights. He meets also an English flier who has been maimed and cruelly disfigured by the war and who yet feels that he is somehow a betrayer of humanity because he cannot continue to fight. These encounters with cynicism on the one hand, and with a spontaneous desire to serve on the other, restore to Slavek his idealism. Once more he knows what it is to feel guilty, but this time the notions of his childhood have been translated into a mature philosophy. He realizes that he has a duty to serve mankind because of its great need. Even if the outcome is doubtful, even if there are many who stand ready to exploit his idealism and turn it against its own purposes, still he can do nothing but fight for what he hopes the new world may become.

Most of the writers of war stories have failed to be effective in their protests against man's inhumanity to man because they have tried to be too objective. They have stuck to the grim facts and neglected the ideas which animate the struggle. Because he has dared to try to deal with the ideas which prompt men to fight against the barbarous Nazi program, Arthur Koestler has succeeded where most of the others have failed. ॐ

But the outcome of Koestler's personal struggle is still doubtful. In his most recently published work, a play called *Twilight Bar,* he presents the spectacle of our sad globe facing an ultimatum laid down by the authority of leaders from worthier planets. It must either justify its existence within three days or be eliminated. In a panic, earth tries the experiment of making happiness its chief value and the experiment works. But very soon earth tires of it and goes back comfortably to its old habit of being miserable. As the final curtain falls, Koestler leaves his audience in doubt as to whether or not the ultimatum will be carried out. That cruel indecisiveness is, of course, an adumbration of Koestler's own gallant, even humorous, but essentially miserable, uncertainty about the fate of humankind.

Mark Aldanov

COMPLETELY and unapologetically a doubter is Mark Aldanov. His cultivated and sophisticated mind has dealt with the problem of man's ability to plan a better destiny and has come calmly to the conclusion that there is little health in the race's collective mind, little hope for its great plans. In *For Thee the Best* he pretends to be considering matters that agitated human society long ago, but actually he is considering the crisis of our own time.

ॐ On the surface this brilliant little novel appears to be the story of Lord Byron's last days, describing dramatically how he became bored with his talent for poetry and went to help the Greeks fight for their independence from the Turks. But I believe Mark Aldanov has slyly tucked another significance into his book. Out of the profound skepticism of his own highly sophisticated intelligence, he has brought the warning that when the great powers of the earth get together in international congresses, their leaders come equipped with weapons to sabotage the high-sounding intentions which the session has supposedly been called to further.

Aldanov is a Russian writer who left his native country in 1919 to become one of its most prominent exiles. He was out of sympathy with its political program. A liberal in outlook, an individualist in the expression of his beliefs, he preferred to develop his own philosophy in the atmosphere of friendly indulgence which Paris has always offered to the homeless. More recently Aldanov has made a second pilgrimage in search of a haven for the intellectual exile. Now he is living in New York.

The gist of his philosophy, as it gets itself expressed between the lines of his new book, would seem to be that even the shrewdest, most discerning of men are too easily seduced by personal desire, too subject to boredom, too readily deflected by their emotional vagaries, to be capable of planning a livable human society.

He writes in this new book about the great figures of the early years of the nineteenth century who met, in an atmosphere of weariness and cynicism after the Napoleonic struggle, pretending that the Congress of Verona was designed to "defend . . . the eternal principles of virtue and of truth." Into the mouth of the Emperor Alexander of Russia he puts these words: "An independent English, Russian or French policy is no longer possible. There must be a coordinated policy that has the good of all nations as its aim." But even while he utters these words, the disillusioned liberal is deliberately destroying that dream and leaving all nations free to follow the policies that seem to serve their own myopic and greedy programs.

Over the shoulders of Alexander and Wellington and Castlereagh and Metternich, beyond the gates of Verona and the limits of the century, Aldanov is looking at the men of our own time, met in San Francisco or in London. Their curiously similar expressions of lofty ideals, he seems to warn us, may have similarly ironic overtones that are inaudible to the general public but quite clear to the masters of statecraft who know where to look for double meanings.

If one reads *For Thee the Best* in the dismal belief that it is meant to offer a parallel to the problems of our day and a translation of the terms of the present debate on international affairs, it is a profoundly depressing book. . . .

Idealism is short-lived even in the warmest heart; behind their masks of dignity and thoughtfulness, superior men hide their collections of wounds and vanities, pettiness, malice, boredom, indifference. And these explosives are enough to blow up any plan for an ordered society.

Aldanov is a disturbing writer because he makes this bleak prospect seem plausible. It is impossible to make the angry retorts one would like to make to his genial and impersonal analysis of the smallness of the human mind. . . . It is impossible not to admire his book and equally impossible not to resent it.

It should be read as a footnote to one of the tragedies of the past, in the hope that we shall learn how to demand better of our leaders and not allow another opportunity to be thrown away as was the world's opportunity at the Congress of Verona. ❧

Georges Duhamel

To THE serene hopelessness of Aldanov and the tempered skepticism of Koestler one may offer as a final comment on

the European mind the stubborn optimism of Georges Duhamel. He tells his stories of man's suffering with the avowed
philosophic purpose of showing that human misery is not, as
Koestler sometimes takes it to be, hopeless or, as Aldanov
seems to consider it, shameful.

⏥ "We walk in anguish in the midst of the incompre-
hensible."

This is the comment made on human experience by the
sober, intellectual, enormously attractive scientist who dominates Georges Duhamel's novel *Cecile Pasquier*. It is more
than a little disquieting to realize that this chronicle of misery,
as seen through the experiences of a French family, ends with
the outbreak of the First World War. In a moment so much
more crowded with anguish and so much more incompre-
hensible, one wonders what the author would say of the present outlook for human life.

Perhaps it may be found in another passage of the same
book when the same observer says: ". . . men may bicker
and quarrel, but thought marches on, nevertheless. The edifice
of knowledge continues to rise in spite of petty warfare. All
the leaves may wither, all the trees may be sickly, but it is a
fine forest for all that."

And again: "Good men! I'm still seeking them; and I find,
yes, here a crumb, there, perhaps something quite substantial. . . . Oh, I'm far from despairing. If some day I should
be too bitterly deceived and disappointed . . . but no, even
so I would rebuild my optimism in the light of my disappointments."

In 1938 there appeared in this country a volume called *The
Pasquier Chronicles*. It contained Duhamel's first five novels
devoted to the fortunes of a family of Parisians. Dominating
the varied, lively, humorous record, which explored many aspects of middle-class life, was the philandering father—always
full of magnificent schemes for acquiring a fortune, always

just managing to keep his family together by his often neglected work as a physician.

The new volume contains three more short novels dealing with the Pasquier family. As a flourish of gallantry, the name of Cecile, the musician, is given to the book. But it is really her brother Laurent through whose eyes we look once more at some of the intricacies, the follies, and the finenesses of social life in France. Largely through his generous, yet shrewdly realistic, eyes we see also the sister Suzanne, who becomes an actress, the brother Joseph, whose field is finance, and the father, who continues to make all the curious and amusing vagaries of the human spirit his exciting province.

The first of the three books, *Pastors and Masters*, has as its chief interest a bitter feud between two great men of science. Chalgrin is an idealist whose philosophy makes room for more than the conclusions of pure logic. His enemy, Rohner, who is "purely detached intelligence," hates Chalgrin for what he regards as his mystical vein.

Each permits the instinctual antagonism between them to take the form of professional distrust, though each in his own way is enormously valuable. They manage to hurt and finally to destroy one another, with the result that when Chalgrin lies stricken, Rohner too is deprived of his objective in life and of his balance. For it "takes a very long time to hatch out and bring to maturity a good, stout hatred."

Laurent Pasquier, who is both biologist and doctor of medicine, has worked under these masters. As he watches their terrible feud, he is forced to see the weakness of the one and the callous indifference to human life of the other. It is the first in a series of tragic experiences with which his education for maturity begins.

The second book, called *Cecile*, describes the curious marriage of a very great artist. Cecile seems invulnerable in the possession of her great and satisfying gift. But she begins to long for an unknown kind of fulfillment. She wants, among other things, a child. She chooses, therefore, as a husband a man with the kind of abstract intelligence which she herself does not have. But Richard, besides being an intellectual and a wit, is a neurotic tormented by his vanity. The marriage is a failure and Cecile ends it without regret and without having learned a great deal. But when she loses her child, she finds the experience devastating and illuminating too. She sums up her philosophy by saying, "I . . . ask permission to suffer without shame and without a sense of hopelessness."

The final book, *The Fight Against the Shadows*, returns to Laurent as its central figure. As head of his department at the Institute, he dismisses a certain objectionable and useless political appointee only to find that he has brought down upon his head a swarm of enemies whose venality disgusts him and yet has the power to destroy his work.

At the close Laurent is still a valiant figure, ready to continue the fight for his own brand of faith when he shall have an opportunity. In the subtlety of his mind, the delicacy of his intuitions, and the breadth of his sympathies, this figure is enormously appealing. ৵

We wait, at the moment, in a mood of tense expectancy to see whether or not the doom suggested by Arthur Koestler's play is to be visited upon us. Such ancient counselors as H. G. Wells have supported Koestler's most dubious view by warning us that life as we have known it in the past is soon to pass from the earth. But if these worst predictions should prove to be less than precisely accurate, if doom should be delayed, then we may expect from the American writers of the next fifty years just such reflections of the conscience of mankind as have been given permanence in the thoughtful books of these eight social philosophers of Europe.

Half-Gods on the Threshold

A<small>N OBSERVER</small> of the literary scene is never in greater danger of seeming to assume the role of Sir Oracle than when he undertakes to anticipate the judgment of posterity by suggesting which ones of the new writers are most likely to achieve permanent place on the library shelf. It is even difficult to define at all accurately the state or condition of being a "new" writer.

A young man or woman who has produced a single book feels exuberantly and exultantly creative. But the cautious critic waits for him to come a cropper with his second book and then to achieve a third before he is willing to admit that the incubation period is passed and a writer has emerged. The question remains of how long "newness" may be said to continue. And, further, is there any age limit beyond which a beginning writer may not be said to be new? It is a little disconcerting to salute a new writer only to discover that he has not been new to himself for some thirty years or more, during which he has written in a frenzy of effort, all of which has been unappreciated.

There are writers who retain the style and originality of youth after two or three decades of uninterrupted productivity. James Thurber, who is several years older than the century, seems always to enroll himself among the promising young men, partly because he has refused to allow his richly humorous talent to be compressed into a mold. As playwright, cartoonist, fabler, and creator of many an enchanting and hitherto unimagined literary form, he has contributed to the literature of our time with poetic utterances that pass as bits of irresponsible frivolity and with pronunciamentos in the cause of truth that are set down as mere whimsies. He renews himself and his gift so often that it is hard not to think of him as a bright young man.

In this he is like E. B. White, another writer who seems to be rejuvenated with each copy of the New Yorker to which he contributes. Mr. White has kept the natural juices flowing in the informal essay during a time when such material has been issued to the large reading public only in a digested and predigested form as unappetizing as K rations. I think he may be credited with keeping liberal ideas alive in many minds that might never receive such stimulation were it not for his subtly seductive contributions to the New Yorker.

Though a writer like Katherine Anne Porter has been before the reading public for many years, she seems always to be just on the point of doing something so much more impressive than she has ever done before that one is inclined to keep her name on the list of new writers. With only a handful of books on her list, she has achieved a kind of luminous prestige for the fastidious simplicity with which she dramatizes a wide variety of human experiences.

So in the matter of prophecy, too, one must dare to be personal and even whimsical, naming as candidates for immortality the writers who take one's own fancy. It is inevitable that one should attempt to prophesy in a postscript to such a book as this. To have sat for twenty years in a quiet and sheltered place watching the pageant of letters seems in retrospect to have been a dramatic experience. In this time of startling change the face of the world has been startlingly altered, and literature is the mirror that reflects the expressions of fear, grief, threatened madness, and hope as they pass over the brow of human society. Having watched the past die in the pages of contemporary writing, a reviewer is bound to attempt to foresee how the future will manage to get itself born in the pages of tomorrow's books.

During the two decades just past we have seen our world rise up and attempt to regain full stature after the crippling experience of a widespread war, stagger immediately into a wild orgy of economic experimentation, collapse to its knees in panic as the wind of depression blew over it, and then, with unexampled courage, rise up again to face the threat of extinction in another world war. And at the end came that terrifying mark of punctuation made by the atomic bomb as it fell, a luridly brilliant exclamation point, the meaning of which is still unclear.

Yet it did not seem like a drama very often as one read and attempted to appraise this day's book and the next and the next. Of the five thousand and more that have been considered by one earnest and indefatigable man in these twenty years, most have been completely forgotten. Many seemed totally commonplace even with the delicious smell of printer's ink still fresh on their pages. The charms of others have withered in the bitter climate of the world's ordeal. In the early 1920's one would have needed the gift of divination to have foretold that only two decades later the talents of Joseph Hergesheimer and James Branch Cabell would hardly seem worth re-examining, while that of Scott Fitzgerald, then a slightly moonstruck exponent of the ecstatic rituals of flapperism, would communicate its disease of neurotic insight to the age.

Standing on the critic's bit of removed ground, one has seen the literary half-gods go, one by one. Some of them have survived their gifts and gone on muttering nearly unintelligible jibberish in imitation of the work of better days. Others have died with their brilliance just beginning to clarify itself and with their potential accomplishments unfulfilled. But the departure of so many has not left the scene empty. Indeed, faster than the old half-gods go, the new ones crowd over the threshold.

The incurable optimism of the human spirit attaches itself more firmly than ever, in a time when the outlook for humanity itself seems dubious, to the saving grace of intelligence.

Intelligence seems to be the comfortingly widespread trait of the new generation of writers. Among those who went to war one discerns no tendency toward lachrymose self-pity, no preoccupation with the personal sorrows of a lost generation. In the temperament of those who were just too old to go to war, one tastes that blend of skepticism and faith which ages so well and produces one of the best vintages of the brain. And in them all—all, that is, who have seemed to ask for serious consideration as artists—there is an unapologetic concern with large themes and sober social issues.

We shall be deceived in some of them, to be sure. The temptation will prove too strong, and they will do up their skills into neat little gift packages for the popular magazines. Skepticism, gaining the advantage over faith, will unravel the talents of others, leaving them frayed and meaningless. One has seen that happen before, and it will happen again.

Yet it is possible, I think, to select the names of some performers who seem to be destined for distinction in the act of the pageant which is presently to begin. Much the easiest way of presenting them in review seems to be that of the drill sergeant; one must divide them up into squads. Perhaps some of them will mildly resent the arbitrary and artificial relations in which they find themselves. But good democrats that they are, they will endure the individual inconvenience for the sake of their analyst and their audience.

For many years the writers of the resurgent South have been among the most important ones before us. It is still so. The men and women of Kentucky, Louisiana, and Virginia keep their world in the steady focus of eyes unmisted by the old delusions of grandeur. Robert Penn Warren, poet and critic as well as creative artist, seems to have gathered up the resources of all these forms and, with a generous but disciplined hand, found place for them in a new kind of philosophic novel. The complexities of *Night Rider* and *At Heaven's Gate* are matters of the mind and heart that have reached their special tension out of the strained economic and social conditions of an old community seeking to renew itself.

Richard Wright, the most distinguished Negro writer of our time, refuses to compromise with the desire of his people to be shown in star parts, displaying their cultivation and charm; he continues to force America to look at the tragedy of wastefulness and degradation wrought by keeping his people in a sordid environment.

Hodding Carter, in an excellent first novel, *The Winds of Fear*, has stated the problem of tension between races as it exists in the small town's intimate, familial group. He has stated it with no less intellectual hardihood than did Lillian Smith in *Strange Fruit*, and Mr. Carter has, perhaps, more of the poise that is essential to a long career as a novelist.

Eudora Welty has been known until recently as a writer of short stories having the pungency and elusiveness of smoke. With her novel *Delta Wedding* she has established herself as a writer of brilliant and solid gifts. Her picture of a way of life that is doomed to die makes the book as memorable as Chekhov's play, *The Cherry Orchard*.

Hamilton Basso shows us the image of the artist as man of the world, and Josephine Pinckney is his feminine counterpart. Both have explored the often bitter comedy of contemporary life in the drawing room, the statehouse, and the picturesquely crumbling plantation of the southern community. Caroline Gordon speaks out of her "forest of the South" in a slightly portentous voice and to a special audience, which is willing to grope for subtleties that are deliberately left shadowed and obscure. Even the historical romancers like Clifford Dowdey and the experts in whimsey like Berry Fleming are concerned with ideas and with values.

In the work of middlewestern writers one discerns a frequently recurring theme: the triumph of essential health over the conditions of adversity. The scattered but pervasive effects of this adversity may be summed up in the word *depression*, and its particular reference in the Middle West is to the economic let-down that almost immediately followed the orgy of the pioneers.

Meridel Le Sueur, a prose poet of the short story and the novel, is obsessed with the class struggle, turning the language of the strike meeting and the grim comedy of the picket line into paeans in praise of the worker. Josiah Greene has made his debut as a serious novelist with a cool, thorough exploration of the background of strife in industry. His title, *Not in Our Stars*, offers in itself a clue to his intention, which is to be judicious and objective in his examination of the psychological, as well as the ideological, distance between workers and employers.

Wallace Stegner in such big, ambitious books as *The Big Rock Candy Mountain* offers a larger banquet of material than he himself seems to have been able to digest. His theme, however, is the significant one of how the "American dream" has faded for the dreamer in the Middle West. In *The Golden Bowl* Feike Feikema has shown how the same illusion of eternal prosperity has dimmed out in the dust-doomed Dakotas. He has testified, however, in *Boy Almighty* that the people of his region have the mental hardihood and the physical stamina to withstand their ordeal by drouth. This second novel, a sort of ardent and juvenile version of *The Magic Mountain*, dramatizes a young man's struggle to put off both the depression and the ecstasy of serious disease and to become whole once more.

Ann Chidester in *Young Pandora* has sought out the un-hackneyed eccentrics, originals, and irrepressibly vital creatures of a dying village. Glanville Smith, speaking for the cosmopolitan way of life out of the mind of an amused and witty Middlewesterner, restates with fine urbanity the truth that all ways of life are worth studying for their blend of idiocy, grace, pathos, and gallantry.

Not all regions of America seem to be represented by anything resembling a school of writers. New England, for example, being old in the ways of literature, has developed nothing so naive as a fraternity of eager-eyed interpreters. Its people tend to identify themselves with traditional themes as John Marquand identifies himself with the theme of the inflexibility of social patterns, as Nancy Hale identifies herself with the theme of the emancipation of women, and as Walter Edmonds identifies himself with the epical theme of historical development.

The Southwest, however, has a representative group of writers who are preoccupied with the powerful effects of scene upon character. Paul Horgan, in novels like *The Common Heart*, has dramatized the genial influences that make growing up in Albuquerque an agreeable experience. Perhaps because the milieu as a setting for American lives is so new, its writers seem to concentrate on boyhood experiences. Marquis James, turning in his middle years from the biographies that have previously absorbed his attention, has produced in *The Cherokee Strip* a wholly admirable example of autobiography, showing, without any injudicious display of self-love, how perfect a sympathy existed between a rugged way of life and his own rugged temperament.

But the region has its bitter tragedies too. In *The Life and Death of Little Jo* Robert Bright has presented the touching and embarrassing picture of the Spanish-American citizen, the rejected child of our hybrid civilization, whose Uncle Sam remained contentedly unaware of his existence until he was needed as a soldier to fight and be snuffed out on Bataan.

New York, being a world in itself, has its own school of writers. The sons of the congested areas of Brooklyn, Harlem, Greenwich Village, and Park Avenue are conscientiously objective and knowing. Reporters like Joseph Mitchell and A. J. Liebling move out of the throng of technically expert writers because, though both have continued to be simply reporters, they appear to have looked more steadily and intelligently into the heart of the human experience than many another bright young man has managed to do. It seems likely that larger works will be forthcoming from them.

The other "boys and girls together on the sidewalks of New York" offer souvenirs of their experience which range all the way from the grossest of melodramas to the most frivolous of social comedies and the most lightly lubricous of fantasies. In such novels as *I'll Never Go There Any More* Jerome Weidman presents dismally persuasive accounts of the meeting between cunning and depravity in a world peopled by creatures the only meaning of whose existence is its utter meaninglessness. In books like *Tucker's People* Ira Wolfert has unfolded scenes no less squalid; yet he has managed, because of his quite distinguished gifts of insight and compassion, to speak out against the cruelty of a society which continues to exploit its Negro citizens as relentlessly in their pleasures as it does in their labor.

John O'Hara, working a wider field, has explored the depressing pastimes of all branches of urban society, occasionally revealing in his contemptuous assaults a trickery and cunning as a craftsman that is not above suspicion of meanness. Ruth McKenney, though in *Jake Home* she has written a bold, ambitious study of the psychological development of a labor leader, appears to be more comfortably at home in her charming sketches. Her admirable series called *My Sister Eileen* seemed to make primroses, in all their fresh prettiness, flourish in the window boxes of Greenwich Village. Though Sally Benson can on occasion be mordant, she has brought the imperishable interest of Jane Austen's material down to date in the stories of *Junior Miss.*

Vincent McHugh has managed to pump the wayward breath of fantasy through the air-conditioning outlets of New York office buildings and apartments. The results, in *I Am Thinking of My Darling*, were not infrequently raffish; yet the persistence with which McHugh gave that emphasis to his report of magical happenings did not detract from the ingenuity, the charm, or the seeming spontaneity of the performance. The pavements of New York would not seem to be a sympathetic habitat for creatures of American folklore, but Vincent McHugh achieved something new in native writing by discovering magic in Manhattan.

A few writers of distinction have made their debuts during the war years wearing the uniforms of soldiers and the stripes, usually, of corporals or sergeants. The much exploited Marion Hargrove may find his way back from Hollywood, now that the war is over, but he is perhaps less likely to write soberly and well on a variety of themes than are other soldiers like Robert McLaughlin and Walter Bernstein. Niven Busch, in his novel *They Dream of Home*, stated better than any other writer has managed to do the emotional problem of the veteran whose home seems no longer to be his home. With this book Busch has made his way to a place of promise among interpreters of soldier psychology. This is, of course, certain to be a theme of persistently recurring interest.

Two hard-working and conscientious neurotics among the women novelists have attracted responsive interest from the more inflammable elements of the reading public. Carson McCullers' two novels, *The Heart Is a Lonely Hunter* and *Reflections in a Golden Eye*, have brought approving gasps from those studios where it is assumed that unintelligibility is next to genius if it is not genius itself. But for the pretensions and absurdities of those books, Carson McCullers has made amends with her no less disturbing, but thoroughly honest and quite unmannered, study of the preadolescent child in *The Member of the Wedding*. With only one book to her literary name, Jean Stafford has joined the sorority which devotes itself to examinations of the more intense forms of mental suffering. In *Boston Adventure* she produced sentences so long and involved that one might suspect her of having cribbed them from Henry James, except for the fact that they sound so much more like bad translations from Dostoevski.

Abnormality in all its more sensational aspects is the pre-occupying interest of these writers. A third woman novelist, Dorothy Baker, joins them in this clinical study, if *Trio* is to be taken as typical of her absorptions. Miss Baker, however, has so strongly marked a taste for drama and so natural an impulse to follow its rules of directness and compression that she manages to be as clear and emphatic as the others are vague and discursive. Yet all three have opened doors which American niceness has hitherto required to be kept firmly closed. Their boldness recommends them for further attention.

There are, in the contemporary circle of American writers, some who quite elude classification. It is, perhaps, from people like them that the most rewarding examinations of heart and mind may be expected. William March, though he has not had distinguished success as a novelist, continues to be one of the best of American short-story writers, taking his themes from no particular region and no fixed or rigid way of life, yet achieving a comment, made always by artful indirection, on some significant feature of the human drama.

Muriel Rukeyser has been a distinguished and passionately honest exponent of a liberal philosophy in poems that show great originality in form. She has also made a surprising debut as a biographer of the almost completely unknown genius of the physical sciences, Willard Gibbs. Miss Rukeyser's adventure in biography seemed a particularly bold and fruitful one because she managed to make it also the biography of America in the period of which she was writing.

A group of voluble and highly opinioned people will demand our attention frequently in the future by virtue of the fact that they speak to their American public as interpreters of the spirit of internationalism. Klaus Mann, son of Thomas Mann, even before he became an American soldier, undertook in *The Turning Point* to offer his personal experience as something that might reconcile the ways of European youth to American youth. No doubt he will write again to attempt a *rapprochement* between two worlds.

Kay Boyle, who has lived the greater part of her maturity in France, continues to be an agent of understanding between societies that must learn to be tolerant of each other's ways. Miss Boyle, having learned after many years of being an extremely precious writer to reconcile herself to the requirements of the chic magazines, may not be the best of available ambassadors of good will. But she will be among them nonetheless.

Martha Dodd, as the daughter of an American ambassador, saw the Nazi world from a favored position within the Reich. Her book *Sowing the Wind* surely did not say her last word on that subject. Her curiosity, intelligence, and facility will suggest many more. In *The Cross and the Arrow* Albert Maltz dared, while the war was still in progress, to urge us to remember that Germans were the first rebels against Nazism. He will take up that cross again.

David Cornel De Jong has offered his talents, as well as his memories, to bridge the psychological distance between America and the Old World. Souvenirs of Holland and of the resolute temperament of its people have existed in profusion in all his work until the most recent novel. *Somewhat Angels* showed how brilliantly a European of high talent may assume a new role as mordant satirist of American mores. But the shadow of Europe is sure to cast itself over David De Jong's work once more.

Angna Enters possesses a dramatic and highly variable talent so widely inclusive that it makes a place for Spain and Greece within the pattern of its sympathies as easily as it makes a place for Milwaukee, Wisconsin. Emily Hahn, the most impudent, unpredictable talent the whole American tradition has to offer, has already written down impressions of Africa, Japan, and China that her worst wishers could hardly call stereotyped.

Peter Gray, in books like *People of Poros*, has dramatized the almost totally unfamiliar lives of the modern Greeks on their least exploited isles. Vincent Sheean's appraising eye takes in a continent at a time and each of the continents in turn. Though he is best known for his work as a wandering reporter of world politics, he has shown an interest in both the novel and the drama. This absorption is likely to bring the large themes encountered in his far wanderings back to the pages of literature.

The scope of these discussions has not been limited to the work of American writers. Therefore a glimpse at the British half-gods on the threshold may appropriately close this experiment in prophecy.

Rumer Godden is a highly creative writer who has explored so many scenes and so many techniques that already her "infinite variety" is established. Sometimes, as in *Take Three Tenses*, her exquisitely written, beautifully tasteful exercises seem to enclose narratives that prove on close examination to be quite commonplace. But when the originality of mind that her earlier books revealed is matched with her delicately perfect craftsmanship, she should produce novels of greater distinction than any she has yet done.

Rosamond Lehmann, writing at a leisurely pace with long intervals between volumes, has done nothing that did not have points of brilliance. The complexity of her gift seems to have a natural attraction toward quite unusual subject matter, as in *The Ballad and the Source*, a study of a woman of death-exuding charm.

Similarly brilliant, similarly decadent, is Evelyn Waugh, whose *Brideshead Revisited* showed him climbing, at Aldous Huxley's heels, into the chilly protection from the vulgar world of a heaven which only the spiritually elect may enter. Waugh has chosen the paradise offered by traditional religion, but he offers his own quite extraordinarily snobbish notion of what the prerequisites for entrance should be. These might not, I think, agree with the beliefs of more completely orthodox interpreters. But Evelyn Waugh is a seductive writer, a subtle intelligence, a fine artist.

Bruce Marshall, working in *The World, the Flesh, and Father Smith* with the theme of religious salvation, has gone the other way around his subject from that taken by Waugh. He comes out of the journey with compassion and identification with the commonalty of human creatures as his trophies. Inevitably his book, considered simply as a work of creative imagination, seems far more attractive than Waugh's.

Richard Llewellyn has written a book that was overestimated, *How Green Was My Valley*, and one that was underrated, *None but the Lonely Heart*. That leaves him in a good position to continue his experiments with settings, styles, and idioms until he has found the one that will prove suitable to the major theme toward which he appears to be making his way. Gerald Kersh seems to have taken his style from Hemingway. But he has made it more securely his own than have any of the other imitators. Margery Sharp, imitating no one at all but listening to the sly promptings of a first-rate intelligence, has created a series of completely original comedies, of which *Cluny Brown* is the best so far but probably not the best of which Miss Sharp is capable.

So the curtain must be allowed to fall on what is clearly an entr'acte in the drama of letters in our time. The casualties of the first act must be removed from the stage and the actors who survive must be given time, now that the Second World War is over, to freshen their make-up.

Twenty years is a long time for one act of a drama to continue. But with the indestructibility that has ever characterized the stage-struck, I have enjoyed it all, good and bad. I ask nothing better than that I should be spared long enough to see the second act to its close.

Index to Authors and Titles